Corporate Chanakya

Corporate Chanakya

Successful Management the Chanakya Way

SPMGROUP SPM Foundation
SINCE 1967

Radhakrishnan Pillai

JAICO PUBLISHING HOUSE

Ahmedabad Bangalore Bhopal Bhubaneswar Chennai
Delhi Hyderabad Kolkata Lucknow Mumbai

Published by Jaico Publishing House
A-2 Jash Chambers, 7-A Sir Phirozshah Mehta Road
Fort, Mumbai - 400 001
jaicopub@jaicobooks.com
www.jaicobooks.com

CORPORATE CHANAKYA
ISBN 978-81-8495-133-2

First Jaico Impression: 2010
Seventeenth Jaico Impression: 2012

Printed by
Repro India Limited
Plot No. 50/2, T.T.C. MIDC Industrial Area
Mahape, Navi Mumbai - 400 710.

The book is dedicated to
My Gurudev Swami Chinmayananda,
who inspired me to study our ancient scriptures that
offer solutions to all our modern day problems.

Contents

- Qualities of a Leader

- Competition

Contents

• People

• To Avoid

Part II — Management

* Employees

* Finance

Contents

Part III — Training

• Trainees

• Boss

Contents

Preface

Let me tell you a story…

There was once a young man in Mumbai who wanted nothing more than to succeed in the world of business. He had studied management in colleges that extolled the virtues of the western ways of understanding this subject. Soon enough, he worked his way up the corporate ladder, but finally decided to set out on his own. After all, who wants to be bossed over by someone else?

His first venture was in the realm of spiritual tourism. Since no one in his family had ever been an entrepreneur, he had to learn everything about setting up a business on his own. By the grace of God, and the support of his business partner, the business began to do well. From being a manager in someone else's company, he had become the leader of his own business.

His next step? Creating a well-known corporate entity. He met people and discussed his ideas and plans with them, learning from people, making copious notes, reading books, attending seminars, and training programmes. And yet, nothing helped. Something vital was missing in his pursuit for knowledge. He was not able to figure out what this missing piece was, for a long time.

The answer was right within him.

Since his childhood, he had found guidance in a spiritual organisation and had been blessed by many spiritual masters. During a spiritual discourse a Mahatma said, "India, our motherland, has great history and legacy. Our *Rishis* were no ordinary men — they have studied and perfected every science in this world. Only if we were to look back into our glorious past we would find solutions to all our modern problems."

This was the divine message he had been waiting for.

Management has been recognised as a science since the 1950s. One of the fathers of modern management is Peter Drucker. But didn't 'management' exist in India even before the 1950s and the Drucker era? As a nation we have over 5000 years to our credit. Did we not have management scientists in our country before the 20th century?

In the ancient Indian scriptures — *Ramayana, Mahabharata*, the various *Upanishads* — he found brilliant discussions of management strategies. Why was it that us Indians, always look at what is *wrong* with India and never appreciate what is *great* about our country? As a nation we have survived the test of time. Even though we are still a growing economy, we are not a failed nation. In the past, our country had achieved the peak of success for thousands of years. How many nations can boast of such a heritage?

He now realised that the missing piece which would help his business grow was to look 'within' rather than outside. The western principles of management are undoubtedly good, but even his own ancestors were extremely good at management.

Thus, one day, while looking for Indian books on management, he stumbled upon *Kautilya's Arthashastra*, written by the king-maker, Chanakya. Who has not heard about this book? Even he had. But hardly anyone from his generation had studied it. He bought a copy.

A few pages into the book, he was upset! He could not

understand anything! He read the pages over and over again, but the message of the book was out of reach. The subject itself seemed dry and boring. He felt the author had made everything seem more complicated than necessary.

He said to one of his mentors, "I do not understand anything in the *Arthashastra*, even though I am trying my best to learn from it." His mentor told him, "In India, we consider the scriptures to be mirrors. They reflect who you are. So if you do not understand *Arthashastra*, do not blame the mirror. As you grow and experience life, you will understand the book better."

That year, he went on a pilgrimage to Kailash Mansarovar, the holy abode of Lord Shiva. One evening, a voice seemed to speak to him, 'Make *Kautilya's Arthashastra* your life-long pursuit. Don't just study it, but apply it in your life. Live the *Arthashastra!*' He could not believe that he was listening to his *own* thoughts, this had to be divine intervention!

He had heard about an ashram in Kerala, dedicated to the research of ancient Indian scriptures. He declared to the Acharya (teacher) in charge of the ashram, "I want to study the *Arthashastra.*" The Acharya was happy to see the young man's interest, but said, "You will have to come here and learn it under the Guru-Shishya Parampara." This meant taking a break from the business and staying in the ashram and studying under a Sanskrit scholar.

This was not an easy decision for a businessman from Mumbai. But, with the help of his partner, he took time off from the business, and studied the wisdom of the Rishis. The time he spent in the ashram changed his life forever.

He realised that each modern management theory had already been explored thousands of years ago in the *Arthashastra*.

With a deeper knowledge of management he now returned to his urban life to apply what he had learned. Immediately, he experienced success! His business grew and people were impressed with his new skills. When they asked him how he had achieved success, he said, "Two things helped me — the grace of my Guru and the knowledge of *Kautilya's Arthashastra.*"

Friends, this is my story. Every word is true. But, the story does not end here. In fact, this is where the story begins....

After I returned from Kerala I applied Kautilya's practical and perfect theories to my own business (Atma Darshan, *www.atmadarshan.com*). Even though Atma Darshan brought me success, something else began to happen. My friends from the corporate world urged me to share this knowledge I had gained.

I was invited to speak at various seminars, conferences, and training programmes in India and all over the world. Businessmen consulted me on several matters. Well-known publishing houses and newspapers asked me to write about how Kautilya's wisdom could be applied to modern businesses. I was also asked to host a radio show.

I met so many people who are interested in Indian management and Indian wisdom. Despite the differences between them with regard to age, nationalities, designations, and industries, all those who participated in my workshops and chose to attend my seminars felt a deep respect for Chanakya's genius.

And then came the support of the SPM Group of companies which allowed me to delve deeper into *Arthashastra*. I am now fully devoted to the cause of the promotion and application of Indian management ideas. Today, I am the Director of the SPM Foundation which aims to 'Make India strong and self sufficient' in the ancient Guru–Sishya Parampara method.

This book is a documentation of all my ideas that I have shared with millions of people from the corporate world, all across the globe, about how to apply Chanakya's practical solutions to solve day-to-day problems in modern businesses.

Corporate Chanakya is not just about me. It's about you and everyone else who wants to practise the principles of Indian Management in their work and wants to be successful.

Chanakya — Who Was He?

Born in 3rd Century B.C. in India, Chanakya was also known as Vishnugupta and Kautilya. Through the centuries, scholars have described Chanakya as a rare mastermind who became an expert in varied and specialised fields like management, economics, politics, law, leadership, governance, warfare, military tactics, accounting systems, and several others. The 6000 sutras have been classified into 15 books, 150 chapters, and 180 topics by Chanakya himself.

He was responsible for bringing down the Nanda dynasty and establishing his able student Chandragupta Maurya on the throne as the Emperor. Hence, he is called a 'Kingmaker'. He is also credited with masterminding the defeat of Alexander in India who was on his march to conquer the world.

As a political thinker, he was the first to visualise the concept of a 'nation' for the first time in human history. During his time, India was split into various kingdoms. He brought them all together under one central governance, thus creating a nation called 'Aryavartha', which later became India. He documented his lifelong work in his book *Kautilya's Arthashastra* and *Chanakya Niti*.

For ages, rulers across the world have referred to the *Arthashastra* for building a nation on sound economics, based on spiritual values.

Arthashastra when literally translated means 'scripture of wealth' but it contains knowledge about every subject under the sun. It's the knowledge of wealth and a wealth of knowledge.

Acknowledgements

When I started on my journey to learn and teach Chanakya's ideas I was not sure about how it would work. It was just an idea, a dream. I took my first step and then thousands of well-wishers joined me and encouraged me along. The number of people who are responsible for making this book a reality is endless. I must acknowledge some of these wonderful people who gave me strength right from the start.

CHINMAYA MISSION I am a 'product' of the spiritual organisation Chinmaya Mission (*www.chinmayamission.com*). I met my Gurudev Swami Chinmayananda (1916-1993) when I was a child. He is my spiritual and management guru. Gurudev said, "A single ideal can transform a listless soul into a towering leader among men." This statement has been the guiding principle of my life.

Today, Swami Tejomayananda, the global head of Chinmaya Mission, continues to give me the same support. He chose the beautiful name of my first company — Atma Darshan (vision of the self).

Among hundreds of Acharyas (teachers) of the mission, some with whom I am closely associated require mention — Swami Sacchidananda, Swami Sadananda, Swami Ishwarananda, Swami Swaroopananda, Swami Mitrananda, have encouraged me to spread the work of Chanakya.

Swami Advayanandaji — the Acharya in-charge of Chinmaya International Foundation (CIF) accepted me as a student of CIF where I learnt the complete 6000 sutras of Arthashastra and this has been the turning point in my life.

DR. GANGADHARAN NAIR, former Dean of Adi-Shankara Sanskrit University, Kalady, Kerala, my teacher and my guru of *Arthashastra*. His wife, Dr. Uma Devi Nair, herself a Sanskrit scholar, was like a mother to me while I was studying the *Arthashastra*.

VENKAT IYER, my friend since childhood and later my partner in the company Atma Darshan. Without his support, I couldn't have spent time learning about Chanakya's work. He also runs a successful venture called Wealth Tree Partners (*www.wealthtree.in*).

MUULRAJ CHHEDA AND SPM GROUP, came as a godsend. Muulraj, is the Director of Swati Energy and Projects Private Ltd, part of the SPM group of companies. SPM stands for Strength, Progress with Maturity, and is also the initials of the three Founder brothers — Shantilal, Pravin, and Mavji Chheda. They supported my research and promotion of Chanakya's works.

Today, I am the Director of SPM Foundation (*www.spmfoundation.in*) the education wing of SPM Group (*www.spmgroup.co.in*) the vision of which is to bring back ancient Indian knowledge and apply it to our modern day problems. The other directors of the SPM Group — Rajen Chheda, Kinnjal Chheda, Niket Shah, Guruvinder — and their spouses have supported me in my search of knowledge. Each day, when we sit for lunch together, I call it my 'classroom' where words of wisdom from senior members have always given me insights into the intricacies of human nature.

MTHR GLOBAL, is More Than HR Global (*www.mthrglobal.*

com). The core team — Rajesh Kamath, Vipul Agarwal, Ashish Gakrey, Rajesh Gupta, and Preeti Malhotra —were the first to christen me 'Corporate Chanakya'. I dedicate the title of this book to them.

MUMBAI UNIVERSITY's Dr. Shubhada Joshi, Head of Department of Philosophy, and her team, give my work on Chanakya the academic outlook it required. SPM Foundation partnered with the Mumbai University for offering joint programmes on 'Chanakya's Management Ideas and Indian Philosophy'.

WORLDSPACE SATELLITE RADIO's Karthik Vaidyanathan, Harish Puppala, Seetal Iyer came up with a wonderful idea for a show called 'Ask Chanakya' on Moksha, a channel on Worldspace. I hosted at least a hundred shows.

Also, I am grateful to my other 'media friends' — Dinesh Narayan, Meenal Bhaghel, and William Charles D'Souza for their support.

Gautam Sachdev promoter of (*www.indiayogi.com*) introduced my first online e-course based on *Arthashastra*. My course now has students from over 25 different countries. I am glad that I can use technology to take Chanakya's message to the world.

Several **MANAGEMENT GURUS** supported my thirst for knowledge. I would like to thank Dr. Subhash Sharma, Dr. M.B. Athreya, Debra and William Miller, Sudhir Seth, and Dr. Anil Naik.

I am grateful to the **POLICE FORCE** — Sandeep Karnik, (IPS) Dhanraj Vanzari, Milind Bharambe (IPS), Satish Menon (Railway Protection Force) — who made me realise that behind the tough looking cop there is a human being who feels just like you and me.

MY FAMLY, especially my parents, C.K.K. Pillai and Sushila Pillai, have my heartfelt gratitude. Coming home late at night, not being sure of a regular income while I developed a business, missing weekends and family time while prioritising professional commitments, my life would never have been smooth without my wife Surekha. Her parents Shekhar and Dhanvati, and her sisters

Sarikha and Chandrika bring joy to my life.

My **FIRST STUDENTS OF *ARTHASHASTRA*** — Mala Thevar, Yogesh Sanghani, Anuraag Gupta, and his sister Seema Gupta, and Anupam Acharya. Their dedication to knowledge has given me the confidence that this good work will continue for many long years after I am gone.

And I must thank Ranjit Shetty, my friend from the Chinmaya Mission, who has decided to dedicate all his time to implementing the ideas of Chanakya.

Notes

• Chanakya, Kautilya, and Vishnugupta are the names of the same person. Either of the names has been used in this book to refer to Chanakya.

• This book does not compare Indian management ideas against western management ideas. In fact it is complementary to western management thoughts. We have taken the best of both worlds.

• In most cases, leaders have been referred to as 'he'. But it also applies to 'she' as well. Since Chanakya has taken the King (male gender) as the leader, the pronoun 'he' is used. Leadership and management skills are not gender-based but they are qualities which can be developed as a 'mind-set'.

• In this book, I have referred to verses or *sutras* from *Kautilya's Arthashastra*. For those who would like to read the verse in the original text, the verse number is written in brackets. The first digit is the book number. The second is the chapter number and the third digit is the verse number. For example,

"He (leader) should constantly hold an inspection of their works, men being inconstant in their minds." (2.9.3)

So, this verse is from *Kautilya's Arthashastra* Book 2, Chapter 9 and Verse 3. The same format has been followed in all chapters.

• The book that readers can refer to for the verses quoted, is the English translation of *Kautilya's Arthashastra* by R.P. Kangle of Mumbai University, published by Motilal Banarasidas. The explanations given are the interpretation of the author. Various other translations and commentaries of *Arthashastra* other than this book are available.

TIP

This book has 175 chapters. The idea is not to read it as a novel but to enjoy its practical benefits. Read a chapter, or a few chapters, a day, apply the teachings in your life, and observe the benefits. It only takes three minutes to read each chapter.

PART I

Leadership

Power

1

Power in the Corporate World

≈୨

The corporate world's search for supremacy over competitors and players from other industries can be summed up in one phrase — the search for power. All CEOs refer to this struggle for power as though it was warfare strategy. No wonder then that the book *The Art of War* by Sun Tzu is often quoted by various CEOs in their strategy plans.

Kautilya's Arthashastra is India's contribution to the subject of warfare strategy. From the 15 books in *Arthashastra*, six books are dedicated to the art of warfare. A deep study of these chapters will give us an insight into the factors that contribute to the making of a powerful organisation.

Kautilya outlines the various factors that lead to true power.

• Intellectual Power

The power of knowledge. The corporate world is today led by knowledge workers. It's the intangible asset of any organisation. Management gurus across the globe are talking about the knowledge revolution that is sweeping through this century. The greatest commodity in the future will be 'knowledge'. No wonder then that the richest man in the world, Bill Gates, is part of the IT industry which is *only* knowledge-oriented. Even the highest paid executives are evaluated on the basis of the knowledge they have gained over the years.

• Man Power

Men are the assets of an organisation. There are two kinds of manpower — internal and external. Internal manpower comprises employees of the organisation, the board of directors and the shareholders. External manpower includes the customers and suppliers. It is because of them that we exist. We have to focus on satisfying our customers. As Peter Drucker, the father of management, points out, "The aim of marketing is to know and understand our customers so well that the product or service fits them and sells itself."

• Financial Power

Financial success ensures the progress of an organisation. A sound balance sheet is the parameter on which employees, shareholders, and stakeholders continue to give their support to the organisation. As Jack Welch, the former Chairman of GE points out, "Nothing succeeds like success." To be financially successful is very essential. It gives a lot of courage to the organisation to not only share its profits, but to also reinvest it in various productive areas like research and development, venture into new projects and ideas, and contribute to social causes.

• Power of Enthusiasm and Morale

This is the most important factor of all. A leader who is

charged with enthusiasm and a high level of morale can create the other three factors. Research has proved that the most productive organisations are the ones that create a very high energy level. The drive to 'get more' is the true sign of progress. Venturing into new markets, scaling high targets, working towards deadlines… all find their roots in enthusiasm. All great organisations have inspired leaders.

2

Power brings Responsibilities

≈੭

All of us remember the ideas and ambitions we would write about in school essays on topics such as, 'If I were the Prime Minister of India'. We would imagine a utopian society and how we would run it. Smartly carving our solutions to fit socio-economic, political and security related problems, we could write about the ideal society endlessly.

But is it easy to get and remain in power? Is it secure and safe to remain at the top?

About the dangers a king has to face, Chanakya says:

"For the king, there is (danger of) revolt in the interior or in the outer regions." (8.2.2)

The greatest danger for a king is revolt. This is what he has to be wary of and protect himself from. What does 'revolt' mean to a business leader? It means dissatisfied employees, shareholders, and stakeholders, who are integral elements of the organisation. There are also external threats from suppliers, customers, and clients.

Even politicians know that if they do not rule the country properly, the dissatisfied voters can overthrow them.

How can you keep everybody happy when you are in command of an organisation?

- Understand The Needs Of The Market

    As a leader, it is important for you to understand the needs of the people in the organisation, as well as in the market and the industry. As long as you are fulfilling their needs, they will be loyal. But while carrying out a 'Needs Analysis' you should also be able to differentiate between need and greed.

- Remember Old Clients While Making New Ones

    Business is not a one-time deal, but a collection of deals over a period of time which makes the business successful. Hence, understanding the requirements of people around you is a continuous process. You should always be on the move. Keep meeting your old clients regularly even when you are in the process of expanding your client base.

- Solve The Problem Immediately

    To curb any revolt, early action is must. Similarly, it is necessary to curb the dissatisfaction of the employees and clients, the moment any issue crops up. When you sense any threat in terms of market or labour unrest, pay attention to the problem and resolve it as soon as possible.

    A good leader knows that only committed employees run an organisation. They also are aware of the fact that only satisfied customers bring good business.

3

The Art of Punishment

≈୭

The CEO, or the leader, of any organisation has a tough role to play. In order to reach the target set by the board of directors he has to tactfully get the work done by his team. Dealing with the employees is not an easy task. He has to consider their problems, understand where they are stuck, and solve their problems immediately so that work does not suffer.

At the same time, he has to be a disciplinarian. He should be very flexible with the employees, but he should not lose focus of the goals and priorities of the organisation — the reason for which he has been appointed.

At times, he has to even use a rod (punishments) to discipline his employees. How much punishment can be given, when it can be given, and why — is an art in itself. This art is perfected by Kautilya in the *Arthashastra*. This is one of the reasons why *Kautilya's Arthashastra* is also called *Dandaniti* — the art, or the strategy, of punishments.

Are punishments required at all? Can an organisation or leader do without it? Punishments are carried out if one steps out of the framework that are laid down in any society or organisation. This is because stepping beyond the framework is harmful for every one. But, what if this framework has not been laid down?

"If the rod is not used at all, the stronger swallows the weak in the absence of the wielder of the rod." (1.4.13-14)

The leader or the CEO is the final authority in the matter of punishments. If he is not disciplining his team from time to time, there is always the possibility of him being seen as a poor leader. More importantly, in his absence, the law of the jungle will take over and disturb the setup and structure of the organisation. The 'bully' in the team will start overpowering the weak as he would not be afraid of the boss, or the actions that will be taken when he returns.

However, the CEO should not just punish employees for the sake of showing off his power and position.

"The king severe with rod (punishment) becomes a terror. A king with a mild rod is despised. The king just with the rod is honoured." (1.4.8-10)

He will become like Hitler if he is too severe and unfair. At the same time, if he is too soft, people will take him for granted. The leader who knows the right level of punishments, carried out in the right manner and at the right time is always respected. He is honoured by one and all. Such a disciplined leader is highly productive.

4

Staying at the Top

It is easy to get to the top, but it's very difficult to stay there. Once you are in the leader's position, the whole dynamics of the game changes. The priority now is to get everything right and maintain your position.

Kautilya was aware of this truth and hence, guides leaders about how to avoid one's downfall, as well as that of the organisation.

He points out:

"Control over the senses, which are motivated by training in the sciences, should be secured by giving up lust (Kaam), anger (Krodha), greed (Lobha), pride (Mana), arrogance (Madh), and overexcitement (Harsha)." (1.6.1)

A leader is carefully watched by each person around him. Apart from the external observers, like the media and intelligence agencies, his team members are also watching every move he makes. All his subordinates look to him as their role model. Such a leader should be every careful in his private as well as public life.

As Stephen Covey says in *Seven Habits of Highly Effective People,* "Private victory leads to public victory."

A leader's success is maintained by controlling the senses. For this, Kautilya pointed out the following six negative behaviours that need to be avoided:

- Lust (*Kaam*)

Lust is the deep hunger for any object which results from over-attachment. People at the top level are carried away by the lust for power. That is why it is recommended that they should identify the new leaders and train them. Leaders should slowly evolve into mentors guiding the new generation to take over.

- Anger *(Krodha)*

Maintaining a cool head is very essential. A short-tempered leader is neither appreciated nor liked by his team members. Such a person is very unpredictable. One should be able to control oneself in all circumstances, mostly importantly in public.

- Greed *(Lobha)*

Gandhiji had rightly said, "There is enough in this world for every person's need but not enough for one man's greed." Satisfaction does not mean complacency. One should be dynamic, yet not get carried away by purely material gains. He should also focus on the social and spiritual contributions he can make.

- Pride *(Mana)*

Even when at the top, a leader should be able to initiate more and more projects. However, a feeling that "I am the doer" should not be entertained. He should understand that, after all, his success is because of teamwork. A highly egoistic leader is sure to lose his team members in the long run.

- Arrogance *(Madh)*

An arrogant leader will always take the credit for every success, while he blames failures on others. Instead, he should share the results of success with everyone. His motto should be, "It is 'we' who have succeeded not 'I'."

- Over-Excitement *(Harsha)*

A leader should never get over-excited. Expressing extreme happiness or sadness has to be avoided. When the whole world is

9

on fire, it is only the one with a balanced mind who can find a solution.

5

Create your Own Law

∽Ɔ

In Sanskrit, 'law' is called *dharma* — meaning that 'which holds'. For example, what holds people onto planet earth? It's the 'law' of gravity. If this law was missing, then everything would be out of control.

Similarly, in every home, organisation, and country, a certain law exists that holds everyone together. In most cases, like in our homes, these laws are unwritten, yet practised. While in organisations and countries, they are documented as rules, regulations, constitutions, mission statements, etc.

Here, Chanakya suggests that if the laws have not been set down in an organisation, the king (the leader) should take the lead in setting them down:

"When all laws are perishing, the king here is the promulgator of laws, by virtue of his guarding the right conduct of the world consisting of the four varnas and four asramas." (3.1.38)

So, if you are the leader of an organisation, you have to take the lead in laying down the rules too. But, before you do that, keep the following in mind:

• A Law For What?

The first question one needs to answer is, why do I require this new law. Until this is clear, we will just be creating something mechanically without any clarity of what we are achieving.

In some companies where I conducted a 'goal-setting'

workshop, I found that rule-setting was merely a formality, not something that 'they' really wanted from the depth of their hearts. Compliance issues and government rules are signed about the setting up of new companies without even knowing why these rules have to be followed. As a leader, it is important to have a clear 'vision' for the organisation.

• Benefit For All

Let's go back to the fundamental principle of *Kautilya's Arthashastra*. What is the duty of a king? "To consider the benefit of ALL his subjects and act accordingly." Therefore, when you are making a policy, take into consideration the benefit of all and not just that of your own. The welfare of all is the foundation on which we build a country, society, and any institute. If this is missing, then the subjects will be disappointed and, in the long run, will either replace their leader, or search for a new one.

• Fit For All

In the verse quoted here, Chanakya says that the king should make laws according to the four varnas and asramas. This means that we are looking at various, deeper aspects of subjects and workers — such as age, talents and natural qualities — while taking various decisions. For example, an economically poor person stealing a piece of bread may be let off unpunished, as for him the act of stealing was a matter of survival, rather than greed. This human perspective is important.

6

Control your Office

≈◗

The office is an integral part of any organisation. Even in the past, it was compared to a fort — or *Durga* in Sanskrit. This was from where the king would rule. Keeping control of the fort was essential for the king.

This is no different from today's corporate world in which a CEO needs to keep control of his office.

Chanakya says:

"He should cause the treasury and the army to be collected in one place, in the fortified city, in charge of trustworthy men." (5.6.7)

This is the prerequisite of a good office.

But, let's look at each aspect of this 'office' in detail:

• Treasury

The head office is from where the treasury is monitored. Only if the treasury is well-managed, can other things be directly controlled. If the treasury becomes weak, problems crop up. Hence, it is essential to keep it full and protected.

• Army

An army includes all the employees — right from the CEO, to the peon and the driver. All of them form a complete unit. There's just no division in teamwork. Each person is equally important. When there is a war, or competition, each person should be able to deliver his best. Thus, a good office has good, talented, skilled, and capable men.

• Trustworthy Men

In every organisation there are key people who run the show. They are the lieutenants to the commander. Such people should be trustworthy and should also be able to trust others. These key positions — decision makers — are the backbone of any business unit.

So, in the above verse, the strategy according to Chanakya is that the the leader should control the treasury (finance) and the army (people) from one place — the fortified city (the office/ plant) — and let trustworthy men (managers) run the show.

On achieving such a setup, the CEO or Director will have

another advantage. The fact that all these components are under one roof makes them easy to monitor on a regular and continuous basis.

Now, since we are already talking in modern terms, let's understand one more thing — the office should also be well-equipped with the latest weapons. This means that the installed systems should be constantly upgraded, the technology should be the latest and the computers and other effective tools should be properly used.

But then, all these technical additions do not guarantee success. Just like in war, the success of any group or organisation depends on multiple factors. But in the end, success depends on the 'brains' of the leader.

As the former Indian Army Chief, General J.J. Singh puts it, "Finally, it is the man behind the machine, who makes you win the war."

7

Leaders have the Edge

The leader, the Chief Executive, or the Chairman of a company, has the most important role to play in taking the organisation ahead. Being at the helm, he has to guide the organisation and help it achieve higher goals and set new trends.

He has to ensure that the organisation is growing stronger, not only financially, but also in terms of the foundation and the value systems set in place by the founders and visionaries. The organisation has to grow from being just a profit-making machine to a contributor to society, an enterprise for the well-being of one and all. To achieve this, the leader has to lead by example.

How does Kautilya define an ideal leader?

"If the king is energetic, his subjects will be equally energetic. If he is slack (and lazy in performing his duties) the subjects will also be lazy, thereby, eating into his wealth. Besides, a lazy king will easily fall into the hands of the enemies. Hence the king should himself always be energetic." (1.19.1-5)

Being energetic is the most important quality of a leader. A self-motivated person, he has to raise the enthusiasm of his team members too. Only if he is energetic, will his employees be energetic too. If he is lazy, the employees will also lose interest in their work and very soon, a sense of complacency will take over the whole organisation.

All great leaders who have set a trend in the corporate world were highly motivated and inspired. The best example from recent times is J.R.D. Tata.

A visionary leader, JRD, as he was popularly known, was largely responsible for making Tata a trusted household name in the country. He not only guided the Group towards higher achievements and helped it grow, but he was also an important part of the process.

JRD was the first Indian to get a pilot license in his early twenties. He was responsible for setting up Tata Airlines — the first commercial airline in the country which is today Air India. The airline was the best in terms of punctuality, service, and efficiency. In Air India's golden jubilee year, JRD flew a solo flight between Mumbai and Karachi. He was always a leader who led from the front.

What if the leader is not every alert and active? With the high level of competition around it is easy for his enemies to overtake him. A slack leader will also cause the company he heads to become financially weak. Fundamentally, a leader should be physically active, mentally alert, and intellectually convinced.

Once Swami Chinmayananda, a great leader, who continued working even when he was very old, was asked, "Why do you go around doing so much work? Why can't you take rest?" Quick came the reply, "If I rest, I rust."

8

Maintain Secrets

A leader holds a very responsible position in any team and hence, also in an organisation. He has to be very careful when he speaks and of the words he uses. If he utters a single, wrong statement it can destroy his organisation.

One of the important factors that a leader should know is how to maintain secrecy.

Kautilya warns the leaders,

"To as many persons the lord of men (the leader) communicates a secret; to so many does he become subservient, being helpless by that act (of his)." *(1.8.9)*

There are various projects and issues that the leader should never talk about openly. Until and unless it is the right time, he should not make these secrets publicly known.

Every project that is executed in an organisation goes through three stages — the conceptualisation stage, preparation stage, and delivery stage. At each stage, there are key 'secrets' that only a leader should know. He should never let others know these secrets.

What if he keeps telling others his secrets? Let's look at two possible repercussions:

• He Has To Bend Down

A leader has to bow down to all the people who know his secrets. If more people know his secret, the leader will have to bend down that much more. A leader should always be in control of the situation, and not allow others to control him. If he has said the 'right' thing to the 'wrong' person, he has to be at the mercy of that person who may not keep that secret. Such a person may not only blackmail him, but also leak the information to competitors and enemies.

- He Becomes Helpless

Having shared his secret with others, the leader becomes totally helpless. Instead of thinking about how to carry out his plans, he will worry about how to protect himself from attacks.

A golden rule in business is, think twice before you speak. Even a tailor is advised during his apprenticeship, "Measure twice, but cut once."

Kautilya's enemies were afraid of him because they could never understand what his next move would be. He always had multiple plans ready. If one plan failed, he was ready to attack with the next, totally surprising his enemies.

Chandrashekhar Azad, the Indian freedom fighter, was another person who was always a mystery to every one. He would never allow anyone to know where he would go to next. Not only the British, but even his own team members, like Bhagat Singh, would not know his hideouts. He believed that he was 'Azad' — the ever free person. If he wanted to be truly free, he had to keep himself unknown to others.

Therefore to be free — keep your mouth shut!

9

The Seven Pillars of Business

A strong foundation is the key to any successful business. Your vision, your commitment, your purpose, all these form the all-important pillars of an organisation, the most essential part of any building.

In his ground-breaking *Arthashastra*, Chanakya lists the seven pillars of an organisation.

"The king, the minister, the country, the fortified city, the treasury, the army, and the ally are the constituent elements of the state." (6.1.1)

Let us now take a closer look at each of them:

- The King (The Leader)

All great organisations have great leaders. The leader is the visionary, the captain, the man who guides the organisation. In today's corporate world we call him the Chairman, Director, CEO, etc. Without him the organisation will lose direction.

- The Minister (The Manager)

The manager is the person who runs the show — the second-in-command in the organisation. He is also the person you can depend upon in the absence of the leader. He is the man who is always in action. An extraordinary leader and an efficient manager together bring into existence a remarkable organisation.

- The Country (The Market/Client/Customer)

No business can exist without its market capitalisation, its clients, and customers. The market is the area of your operation. The place from where you get your revenue and cash flow. You dominate this territory and would like to maintain your monopoly over this segment.

- The Fortified City (Head Office)

You need a control tower, a place where all plans and strategies are made. It's from here that your central administrative work is carried out. It's the nucleus and the center of any organisation.

- The Treasury

Finance is an extremely important resource. It is the backbone of any business. A strong and well-managed treasury is at the heart of any organisation. Your treasury is also your financial hub.

- The Army (The Team)

  When we go to war, we need a well-equipped and trained army. The army consists of your team members. Those who are ready to fight for the organisation. The salesmen, the accountant, the driver, the peon — all of them add to your team.

- The Ally (Friend/Consultant)

  In life you should have a friend who is just like you. Being in the same boat, he can identify with you and stay close if you need help. He is the one you can depend upon when problems arise. After all, a friend in need is a friend indeed.

Look at these seven pillars. Only when these are built into firm and strong sections can the organisation shoulder any responsibility and face all challenges. And while building them, do not forget to imbibe that vital ingredient called 'Values', speaking about which, the author of the book *Build to Last*, Jim Collins, has said, "Values are the roots from which an organisation continuously gets its supply as well as grounding — build on them!"

10

Three Aspects of Success

≈9

Who doesn't want to be successful? Forget the intensely competitive corporate world, today even children studying in schools and colleges crave success. So do folks in their own homes and societies.

Workshops and seminars are conducted on how to be successful. Entire organisations spend huge amounts of time, money, efforts and energy in becoming successful, and making their teams successful.

But what exactly is success? And how does one really become successful?

Well, success is a relative term.

The parameters for success change from person to person. However, when we study the lives of successful people, we come across some core values and actions on the basis of which they succeeded. Learning these core principles will help each one of us succeed too.

Even our own Indian hero Chanakya had delved deep into the subject of success.

He said:

"Success is threefold – that attainable by the power of counsel is success by counsel, that attainable by the power of might is success by might, that attainable by the power of energy is success by energy." (6.2.34)

Let us look at each of these separately:

• Success By Counsel

Every person needs an advisor. The better the advisor, the better one is guaranteed to succeed. In fact, one should aim at having the best advisor all the time.

Chanakya, in another chapter of the *Arthashastra*, had said, "Any undertaking that one takes should be with the help of advisors who are specialists in that particular field."

If you ever have a choice between a mediocre teacher who charges less, and the best teacher who charges more, choose the second option.

You would, thus, minimise possible risks and also reach your goal faster.

• Success By Might

Muscle power is strength too. But might also means what benefits one derives due to one's position, or the chair that one holds.

A mighty person can take many quick decisions based on his authority and his execution capacity. Apart from holding such a high and responsible position, another way for becoming mighty is to associate with someone mightier than oneself.

• Success By Energy

This is called will-power. A person can achieve success on the basis of the enthusiasm and the passion he shows.

A highly inspired and energetic person is very contagious. Anyone who meets such a person also feels charged up. Great leaders had this power. They were those who could mesmerise masses with their oratory skills. Such energetic people can also make the most lethargic person productive.

This is akin to what Napoleon once said, "It requires a stroke of genius to awaken the mass consciousness. In any given century, only a few can do that!"

11

Power Management

A scholar had once defined Artha as 'power' in the ancient Indian texts. This gives us a different, yet an apt meaning of the word *Arthashastra*. Thus, Chanakya's *Arthashastra* can be taken to be a book on 'power management'.

Such a book would be extremely useful for a person who holds a top leadership position and who should know which card to play at what time. Chanakya was a master in the field of power management and, throughout the *Arthashastra*, various options are given to the king.

In the seventh book of Kautilya's *Arthashastra*, Chanakya defines six situations and six different measures for handling them.

He says:

"These are really six measures, because of differences in the situations."
(7.1.5)

Why does Chanakya promote alternative moves to deal with different situations?

The reason is simple — no two situations are the same and a unique 'strategy' must be applied for every situation.

If we understand just this, we will understand how to manage power. Let us take up some of the most common situations a corporate leader could come across:

• People Situations

As soon as a person attains power, the first thing he has to handle is the people working under him. In fact, the success of his career depends on not only how he will handle his own people, but also those who work for the competitor.

Each person is different, and it is important to understand how human beings act and react in different situations.

There have to be alternative strategies for every person and group. A study of human psychology will prove helpful in this very important task.

• Knowledge Situations

As the world moves towards a 'knowledge economy', the competitive advantage will be held by people who are ahead of others in the information sphere.

Today, companies are investing in research and development globally. You can either predict the future, or create it.

The future belongs to those who can not only think differently, but also create products and services that people will seek in the future.

• Material Situations

Here, material means money, machines, and even technology.

21

The way business is done is changing drastically.

So what plans does a CEO have in place to handle rising costs, rapid technological changes and financial instability? A leader has to analyse each issue and create alternative and back-up plans.

There are always two routes — either let the situation come up first and then change accordingly. Or study and understand the situation even before it comes up to be ready with the right alternatives. In other words, being prepared for the inevitable change.

So, get into the habit of creating alternatives in every given situation. This is how one can manage power efficiently.

12

Bosses are Answerable

All salaried people have, at some time or the other, given into wishful thinking — 'If I were the boss, I would have done this...' The general feeling is 'Had I been the boss myself, I wouldn't have to report to anyone. I would be the ultimate — no questions asked!'

This is simply not true. Every boss has a boss above him. Every leader is answerable to someone else. Well, who is this someone? If I am the chairman of a company, then there should be no one above me, right?... Wrong!

Chanakya had said:

"Only, the king, behaving in this manner (following the rules given to a king), obtains heaven, otherwise hell." (3.7.38)

According to him, every king is given a code of conduct (written or unwritten) and the duties and responsibilities that have to be borne.

If the king follows this code, he becomes a good leader and need not fear hell. Basically, this refers to moral control. But who exactly bosses over our boss? Is he responsible to anyone? The answer is yes.

• To Stakeholders

Usually, it is understood that the person at the top is answerable to only those from whom he has taken money, like financiers and lenders. However, this is only partly true.

Modern management theories have evolved from being responsible not only to shareholders, but also to all 'stakeholders'. A stakeholder is not just one who controls shares, but also others like the employees, suppliers, and all partners in the business.

• To Government And Society

Every company is governed by certain laws. It can be the law of that particular nation, defined by the government through corporate and company laws. It can also be laws of industry associations that establish common standards which all members are supposed to follow.

But, most importantly, each company is also responsible to the society of which it is a part. Today, Corporate Social Responsibility (CSR) is a driving force in many businesses. Every company has to be socially responsible.

• To Self

Well, one may not follow others. One may not even like government policies, the industry standards or existing social rules. But the one person that you cannot run away from is 'yourself'.

You are still answerable to your parents and your teachers. More than anyone else, a leader is supposed to be reporting to himself. So ask yourself these questions and take stock — "Have I done my duty well?", "Am I following what I am supposed to do?"

After all, at the end of the journey, you and only you are left alone. And, as all religions and scriptures say, "Finally, it is between you and God."

13

Applying *Arthashastra* in Business

∼୬

Whenever I offer training sessions on *Arthashastra*, the first question I hear people ask is, 'Chanakya and *Arthashastra* existed in the past, but what does *Arthashastra* have for me?', 'What are the benefits I will get by studying this?'

Well, as Chanakya himself said about the benefits:

"This science (of Arthashastra) brings into being and preserves spiritual good, material well-being and pleasures, and destroys spiritual evil, material loss, and hatred." (15.1.72)

• Protecting And Expanding

If one has achieved something, it has to be protected. If you earn a few lakh rupees, it has to be saved and protected. You should not let anyone steal it. At the same time, we should think of how to expand these lakhs into crores. This is where 'investment planning' comes in.

Similarly, studying the science of *Arthashastra* helps one accomplish as well as preserve spiritual good, i.e. the goodwill and ethics that one has cultivated, along with material benefits (financial and lifestyle).

In addition to achieving, *Arthashastra* even gives us strategies on how to expand and improve on these.

• Destroy The Wrong

Only protecting and expanding the good is not enough. One has to destroy the evils also. This is a two-way street. *Arthashastra* destroys spiritual evils like laziness and lethargy.

It also helps in destroying material and monetary losses with the help of good planning and implementation. Best of all, *Arthashastra* helps in destroying even hatred. You see, hatred is a negative emotion that is self-destructive.

As the saying goes, "A man who is angry destroys himself first." Even in a war, one should respect the enemy and not fight because of hatred alone.

* Expansion Of Knowledge

By studying the *Arthashastra*, one increases knowledge and experience. How, you ask? Chanakya's treatise may be theoretical, but studying it automatically translates into practical application in daily business life — the best way to gain wisdom.

But its most important lesson is that one learns by teaching, i.e. sharing wisdom with others. So do not forget to do this as it will help and support your peers just as it did for you.

14

Inherited Company

∽౨

There are first-generation entrepreneurs, and then there are the 'businessmen' who have inherited their parents' creations. What matters in both these cases is how the person manages the business.

While most of the work has already been done by the parents, Chanakya still had advice for children born with a silver spoon in their mouth:

"In the case of inherited territory, he should cover up the father's defects and display his virtues." (13.5.23)

All establishments, inevitably, have their negative points along with various positive aspects. Chanakya advised those benefiting from an inheritance to look at the positives of the business and change the negative points with their own positives.

- Identify The Positive Aspects

As far as inheriting a business is concerned, we find that the previous generation did the worst work — starting up, sales, capturing the market, etc. They went through some real hard times when there was no capital, uneven cash flows, when even such basic necessities like infrastructure and other comforts were not available.

At the end of the tunnel, they saw the light, and eventually started making money. But, more than the money, it's their original experience that makes the most valuable inheritance. This knowledge will prevent people from repeating mistakes.

- Neutralise The Negatives

Earlier generations lived in different times. The market conditions were different then. Economic conditions were different. Even government policies and structures were unique then.

Everything, right from technology to travel, and even communications, was slow. However, we should study these situations as next-generation leaders striving to fill top positions. Only then we will be able to see the business from a new perspective.

- Be a 'Positive' Change

After getting the power to make decisions, move your company slowly to the next level without giving any serious jerks to the existing system. In other words, install the required new systems and processes, but do so while maintaining relations with your previous clients, and employees while growing your business too.

Basically, you should come across as a new-age leader who is also grounded in the traditional values on the basis of which your seniors built the business.

And when you finally commence operations in your new capacity, remember this — "What I have, is my father's gift to me. What I do with what I have, is my gift to my father."

15

A Public Awakening

History has time and again proved that people and their opinions cannot be suppressed for too long. The oppressed people may not openly revolt against their rulers, but only till a particular point. After that the frustrations will build up and a revolution will break out.

Even in the modern day democracy we find that public awakening is dangerous for the government. Once the public loses its patience and takes to the streets, even the most powerful rulers will crumble. After such demonstrations, several tainted ministers have had to resign.

Chanakya had clearly pointed out how to avoid such a situation:

"In the happiness of the subjects, lies the benefit of the king, and in what is beneficial for the subjects, is his own benefit." (1.19.34)

If a leader is not able to keep his people happy, and instead thinks of his own benefit all the time, he will definitely end up being dethroned. Just look at the way the top politicians have had to bow to the popular opinion of the citizens and give up their positions.

It's a 'perform or get out' environment. Gone are those days when people could take things for granted. One has to be at their best and deliver results. If not, the people's wrath will be awakened.

- **For Politicians**

According to me, politicians need to get one thing straight — from now onwards, you cannot continue to operate in a loose manner. You need to learn better management skills.

And to all those politicians who are reading this, in case you still don't know about political management, learn from the *Arthashastra* about how a state must be governed.

- **For Citizens**

Be an enlightened citizen of the nation. If you have a problem and you can see that things are not getting done, make sure you do your bit. The fuel for any revolution is continuity. Follow up till you get results. Make use of the power of democracy and of your precious vote.

There are two things every citizen has — duties and rights. Fulfill your duties as a citizen first, then demand your rights and, more importantly, ensure that you get them.

- **For Youngsters**

I was in Pune and Nashik, conducting leadership training programmes. To my pleasant surprise, I found more and more youngsters attending these sessions. One of them asked me, "Sir, why not start a new political party?"

I replied, "Good idea my boy, but convert your idea into action." It was not a mini-sermon. Rather, it was my belief in the potential of a youngster to channelise his energy positively.

As Swami Chinmayananda said, "The youth are not useless — they are used less. The youth are not careless — they are cared for less."

Qualities of a Leader

16

Total Alertness

∽๑

The Central Vigilance Commission of India has declared that various government organisations and Public Sector Units must observe a 'Vigilance Awareness Week', every year. This week coincides with the birthday of Sardar Vallabhai Patel — the Iron Man of India.

Sardar Patel had a very important role to play in the building of modern India by overpowering the princely states and uniting them successfully under a central governance. This had been done by Kautilya in the 3rd Century B.C as well. He had united the various kingdoms under a central governance led by his student, Chandragupta Maurya.

Kautilya was the first person to have systematically given

'vigilance' a very important dimension in a state organisation's management structure.

The Oxford English Dictionary defines *vigilance* as, 'keeping careful watch for possible danger or difficulties'. From a corporate standpoint it gives us two perspectives from which to view the same subject. One must protect oneself from external threats as well as from internal mismanagement.

At the external level, an organisation has to be alert about such dangers as competition and takeovers. For this, it needs to have a very powerful intelligence network. In most companies today, market intelligence is a very important activity. There is special technology for getting valuable information.

However, being vigilant 'internally' is more important and very difficult. The problems within an organisation are much more difficult to manage, as we deal with our own people. An army commander may be able to fight and withdraw the enemy troops at the borders, but may not be able to handle a revolt by his own young son.

Important information about accounts, customer databases, and management strategies are very critical to an organisation. These need to be protected from being leaked.

How does one do this? *Arthashastra* guides us about handling these problems. Kautilya says,

"He (leader) should constantly hold an inspection of their works, men being inconstant in their minds." (2.9.3)

It is the primary responsibility of the leader to continuously check all important data as well as the activities in one's organisation. The leader has to be very alert about the movements of his employees.

He has to give the employees targets and deadlines to keep them focused on their work. Secondly, he has to continuously monitor their work.

Why is it so? Because the human mind is very fickle. Employees have a tendency to slip into laziness if deadlines and targets are not set. There is also a possibility of one getting influenced by corruption if the fear of punishments is not strong enough.

As Akio Morita, the founder of Sony Corporation said, "I am dealing not just with my employees but with the *minds* of my employees." Therefore it is important to understand the employees at the level of their minds, to prevent corruption as well as to ensure productivity from each of them.

Thus, vigilance is 'total alertness' on both fronts — internal and external.

17

Advice to Entrepreneurs

Starting your own business and running it is no easy task, especially when you have no previous business experience. But that is how entrepreneurs are born. They start with an 'idea' and a dream to succeed. Most of them do not know the path they need to take, but the confidence they have takes them through all the ups and downs till the final destination where their idea is finally converted to financial success.

The most critical period in an entrepreneur's life is when he has already experimented with his idea a little, and struggled the most, but money has not yet filled his pockets. Now, he sits down and wonders what went wrong. All his near and dear ones are taking the opportunity to prove that he was wrong to have taken this path.

Hold on, says Kautilya, do not get into a mental trap at this stage:

"Wealth will slip away from the foolish person, who continuously consults the stars; for wealth is the star of wealth; what will the stars do? Capable men will certainly secure wealth at least after a hundred trials." (9.4.26)

Your final *big* financial leap in business may be just round the corner. But getting frustrated after such a long period of failure, it is natural for one to wonder if fate and luck has really been on one's side.

That is when we turn to fortune tellers, astrologers, and palm readers. You start to consult the zodiac, the sun, and star signs. But remember, your constant efforts are the only way out. Do not consult the stars. What will those innocent looking balls of burning gas, which appear as glowing points in the night sky, do? Wealth alone is the star of wealth. You have already put in a lot of efforts, time and money into the 'idea' you truly believe in. Just continue doing this.

Capable men will finally convert the whole idea into an 'amazing balance sheet'. The final leap may come in any manner — a big order, a turnaround client or a big investor. But one needs to keep undergoing these trials — a hundred times.

This is the path followed by Bill Gates. Who thought he would become the richest man in the world in such a short time? This is the route taken by Narayan Murthy, or any other victorious entrepreneur, before they touched the success called 'wealth'.

Madam C.J. Walker, creator of a popular line of African-American hair care products and America's first black female millionaire said, "I had to make my own living and my own opportunity! But I made it! Don't sit down and wait for the opportunities to come. Get up and make them!"

18

Multiple Tasking

≈୨

The success stories of great organisations start with the dream and will of one single person. Once the dream starts becoming a reality the little stream becomes a massive flow.

As the organisation grows, work also grows and more and more people join in. From a one-man army, it becomes a full-fledged army with its own dedicated lieutenants and soldiers. Finally, all the teamwork helps the organisation reach the summit of success.

Hence the key to success for a leader lies in effective delegation.

Why is delegation required? Kautilya says,

"Because of the simultaneity of undertakings, their manifoldness and their having to be carried out in many different places, he (leader) should cause them to be carried by ministers, unperceived (by him), so that there is no loss of place and time." (1.9.8)

Delegation is required due to the following reasons:

• Work Happens Simultaneously

In an office, various departments work simultaneously at the same time. Each of them is specialised in a particular area. Sales, accounts, marketing, HR, R&D, and many other processes go on continuously.

• Work Happens At Various Places

These multiple tasks are carried out not only by various people, but at various places. Some of the work happens inside the office, while many others tasks are carried out outside the office. In a big organisation, work happens in various branches, and also in various countries.

Decision-making should be decentralised and given to various managers. The benefit is the saving of time and place. As they say, "In business — time is money." Delayed decisions lead to loss of time and opportunities.

A few tips for effective delegation are:

- Selection

  Good decision makers should be made managers and department heads. An effective manager does not get stuck while taking decisions. He may make mistakes but after correcting himself, the work goes on at the right speed.

- Setting Up The MIS

  The head of the organisation needs to set up a good reporting system. In corporate language this is technically called the Management Information System (MIS). Many software tools are available for this, or an organisation can create one for its own use.

- Training

  The decision makers have to be trained to report all activities by using the MIS. This training ensures that everyone in the organisation can effectively use the reports. With the internet revolution, one can access these reports anytime and anywhere. It is also cost effective.

- Control

  The leader can keep track of the various developments and the shortcomings in each area on a daily basis. He can control the whole organisation with the help of a well-planned system.

  Peter Drucker, the father of modern management once said, "Initially delegation is not easy. It gives a feeling of insecurity. However, one realises that it leads to freedom."

19

Open-Door Policy

The leader of an organisation has to be very alert and vigilant. He has to be aware that he might receive wrong as well as manipulated information from various sources. He has to be most wary about his own 'middle-men'.

Middle-men for the senior management would be the junior managers and those who deal with the lower staff on a daily basis. These middle-men report to the seniors all that happens at the lower end.

However, being totally dependent on the middle-men can be dangerous. If one gets too dependent they can change reports, encourage corruption, and also leak important data.

Therefore, Kautilya advises an open-door policy right not only for those at the junior-most level in the organisation, but also those in the senior management.

"He (leader) should allow unrestricted entrance to those wishing to see him in connection with their affairs." (1.19.26)

Any person who wants to communicate with the seniors about their affairs should be encouraged as it helps bridge the gap of communication.

Unrestricted entrance means middle-men cannot restrict, or control whom you meet and share information with. In various organisations; one has to pass through secretaries to get the work done. Secretaries are required to leverage your work. But the moment one becomes dependent on them and they start taking decisions concerning 'people' for you — watch out!

A few benefits of an open-door policy are:

• Direct Information

Many officials, especially from sales and marketing directly deal in the market as well as with the outside world. They are the eyes and ears of the company. The senior management can keep a finger on the pulse of the market and competition by communicating with them directly.

• Avoiding External Threats

When employees are assured that they are 'listened' to, they will not feel the need for external supporting agencies such as labour unions and political parties. Most of the external threats to organisations stem from 'internal' insecurities felt by their own people.

* Faster Decisions

Important decisions do not get delayed when problems are fixed as they occur. Decisions taken at the right time avoid confusion and misunderstandings.

* Emotional Bonding

Subordinates begin to feel a deep emotional bond with the leader who makes it clear, usually by example, that he will be by their side in tight situations as well as when there are joys to share. The presence of such a leader builds a sense of security and faith in the team.

One of the basic human requirements is to have someone who can 'listen' to your problems. Effective leaders understand this psychological need. Therefore, successful leaders always communicate to their team, "Okay, I will be there whenever you have a problem."

20

Ethics in Business

≈?

There is a huge misunderstanding about Kautilya, also known as Chanakya. People generally believe that he was a shrewd and cunning person. That's just a myth.

While training his students in the management of a kingdom, he emphasised the importance of having a sound philosophy in order to become a good leader. Ethics and morals were top priority for him. In the very first chapter of *Arthashastra*, titled *The*

Topic of Training, he outlines the importance of a spiritual foundation.

Therefore he says in the *Arthashastra*,

"Philosophy is ever thought of as the lamp of all sciences, as the means of all actions (and) as the support of all laws (and duties)." (1.3.12)

The root of any business lies in its core value system — its philosophy. This was also pointed out by the father of modern management, Peter Drucker. He said, "Profits are by-products of business, not its very goal." In the above verse, Kautilya brings out the finer points of the importance of ethics in business.

• Guidance

The value system created by the founders of an organisation always becomes the guiding force for the organisation. Even during calamities and difficult times, these values become a lighthouse, providing direction. Like a lamp, it guides us through darkness.

• Decision In Action

How to proceed, even when drawing up a plan, is always the big question in business. Either one can take the easy route where success is quick and, yet, short-lived. Or, one can take the road less travelled where success is delayed, but is everlasting. Only an ethical person can easily handle these tough decisions.

• Adhering To Law

A good businessman is not just law-fearing, but also law-abiding. He follows the law of the land as set up by the constitution. At the same time, he also understands the higher universal law of nature. His thoughts become very powerful. Such a businessman contributes to society and brings great economic prosperity to all persons connected with him.

• Doing One's Duty

For such a person, duty is a priority over rights. He understands the importance of giving more than what is taken and producing more than what is consumed. His work and duty is not influenced by pressure, but is born out of joy and service.

Once, an Indian company which believes in ethically conducting business was asked by a politician for a small bribe to clear a huge project. The sum was small compared to the size of the project. However, the philosophy of the organisation did not support bribing. The result? They dropped the project. The gain — it still continues to be the most trusted company in the country.

Kautilya would have called such a highly spiritual leader and businessman 'Rajarishi'.

21

Start Now

~～೨

The Indian economy is currently functioning at its best. Foreign investors are pouring money into India. Job opportunities have opened up. Starting a new business is no more limited to the rich class.

In today's corporate scenario, there are multiple opportunities for anything you want to do. Yet, we find people sad, stressed, and worrying about the future.

Kautilya suggests,

"Having found a matter for consideration, he should not allow time to pass." (1.15.45)

Do not wait for any 'golden' moment to start what you always wanted to do. The best time is not the *muhurat* the pundit suggests, nor even the 'right dates' that come up in a calendar. It is right here and now!

After having considered a matter, start work on it immediately.

Remember always that the journey of a thousand miles begins with the first step.

While starting any project or assignment, a few tips from the *Arthashastra* would be helpful:

• Self-Effort

There is always a problem when it comes to starting anything. Maximum energy is required at this point. You need to challenge yourself to shake off your laziness. Do not procrastinate. A job started is a job half-done. Just start!

• Prepare A Plan

Starting does not mean just getting excited. You need to have a direction for how you are going to reach your goal. Take a piece of paper (or open a new file in your computer) and jot down the points. Give shape to your thoughts. Prepare a blueprint of what you want to do. Begin with the end in the mind.

• Consult An Expert

If you are not sure if your ideas are practical, ask an expert for advice. Take the help of someone who can guide you to make your dream a reality. It very important not to go to people who say, "It will not work." In the initial stages, such negative energy must be avoided. You will kill the child even before it is born. Your consultant should display a positive attitude and should be successful in his own field.

• Work Out Your Plan

All said and done, you have to work out your plan. Do not spend too much time trying to make your plan perfect. Plans are theories that can be successful only if they are given the wings of practical application. Once you start, the help, and required resources will come your way. You will learn a lot as you keep putting more and more efforts into your dream. You can keep improving your plan along the way.

However, it is important to complete what you have started to achieve. It is not important how many new things you have started. What is important is how many of them you have completed. Complete what you have started. And, then, start again after you have completed!

22

Knowledge for a Leader

≈೨

Swami Vivekananda had once predicted that India would rise on the basis of its knowledge. True enough, knowledge has become the greatest asset of our country. As more and more projects are being outsourced to India, we have to focus more on the strength of our knowledge.

Whether it is KPO (Knowledge Process Outsourcing) or R&D (Research and Development), India has great advantages over its counterparts.

However, this knowledge cannot be restricted to just hiring intelligent managers from the top B-schools. The leader or the Chief Executive Officer (CEO) of the organisation himself should be a knowledge seeker.

Kautilya advises,

"Just as an elephant, blinded by intoxication and mounted by an intoxicated driver, crushes whatever it finds (on the way), so the king, not possessed of the eye of science, and (hence) blind, has risen to destroy the citizens and the country people." (1.14.7)

The CEO of an organisation holds a position of power and is the commander and the decision-maker. However, if he gets intoxicated by his power and position alone, it will definitely not be long before he loses his chair, and may even destroy the organisation itself.

This is where we need Kautilya's advice about focusing on knowledge. A leader should focus on making his organisation a knowledge organisation. But, first he has to start with himself.

The *Arthashastra* offers some advice on this:

- Gather More Information

A CEO should have his information-gathering systems in place. He should get any information he requires at the speed of thought. He can use technology to gather information quickly. But always remember — information does not mean knowledge.

- Study The Information Acquired

It's very important for a leader to study and analyse the information he gathers. He should spend at least an hour per day reading books and learning something new. He must meet experts from different fields, at least once a week.

- Experiment

What the CEO has learnt should be applied in the organisation. Try a new method, invest in a new technology. Take measures. Calculate risks. A part of the budget should be allocated for research and development.

- Train

Next, he should train his own staff and team members about the new knowledge. No leader should be afraid that he will lose his position and authority if his subordinates become better than him. That only shows insecurity and ego. Learn to delegate and trust your subordinates.

Today, we require more and more knowledge-oriented CEOs. As Rabindranath Tagore wrote in the *Gitanjali*,

"Where the mind is without fear and the head is held high,

... where knowledge is free...,

....Into that heaven of freedom my father let my country awake..."

23

Decision-Making

≈୨

To become a leader you should *think* like a leader. Sit down and observe what qualities good leaders have. And then start practising them. One of the important qualities of a leader is good decision-making.

Chanakya says,

"He should hear (at once) every urgent matter, (and) not put it off. An (affair) postponed becomes difficult to settle or even impossible to settle." (1.19.30)

There is a lot of work that cannot move forward without the leader's final sanction. Thus, Chanakya suggests that if a subordinate comes to him with an urgent matter, he should listen to him at once. If he postpones a decision, the pressure gets piled up and then the situation gets out of control.

A leader has to be a fast thinker, a fast decision maker, and a fast implementer. He has no time to waste. Analysing is good, but moving ahead is more important.

How can one become a good decision maker?

- Do Not Be Afraid To Make Mistakes

In an interview, a CEO was asked the secret of his success. "It is by taking timely decisions," he replied. "How do you know if your decisions are correct?" he was asked. The CEO snapped, "By taking wrong decisions."

Every child has to fall before he learns to walk and run. Do not be afraid of making mistakes. But what is important is to learn from these mistakes. At the same time, do not keep making mistakes eternally.

• Set Up A Time Frame

While you are planning and thinking about an assignment or project, give yourself enough time to think about various possibilities. But there must be a time-frame by when you will have to take some action. Only then will theory meet practice.

• Encourage Others To Take Decisions

Work gets stuck when it is dependent on a single person. Learn to delegate smaller decisions to your subordinates. Your organisation should become a self-managed mechanism. Train others and make them responsible. You should only be dealing with the important matters at the top.

The game should be bigger than the player. The organisation should be bigger than the employees. The purpose should be bigger than you and me.

24

The Spiritual Side

The head, or the boss, in any organisation has an additional responsibility these days — being an important contributor to society.

After all, modern businessmen provide employment, create revenue for the government, and are socially-contributing entities. If the head of an organisation works with the right attitude, the king (leader) not only experiences its benefits in this world, but also in the next world.

Chanakya says,

"Carrying out his own duty, the king, who protects the subjects according to law, leads to heaven; one who does not protect or who inflicts an unjust punishment, his condition would be the reverse of this." (3.1.41)

Now, please remember that Chanakya did not literally mean 'heaven' or 'hell'. Both are states of mind. When you are happy and satisfied, that mental state is heaven. While, stress, tension, uncertainty is hell for any human being.

So how can we transform our work place into heaven?

- Carry Out Your Own Work Well

The prime duty of a leader is to protect and take care of his subordinates. Instead of thinking about 'my gain', he has to think about 'our gain'. This is an attitude that no business school can teach. It comes with a sense of responsibility and commitment. Great leaders have strong shoulders and a big heart. As you practise this, you will realise the depth of the age-old adage — work is worship.

- Respect The Laws Of The Land

In the course of your duty, abide by the law. The law of the government and its policies have to be carried out properly. No illegal work can give any person satisfaction. It only makes you insecure. Remember, many organisations have ruined themselves by getting into illegitimate work. Pay your taxes, and be a company that also plays a role in social development. Also, understand the laws of nature. Enjoy life but never over-indulge in anything. A sense of balance needs to be maintained.

- Be Just

As a leader, you are a law unto yourself. If there is a conflict, your subjects (employees) will come to you seeking justice. At such times, your integrity can help resolve issues in the just and right manner. Chanakya said in the *Arthashastra*, "A king who is severe in punishment becomes a terror. The one who is too mild is taken for granted. However, the king just with rod is honoured and respected."

This art has to be developed.

In the olden days, the king was considered to be God. In fact, there is an Indian saying — *Raja Pratyaksha Devata,* meaning a good king is God himself. Hence, all business leaders can create heaven, or hell, in their companies all by themselves!

25

An Eye for Detail

~9

Understanding the growth of any business entity is a beautiful study in itself. Most corporates usually started with one man's dream. Then, a like-minded person decided to become a partner, and provide support.

The next step involves a group of people joining the vision and, finally, the firm gradually expands into a large corporation.

When a company keeps growing in terms of sales and revenues, the number of transactions it does also grows. Now, that's something that the leaders and founders may not have the time to keep an eye on, as they have to focus on the larger picture.

At such times, we require supervisors from different departments to look into the details of all transactions and activities.

The advice given by Chanakya to the commodity stores supervisor gives us an insight into how important micromanagement is for large corporations.

Chanakya says,

"He should personally observe the amount of increase or decrease in the grains when pounded, ground, or fried, and when they are moistened, dried, or cooked." (2.15.24)

So for every small task, there should be systems in place to monitor and supervise it. And, since these systems alone cannot be helpful, the department in-charge should also 'personally' observe the details.

Now how can the Head of a Department (HoD) do this? Here are some tips:

- Create A System

Firstly, create a system to regularly record transactions. The first step in creating a system is to list down what is necessary to know. Do not try to make a perfect system on the first day itself. Take one step at a time. Your system could be just a notebook, or a simple Excel file. As your requirement grows, you can invest in better software programs, or even an ERP program. But first, start from where you are.

- Daily Monitoring

Creating systems isn't enough. You have to also control the systems. No system is complete without a person monitoring it from the top. Therefore, the next step is to arrange for daily and regular supervision. In the initial stages, you will have to give more of your time to understand whether your methods work. Then, as you get a grip over the methods, monitor them from time to time.

- Conduct Surprise Checks

This is the best way to keep people on their toes, and has remained so for years. This method is not only for companies, but also for schools, homes, and all those places where you have to lead a group of people.

Always remember that you should never leave the game till you win it completely. So, define your parameters for achieving victory. The best way to be in the game is to keep raising the bar every time you reach it.

26

Being Energetic

ॐ๑

Before you start on any task, the first requirement is you should be optimistic. If you mix this attitude with the right amount of dynamism and energy, you're set for success.

Why else do you think all the 'motivational speakers' are so well-received globally? It's their workshops that transform a person who is feeling low into an enthusiastic contributor to society.

Chanakya outlines similar qualities in the *Arthashastra* as well:

"Bravery, resentment, quickness, and dexterity — these are the qualities of energy." (6.1.5)

In one line, Chanakya tells us how, in addition to enthusiasm, energy is important too. He has gone into great detail to make us understand what energy means in the above verse.

These points are also leadership qualities that should be developed by any person who aspires to be successful not only in the corporate world, but also in life:

• Bravery

Literally speaking, bravery means 'facing something frightening, or unpleasant in a courageous way'. A brave person is ready to face life's unpleasant events with a strong heart and tremendous will-power to carry on.

He is ready to fight and win challenges enroute his goal. This is also the most important quality of a Kshatriya — the warrior described by all Indian scriptures as well as the *Arthashastra*.

• Resentment

Resentment means anger, hatred, and yes, even bitterness.

Now this may sound negative. However, understand that being a little unsatisfied with our current status can push us towards achieving the bigger things in life.

So, be angry with yourself for thinking small. Hate the low mental and vulgar values that we entertain. Be bitter about the comfort zone we get into.

Push yourself to the next level. This 'positive' negativity adds spice to life.

* Quickness

Time is an important ingredient for success. A person who aspires to be successful needs to be quick and fast while taking decisions.

When a leader was once asked how to develop the skill of quick decision-making, he answered, "Be around people who are not afraid of making mistakes." So, move on in life as quickly as you can.

* Dexterity

Here, it means the ability to adapt and continue. It's best defined by the famous saying — When the going gets tough, the tough gets going. We all start on a journey, but only a few adapt to the changes and overcome problems.

Swami Chinmayananda said, "There are three kinds of people — first, those who do not start work because of the fear of obstacles. Second, those who start, but stop when they face obstacles. And, third, those who work inspite of obstacles and overcome it!"

Now, you decide which kind of person you are.

27

Improve what you Inherit

≈୬

An entrepreneur was once told by his mentor, "When you start a business, you will have to struggle a lot. The success you finally get will be enjoyed by your children, not you!"

Every generation benefits from the struggle of its predecessors. However, thanks to the human mindset, we always tend to look for what was built incorrectly, rather than what was built right.

This is where Chanakya comes in:

"In the case of inherited territory, he should cover up the father's defects and display his virtues." (13.5.23)

Even Swami Chinmayananda had similar advice — every generation has got two responsibilities: to correct the mistakes of the past, and to create something for the future. But how do we apply this in our careers and family lives?

• Look At The Positive Side

When we inherit something, like a car, we immediately think, 'Oh, what an old car. I wish I could get a new one.' But train your mind to look at the positive side. "So what? It's better than having no car."

Similarly, when you get an old computer to use as soon as you join a new office, be thankful that at least there is a computer for you to start working on. These steps will tune your mind to look at the bright side of what our elders provided, without any effort.

• Understand What Is Missing

With their limited vision or resources, our elders gave you whatever you now have. Surely they must have wanted to give us something better, but their conditions must have been different. They missed the luxury that our generation can access with ease.

If, by chance, our seniors did a mistake due to short-sightedness, try to understand the reason. Instead of condemning them, 'empathise'. Put yourself in their shoes.

Even in your company, you should study what is missing instead of blaming the management. Try to 'understand' the reason behind present circumstances and then try to improve the situation.

• Create Something New

Be the change you are seeking. If something is not available, create it yourself. Put in some efforts and do the needful yourself.

If you find that systems in your firm are not updated, study the technology yourself and apply them. Basically, you should convert your tendency to blame others, into a tendency to be thankful.

A young boy once told his father, "Your generation doesn't understand anything. You did not have mobiles, computers or the Internet."

The dad replied, "Yes, it's true. So our generation created the mobiles and computers for you to use. Now let's see what you will create for your children!"

28

Setting an Example

❧

Being an expert in political science and even statesmanship, Chanakya emphasised the importance of discipline in a governance system. However, he also knew that the ministers and bureaucrats would have to follow the rules themselves.

Therefore, Chanakya had said:

"The administrator and the magistrates should first keep in check the heads of departments and their subordinates." *(Book 2 & 3)*

Let us see why this is necessary and how it applies to our offices and organisations:

• Discipline Starts From The Top

If you are the boss, you are the sole rule-maker. But then you should be the first follower of any rule. One cannot create policies and just insist that others follow it. Discipline starts with you. When you become self-disciplined, others tend to fall in line automatically.

• Leaders Are Followed

A leader's position is very critical and sensitive. Your subordinates do not just do what you say — they follow your every action! You are always observed minutely by people around you.

If the leader is highly enthusiastic, the subordinates will also be enthusiastic. If the leader is lazy and slack while performing his duties, so will his subordinates.

The same thought had been brought out in the *Gita* when Lord Krishna said, "Whatever standard the leader sets, others follow." So set high standards, and make sure you follow them yourself.

• An 'Unforgivable' Mistake

Always remember one thing — small mistakes are not small if committed by people at the top. That's because such actions impact the entire organisation.

Chanakya went to the extent of saying that if a common man commits a mistake, the punishment is one unit (like one year). But if the same mistake is committed by the leader, the punishment is four units.

This is because if the leader makes a mistake, it is akin to the entire group making a mistake. Hence, a leader should think twice before taking any decision.

A leader with a vision is the prime requirement of any good company, organization, or society. The next step is to transform his visions into reality.

This happens through hard work and the ability to inspire others to pitch in and dedicate themselves to the eventual goal. And all this is possible with self-discipline.

29

Work through Problems

Swami Chinmayanandaji had once said, "In any work, problems are unavoidable. It only ends when we are in the grave."

Thus, life can be said to be a continuing series of problems. But, you should remember that people become successful when they learn to handle these problems, instead of allowing it to overpower them.

It helps to know how problems are created. Chanakya offers some important information:

"Internal (hindrance) is hindrance by the chiefs, external is the hindrance caused by enemies or forest-tribes." (8.4.48)

All of us must have experienced such 'hindrances', especially when we want to start something new. We should understand how these hindrances begin and how to avoid them. Chanakya said there are three kinds of problem creators:

• The Chief

Quite often, the boss himself becomes a problem-creator. One experience of this is enough to make us hate our bosses, especially when they reject what we think is a good idea. But don't be discouraged.

Enquire about the reason for the rejection and see if they are justified. If you are the boss yourself, then become an ideal leader by developing leadership qualities and understanding your workers.

• The Enemies

The enemies are our competitors. When we have a plan to execute, they almost immediately have a counter plan. This is apparent in the advertising industry which goes to great extremes to prove that one's own client has a product that is much better than that of the competitor.

But remember to respect your enemies as well. Even when at war, your actions should not be driven out of hatred or anger. This is because the best warfare strategies are devised by those who remain calm.

• The Forest-Tribes

A firm normally encounters opposition from local groups when entering a new territory or market (forest-tribes in the time of kings). Always remember that this particular opposition arises even if you are doing something for the greater good. The insecurities of the people who already live there will create problems for you. So, the first step is to win their confidence and ensure that it's a win-win situation for all.

30

Respect and Protect Women

≋

Bhishma, the warrior hero in *Mahabharata*, had once advised Yudhishtira — "A society that does not respect women will perish." It was this lack of respect towards the fairer sex that caused the two great wars in our Hindu epics — the 18-day battle in *Mahabharata* after Draupadi was humiliated in front of all the men and in *Ramayana*, the war in Lanka when Sita was kidnapped by Ravana.

Even Chanakya refers to the priority that must be given to women during a crisis:

"From a dangerous situation he should move away with effort, after removing the womenfolk." (7.5.46)

In other words, even when one has to run away from disaster, or a dangerous situation, he should do so only after rescuing the women. One may ask, where is the need for such lessons when there's so much gender equality?

Well, ask your own female friends and relatives whether they feel equal in society, and if any harassment aimed at their gender has ended completely.

Base your own decision on their answer. And if you believe a change in mindsets is a must, read on to see how we can respect and protect women in our daily lives:

• In Our Work Places

Today, the number of working women has increased in all areas. Be it in the field of business, education, or civil services.

All of us have to interact with women. Remember that men and women think differently. It's a basic psychological difference.

When men and women work on a common project together, they bring in different perspectives. Now if you are the boss, see to it that there is a gender mix in every project. If you are an employee, inculcate not only respect towards women, but also a receptiveness to their point of view.

• In Our Homes

While a house is incomplete without a woman, the women in our family also have talents that need to be given wings.

Identify their talents and give them freedom to explore their potential, regardless of whether it's your daughter, wife, sister, or mother.

• As A Nation

Even though women have proved themselves in every field, we still have a long way to go. Just look at the number of female infanticides we still hear about, the low percentage of girl literacy, the prevailing evil practice of dowry, etc.

No social work can be complete till women are empowered. We refer to our country as 'Mother India', but hardly allow her to have any daughters.

Swami Vivekananda had rightly said — "Educate the girl child and the nation will awaken."

31

Don't Forget Your People

Freedom fighters and soldiers fight to protect their countries. But when we finally become victorious, it's our duty and responsibility to free the Prisoners of War (PoW) who have been captured by the opponents.

Chanakya had said the same thing:

"When grown in strength, he should bring about the liberation of the hostage." (7.17.32)

In the case of the Indian freedom struggle too, several members of the Indian National Army (INA) were held in prisons in the Andaman Islands. When we achieved freedom, they were rescued and also given awards and other national benefits.

It was the right thing to do, especially after the country had become victorious in her struggle for freedom. Now, how do we practise this in our organisations?

• Know Each Person And Group

The head of each organisation should be aware of those who fight for him. Keep track of the people who have been with you through difficult times. Spend some time with them and their families too.

You will be surprised to know of the sacrifices your employees and their families have to make sometimes. In the case of a large company, or nation, the leader should keep track of groups of people who have fought for him or her — communities, local committees, religious leaders, etc.

• Freedom Is A Responsibility

After achieving the target, leaders should not think only about enjoying the resultant power. Instead, they must immediately meet with the people who fought for them. In companies too, when we have gone through a difficult phase — like a financial setback or a recession period — meet with those who have stayed committed and loyal.

So when you rise in life, understand that this freedom brings new responsibilities. Also, if someone is held hostage (or down with problems), immediately release them (solve their problems).

• Stories To Tell

Finally, never forget the most important task — making sure that the sacrifices made by your followers do not go unnoticed. Bring the heroes into the limelight and let them tell their stories. Document their struggle and let others get inspired.

These heroes are the pillars of any institution and should be rewarded. If any generation has to look back and it does not find any inspiring martyrs, they will take your hard-earned success for granted.

So, ensure people know what it took to reach where you are

now. And the best way to do this is to recognise those who helped you become victorious.

32

Passing the Mantle

~~♥~~

I was once conducting a session for management students who were specialising in family-managed businesses. The students were second-or third-generation businessmen who hoped the course would help them take the businesses, started by their parents and grandparents, to the next level.

This reminded me of a verse from the *Arthashastra*:

"The kingdom continues in the succession of his sons and grandsons, free from dangers caused by men." (5.1.56)

One of the basic aims of Chanakya was that every kingdom should continue from one generation to the other, free from any danger. For this, he stressed the importance of good planning and training to make the inheritance of a kingdom fool-proof.

One extremely huge advantage of such an inheritance system is that the king gets to pass on the mantle on his own terms — choosing to make his exit, before being booted out!

Now, how do modern businessmen apply this thought to their own legacies?

• Train Your Children

The first and foremost task for any organisation's founder is to acquaint the next-generation with the firm's systems. There is simply no alternative to training your children in your own business. But, at times, it does not work well because the father may have very high expectations from his own children in business. And children may take a lot of their parents' good

57

advice for granted and ignore them.

One solution adopted by many communities is to impart the requisite training to the children under the watchful eye of the founder's brother. Thus, the child gets trained while the family retains control over the business.

• Emphasis On Education

It's a fact that each generation has more opportunities for better education than the previous generation. So, seniors should capitalise on this and make it a point to educate their children by enrolling them in the best courses available. Education, even in business, should never be treated as an expense, but an investment which will have very high returns in the future.

• Exit In Time

Once you know your children are ready to take charge, make sure you exit from the business in time. Leave before you are kicked out by someone else! Now, this may not be easy for a person who has started the business from scratch. But there is no alternative to it. The best way is to give up power slowly and smoothly.

Remember, even the most iconic businessmen like Bill Gates and Narayan Murthy exited before time — although their exit did not mean 'retirement'. All they did was change their role.

And you can do that too — changing your role from running the business to mentoring it. You will be more valued and respected then.

Competition

33

Handling Competition

≈

The days of monopoly are over. Competition is 'in'. No longer can Public Sector Units (PSU) relax, nor can traders and middlemen think that their huge profit margins will continue for long. With the world becoming a global village and technology reaching the remotest corners of each country, competition has opened up like never before.

Therefore, as new projects are started, bigger brands are launched and new markets are explored, a strategy to meet the challenges from the existing players, or future competitors, is needed. Hence, a carefully researched, planned, and calculated move is necessary in every field today. Kautilya helps us plan a strategy to handle competition.

"After ascertaining the relative strength or weakness of powers, place, time, revolts in rear, losses, expenses, gains and troubles, of himself and of the enemy, the conqueror should march ahead." (9.1.1)

Let us look at each of the aspects of the strategy, which must be evaluated before making our move in the market. Both, from one's own view point, as also from that of the competitors.

• Power

Power comes in various forms — knowledge, money, and also enthusiasm. Some of the most successful projects are the ones that are deeply studied and well-researched. Remember, the foundations are important for the structure to last.

• Place

The right place is very important. The place should be conducive for the product to sell. The right market should be found even for carrying out the experimental process. One cannot launch an agriculture based product in an urban shopping mall. The right place for it is in the rural segment.

• Time

Every product has a season — just hit it at the right time! The cold drink companies will have their marketing strategy built around the summer season. While the paint industry will advertise just before the festival season.

• Revolts In The Rear

Unknown to us there are possibilities of being stabbed in the back! Our distributors, retailers in the market as well as our very own staff can be targeted by our competitors to capture our market share.

• Loss

One should be aware of the losses that can happen in the process — not just financial, but also loss in time, material, and efforts.

- Expenses

    A budget should be worked out before the whole project is started. In most cases, the budgets shoot up as the process commences. A buffer for extra and miscellaneous expenses should be considered.

- Gains (Profits)

    How much is one finally going to get at the end of the whole exercise? A few projects could be one-time projects with immediate gains, while others could reap their fruits in the long-term.

- Troubles

    A lot of troubles will crop up. The best way to avoid or reduce troubles is to be aware of the maximum possible problems that can arise and have a backup plan to solve them all.

    Only after taking all these into account, should one march ahead to conquer the market.

34

Army and Treasury

First things first, let us make leadership simple. Why go beating around the bush, reading a lot of books and doing various courses to understand what management and leadership really is?

Management is all about focusing on how to take your organisation forward. Even in the good old days when the concept of a company or a corporation did not exist, we had efficient managers — the ministers and the kings.

What message did Chanakya have for the leaders?

"The king brings under his sway his own party as well as the party of the enemies, by the (use of the) treasury and the army." (1.4.2)

As Chanakya pointed out, in order to control and lead an organisation, one needs to focus on just two things — treasury and army.

- Treasury Or Finance

The success of any county, state, organisation or association, is chiefly dependent on its economic and financial condition. If the balance sheet is good, cash flow is regular, profits are shown year after year and reserves and investments are in proper places, you will then be termed a financially stable firm.

So, the leader needs to make his company financially strong. Everything else will fall into place.

- Army Or Manpower

The second most important aspect is the army, or the kind of men the company possesses. The more efficient, skilled and professional your employees are, the better is your productivity. The leader also needs to keep his employees from leaving his organisation.

Even in a non-profit or a voluntary organisation, including spiritual organisations, success is dependent on the number of volunteers and workers it can attract and keep.

Even though the above two seem to be different, they are interconnected. A financially strong company can easily attract better employees. And, only an efficient team can make a firm profitable.

So how does the leader achieve this? According to Chanakya. the following are some time-tested tips:

➤ Recruit the right people

➤ Invest in people — train them and pay them well

➤ Focus on developing quality in your products and services

➤ Keep continuous track of your finance

> Ensure that you make your company profitable

In the above sutra, Chanakya says that if these tips are followed, the King (leader) will automatically bring under his control not only his own group, but also that of his competitors.

Al Ries, a marketing strategist, wrote a book called *Focus* which includes various case studies and the analysis of successful companies.

He says, "Focus — the future of your company depends on it." Nothing beats this statement when we consider the treasury and the army.

35

Protection from Enemies

≈⊃

Starting a business, any business, is tantamount to declaring a war on the existing players. As your business grows, either of two things can happen. You may just remain another small player in the market, with steady growth. Or, the business will grow exponentially.

In the latter case, you become so big that the size you attain is one you would have never imagined in your wildest of dreams. Bill Gates, when he started Microsoft, never thought that he would become the richest man in the world and stay so for many years. Neither did Lakshmi Mittal think he would be listed among the top five in the list of richest businessmen.

Why does this happen? At a certain point, business grows at a rapid and irresistible speed — unimaginable and unthinkable.

However, like adversity, prosperity also brings its own problems — enemies.

Kautilya's Arthashastra offers advice on tackling one's enemies:

"The enemies should not come to know of his secret; he should, however, find out the weakness of the enemy. He should conceal, as a tortoise does his limbs, any limb of his own that may have become exposed." (1.15.60)

In any given industry, there are a maximum of five players at the top. Once you are amongst them, you have to be extremely alert and careful. From this point onwards, all new activities should be carried out secretively with complete detailed planning.

- Keep Your USP A Secret

Your competitive strength is all about a formula of your own making. Your USP should stay just that — your Unique Selling Point. Something special in your service or product that only you have. Keep developing those strengths. Even if the enemy knows about it, they should not be able to replicate it.

- Find The Enemy's Weakness

Be alert, very alert. You should be aware of the various moves your enemies are planning and/or making. Have a market intelligence team. You need not be the first to attack at all. But if attacked, you should know how to strike back. This would be easier if you are aware of your competitor's weaknesses.

- Protect Yourself

Learn to protect yourself. Just as a tortoise withdraws his limbs into its shell when threatened, you too should withdraw if someone comes to know your secrets. If the vital areas of your business are exposed, try to protect them.

But this does not mean you should always fight with your enemies. If required, one should also help one's enemies for the overall improvement of the industry. After all, competitors in the same sector form associations all the time.

Remember, the golden statement by Don Vito Corleone in the book *The Godfather* — "Never hate your enemies; it will cloud your judgment!"

36

Right Opportunity

Is success in business a matter of 'luck' or 'self-effort'? It's a question often asked, especially by those who are struggling to build their companies.

There's this saying about success being 99 percent hard work and 1 percent luck. But, remember, you will never get lucky till you put in the best of your efforts. Only then will opportunity knock on your door.

Chanakya says that when such an opportunity finally comes, potentially bringing the success you aim for, you should be alert enough to grab it.

"Time comes but once to a man waiting for an opportunity; that time is difficult for that man to get again when he wants to do his work." (5.6.31)

You might have heard the adage that talks of opportunity not knocking twice, but here's another interesting one for you — "When opportunity knocks, either we are out or sleeping in!"

Still, we have to understand that it is not only about the opportunity itself but about the 'right' opportunity at that. So how does one recognise this so-called 'right opportunity'?

Here are some steps to follow, according to Chanakya:

• Nothing But The Best

Usually, people who are learning the tricks of the trade feel every opportunity is the best opportunity. This is simply not true. You will have to struggle for a few years and put in your best efforts before you develop the 'knack' to differentiate between right and wrong, good and bad, and even the simply 'better' from the very 'best'.

- Learn To Say 'No'

It's quite a temptation to say 'yes' to every event that 'seems' to be an opportunity. When an opportunity comes — stay calm. Think it through — is it a profitable venture? Plan a strategy and then decide to capitalise on it.

- Jump Into It

Once you have thought it through, jump into the field right away. Do not think too much after this stage. Just go out and perform your best. You never know if such a chance will come again.

People only see the success a businessman has achieved; they never recognise the hardships that he has gone through to become successful.

Ray Kroc, the founder of Mc Donald's, was once asked in an interview, "Sir, you were very lucky! You became an overnight success." Ray remarked, "Yes, that is true. But you do not know how long the night was...!"

After putting in your time, energy, and efforts to build your dreams, do not quit when success is just right round the corner.

As Swami Vivekananda proclaimed, "Awake, arise! Stop not till thy goal is reached."

And for all this, remember, it's all a matter of timing.

37

Win-Win Policy

~♥

India is a very attractive destination for investors. The Foreign Direct Investment (FDI) coming into our country is growing day by day.

One of the ways through which we get FDI is through Joint Ventures (JV). This is where a foreign company ties up with an Indian company for business opportunities. Both of them come together to gain from the partnership.

Chanakya has a word of advice for these situations too.

He says, that for such JVs to succeed, there should be a win-win situation between the two partners:

"In a work that can be achieved with the help of an associate, he should resort to a dual policy." (7.1.18)

A dual policy means a win-win policy.

We require funds for new business opportunities. Thus, an investor becomes an associate.

Any one of the new, private insurance companies could make a perfect illustration for understanding JVs. These young insurance firms are pure joint ventures between an Indian company and a foreign one. Both came together in the field of insurance when the government opened up the sector for FDI.

The Indian partner in the JV has the experience of Indian customers. While the foreign investor is an expert in insurance. As India is a new market for the latter, it gains knowledge of the market by tying up with its Indian counterpart. The domestic firm benefits from venturing into another business field, riding high on the years of experience of its foreign backer. This is a win-win situation.

Here are some tips on how to get into successful joint ventures:

• Be Sure Of Your Expertise

Your organisation should be good in one area at least. You should be an expert in that field with a proven track record.

• Make A Business Plan

Make a business plan in order to approach a possible investor for expanding your current business. Make sure that, when you approach him, it is a win-win situation. You get the investment and he gets your expertise.

• Find Like-Minded Partners

Just getting an investor does not solve your problem. Both need to trust each other and should be able to see some value addition made possible due to the partnership.

Both partners should support each other while running the business.

"Finally it's not whether we lost money in our JV that counts," said an investor, "rather, it's if we bet on the right person."

Be that right person!

38

The Winning Weapon

≈∽

Think before *they* think — that is the rule of warfare. Even in the game of chess, every move made by the opponent is studied, analysed, and carefully thought about before you make any move. If you are the first to make a move, first make a plan.

And it is this plan that needs to be protected from prying eyes. It goes without saying that businessmen should be alert. Very alert. While taking up new projects or while executing the projects in hand, a high level of secrecy should be maintained. Thus, secrecy is the most important weapon.

Chanakya advises,

"Others should not know about any work sought to be done by him. Only those who undertake it should know (about it) when it is begun, or even when it is actually completed." (1.15.17)

What you are doing, what you are thinking, and all your moves should not be known to others. One needs to create an aura of secrecy around himself to move ahead, way ahead of the others.

In professional and powerful organisations like the Police, the Army, the Central Bureau of Investigation, till the last moment, no one knows what the next order will be. Only a handful of people work on a strictly-enforced 'need-to-know' basis and it is these people who, in turn, co-ordinate with others who are supposed to execute subsequent orders.

The call is made at the last moment and is quite sudden for those being asked to go into action. Till the moment the order is given, the seniors keep the plan entirely to themselves.

A golden rule to remember in business is that there is a big difference between planning and execution. Make your plan perfect, then execute without delay. There is no point in planning when the time has come to execute.

But let's face it — keeping secrets is tough. However, there are some tips that can help:

• Postpone

Whenever you feel like disclosing a plan to someone, remember to postpone this act.

Give yourself at least a day. Once you have done that, your self-control will improve. By practising this, you will slowly but surely get the confidence to keep things to yourself. Also, learn to observe silence for at least half an hour every day, this will enable your thoughts to rule over your talkative nature.

• Execute And Then Speak

Do not speak and then execute. It should be the other way round. The biggest danger in revealing your plans is that you give the opponent an added advantage to think before you.

• Think Ahead

On achieving success in any endeavour, we feel like talking about it to others. Rather, we feel like bragging! The best way to avoid this is to start new projects immediately. Always keep yourself busy with new plans.

Swami Shivananda, a dynamic saint and the founder of the Divine Life Society, put it best when he said, "The only way to keep yourself productive is by having at least a month's work in front of you."

Follow this advice!

39

Win the War

≈⊃

Whether it's in our personal, or professional, life, we always face competition and hence, enemies too. We do wonder about how much stronger than us the enemy could be. Does this mean that we are going to lose the battle?

No! Chanakya never accepted defeat. However, he was practical. After all, he was an expert strategist while each person around him was playing games with one another all the while.

He believed that one must not mind losing the battle to win the war. Chanakya knew how to win over the enemy in the long run, if not immediately.

He said,

"He should seek shelter with one whose strength is superior to the strength of the enemy." (7.2.6)

The above sutra is a simple, yet excellent, gem of management, and even in real life for that matter. When faced with an enemy who is stronger than you, the best situation is to have an even stronger friend on your side.

Why does Chanakya say this?

* Strength

Former President of India A.P.J. Abdul Kalam, the missile man, once said, "Only strength will respect strength." We should be more powerful than the enemy by acquiring greater strength. If not, like Chanakya said, making friends with a much stronger ally would help counter competition.

* Experience

A stronger ally will have more experience in fighting wars. It can guide you and shelter you, even help you during calamities. When the alliance gives you advice, it is bound to be relevant because it is derived from experience.

* Long-Term Approach

One of the most important things to remember is to keep your ego in check during a battle. Do not think, for even a second, that you can win against an enemy by just sheer power. Think of the long-term, lose your ego and 'surrender' to a person superior to your enemy so that you get the required help. After all, you can defeat the enemy only if you survive through the turmoil in the long run.

Battles may be lost, but the war must be won!

Win with the wisdom your superior alliance gives you, rather than losing with your personal logic.

Remember Amitabh Bachchan's dialogue in the movie *Sarkar*? *"Taakat judne se aati hai tutne se nahi."* He meant exactly what you should remember always — strength lies in making friends, not losing them.

40

Win-Win Situation

∾♀

It was management guru Stephen Covey who first coined the term 'win-win situation'. Now it is a commonly used terminology in the corporate world.

But what does it mean? Can there really be two winners in a game? Well, yes! It is a paradigm shift in management thinking, based on the principle of 'live and let live'.

In fact this policy of avoiding war was written by our own Chanakya:

"In war there are losses, expenses, marches away from home and hindrances." (7.2.2)

When competition sets in, and if it's not tackled carefully, both the parties can end up fighting a brutal war that causes heavy losses of time, energy, and also resources. Huge expenses are encountered when we find one party trying to outdo the other.

Now the real question is, how does one even begin to think about 'win-win' when war is unavoidable. Think about the following points carefully:

• We All Can Share

The biggest prize in the corporate world is the market. But, remember, however hard you try, no single company can win 100 percent market share. That has never happened in the past and will never happen in the future.

So it is important to think about how one can expand the existing market, instead of thinking how much market you can capture. We can all get a bigger share, if the pie itself expands.

- All Of Us Can Teach

It may sound strange, but it really is important that the business leaders should get into the teaching mode. A business leader has a lot of roles to play — teaching being one of the most important. Therefore, with years of experience that have already been earned, the top players should start teaching others.

They need to create an awareness of their own company and industry in potential markets. They should offer guest lectures in business schools, mentor youngsters in their own companies, and also chair sessions in their industry associations.

- Create More Winners

The best way to think 'win-win' is to create more winners like yourself. As some people say, "A leader is the one who can create more leaders." Invest in the 'generation-next'.

Keep looking at various sources from where you can tap potential leaders.

India Inc. today is rapidly changing. As Divya Dayal, the Vice-President (Human Resources) at a Japanese bank, Mizohu, pointed out, "In the next ten years, one of the basic problems we will face as a country is the lack of good leaders."

To tackle this scenario, many Indian corporate giants are now setting up world-class leadership and management training institutes.

This would go a long way in not only helping the industry itself, but also the markets and the entire country. After all, if India wins as a nation, all of us will be winners — the best win-win situation!

41

The Key to Success

While devising a corporate strategy, there are certain associations and relationships that one needs to keep secret from others. And there are some that need to be discussed openly with the public. Learn to differentiate between the two.

For example, the brand ambassador of a company should be openly exhibited/used in order to achieve the desired branding and sales target. But the names of the people being used within the corporate structure — like the key technicians or consultants — should never be publicised.

Therefore, to succeed in any project the key to success is silence.

Chanakya suggests,

"In case of secret associations, those concluded in secret shall succeed." *(3.1.11)*

Every business leader has friends, strategists, associates and market intelligence experts from whom he takes advice and to whom he even gives information. These are his resources for thoughts. Until and unless it is required, he should never make them public. Only after understanding the importance of this, can he succeed in reaching his desired results.

Here are some steps for maintaining secrecy in a project:

• Let The Idea Evolve

Many people get excited when they come up with a 'billion-dollar' idea. They go and tell others about it. They feel they have hit on a goldmine and others will buy this idea. However, it's just a matter of time before someone else (including your competitors) takes the idea away from you and may even profit from it. So please let the idea mature in your heart and mind before you tell others about it. Give yourself time.

• Experiment Quietly

As your ideas take shape, talk to a few people — just a few who can help you make your idea practically viable. Think about all the aspects of a project that must be worked upon to achieve success — such as the research involved, finance required, the people needed, the technical expertise, time to complete the project etc. Then, before you start with the final project, do a pilot project. Thus, you will know the difficulties you are likely to encounter. Remember, a sculptor always makes a six-inch model before the actual 60-foot statue!

• Execute Effectively

You should make your moves very quietly till the time to attack comes. Most importantly, you would keep all plans hidden from your competitors. However, when you do execute the plan, make sure that it is complete and perfect. As the saying goes, "Never give your opponent a second chance; you may not survive the counter attack!"

42

Game Theory

∞

Chanakya's treatise *Arthashastra*, talks about one very important aspect of conducting business — the 'Game Theory'. All management personnel and economists are familiar with this, and use it very often to analyse situations and, especially competition.

Chanakya was a pioneer of the Game Theory. In *Arthashastra*, it is called the 'Mandala Theory' (Circle of Kings). It consists of various multiple permutations and combinations of dealing with the enemy, or the *Shatru*,

In a battle, when face-to-face with the *Shatru*, Chanakya says,

"If near him (enemy), he should strike in his weak point." (7.2.12)

But how does one strategise and make this move against the enemy (competitor) in today's corporate world? Some tips:

• Study The Competition

Before attacking, one should always know everything there is to know about the person or the entity that needs to be countered. Remember, war is 99 percent preparation and 1 percent execution. So, prepare well before you make your move. Accurate information should be gathered about the competitor, his plans, and objectives.

• Practise Well

Never ever go rushing into the market (or your own office, for that matter) seeking a direct conformation with the BIG guys. Gain experience first by practising well in your own region and tasks. The bigger the competitor, the more you need to prepare. In fact, it would pay to seek counsel from an experienced person. His advice can turn things around for you.

• Know The Rules Of The Game

This is the most essential part! The rules of the game are the framework within which you conduct your business, or day-to-day affairs. It would be highly rewarding if you understand them well. Think about it — it's only when you have become well-acquainted with the rules that you can change them.

Just look at how the Indian hockey team was tackled. They had become invincible at the Olympics for years together. Then the competition studied the rules. They understood that the Indians were unbeatable on grass. They changed the rules of the game, and the 'turf' it is played on, literally! Since, then, even on modern-day 'Astroturfs', it continues to be a struggle for Indians.

All said and done, when the time comes to counter your

competitor's moves, do not sit back. Execute. And during execution, do not strategise. The best performers have always defeated their competitors in a single move! It will work for you too.

43

Winning over Friends and Foes

≈∘୨

Most of us must make resolutions every new year. But do we contemplate how to better our dealings with others and be a winner in the game of life?

This is an extremely important art in today's corporate world where one should not only win and make friends, but also win over enemies.

Chanakya says,

"He should win over those of them who are friendly with conciliation and gifts, those hostile through dissensions and force." (11.1.3)

There are two categories of people each one of us has to deal with in life — friends or enemies.

• Dealing With Friends

We have to accept that friends bring sunshine into our life. Can we live without those buddies who stand by us through thick and thin? But the first rule when it comes to having a friend, is to become a good friend yourself.

According to Chanakya, the way to deal with friends is through conciliation and gifts. So, be there when they require you. The best investment in any friendship is your 'time'. Listen and guide them when they are confused and frustrated.

The other way to win friends is with gifts. No person in this world is unmoved when they receive gifts. It's human psychology to expect gifts. Always put some thought into the gift you are giving. Select something that would not only be useful, but also likable. And give it with a smile and genuine joy in your heart.

• Dealing With Enemies

It's ideal not to have enemies. But let's face facts — they are all around us, even if we do not want them. Whether in the guise of competitors, or full-blown foes, they are eternally around for us to contend with.

But the biggest problem with most of us is that we try to fight the enemy alone. This almost guarantees that you will lose the battle. You should, on the contrary, have your own team before you start the fight.

In the *Upanishads*, a student asks the teacher, "Why does the evil win?" The Guru replied, "Because the good are not united!" Once you have a strong team, it's easy to win over competition. You could even create a split in the enemy and then attack them with full force.

Whatever the case, maintain equanimity while dealing with both types. Win over yourself and then win over the others. As our scriptures say, "He who is even-minded with friend and foe is considered a wise man."

44

Respect Your Enemies

～೨

Oscar Wilde once said, "I choose my friends for their good looks, my acquaintances for their good characters, and my enemies for their good intellects. A man cannot be too careful in the choice of his enemies!"

The fact is that often, we do not create our enemies intentionally. But the reality is that they will exist despite us not wanting them to, whether in battle, or business.

But while we may not have a choice when it comes to choosing our enemies, we can surely choose how to deal with them. It is like playing any sport — you need to have a strategy in place to win the game with the competitor.

Chanakya also respected his enemies. His advice was,

"He should enter the enemy's residence with permission." (1.16.10)

In other words, always show respect to your enemies. Even though we may fight, let it be a 'good' fight and in the right spirit.

But how do we do this? Here are some tips to deal with your competitors and enemies:

• Never Take Them For Granted

The competitor is as intelligent as you are, if not more. So do not take him for granted. Be alert and very careful about his moves. You never know when he may attack. And you should not attack him — certainly never if you believe that he will definitely lose.

• Study Him Completely

One of the reasons for the success of the Australian cricket team is that they spend a lot of time closely studying the players of the opposite teams. They watch videos, find the weaknesses and strengths of the players they are watching. With such a perfect analysis, making a game strategy for beating the opposition becomes very easy.

• Practise, Practise, And More Practise

Just because I have a good weapon in my hand does not mean I will win the war. I should be able to use it effectively off the field before I use it in an actual war. The best warriors practise for hours every day, even in times of peace. Similarly, you should also polish your presentation, or product demonstration.

• Be Cool

Being prepared for war does not mean you should go and fight. War should always be the last option as it's destructive and expensive. Therefore, even if your competitor tries to provoke you, be calm. Never hate your enemy as it kills your ability to think logically. Even in the political field, there are 'peace' talks before the war. So give room for peace in your life as well.

It's all about being prepared like the defence force of any nation, prepared for an attack at all times. But, if war does take place, do not hesitate to fight it to the bitter end!

45

Strategy vs Tactics

∾᠀

Strategy. This is the most misunderstood word in today's business scenario. Many managers cannot differentiate between 'strategy' and 'tactic'. But there are some basic differences — strategy is long-term; while tactics are short term. Strategy is forward looking; tactics are situational. Strategy is vision-based, tactics are need-based.

Of course, linguistically speaking, strategy refers to the game plan for attacking and counter-attacking the enemies during war. However, it has become a core subject in the field of management and leadership. Most heads of an organisation now work on 'Strategic Management'. Still strategy is not all about warring. There is a human angle to it too. Just to illustrate this point, I will address the issue of tackling employee problems and winning their hearts.

Chanakya says,

"Strife among subjects can be averted by winning over the leaders among the subjects, or by removal of the cause of strife." (8.4.18)

Let us consider a situation where a company has gone through a lock-out due to dissatisfaction among the employees. This is reminiscent of the 1970-80s when unions used to actively represent employees.

To handle this situation, we find that Chanakya's practical three-step insight is invaluable:

- Winning Over Leaders

Every group has a leader. This leader is generally involved in highlighting the concerns of his subjects in front of the decision-makers. It's easy to win over the whole group of subjects if you just convince the leader. However, what is important to note is whether the leader is more concerned about himself, or his people. This is where your smartness lies — to diagnose the group leader before you start negotiations.

- Remove The Cause

Even when the union used to be strong, there were companies that did not face unionism. How? Because these companies successfully solved problems even before they ever arose. I remember talking to an employee from one such organisation. He said, "Our Chairman knew our concerns even before we spoke about it. If there were genuine demands, they were fulfilled without an outsider intervening."

- Give Them 'Purpose'

One topic which management consultants love to concentrate on is 'problem analysis.' This HAS to stop! If you look for problems you will end up playing the blame game. Instead, define a purpose for your organisation and its people. Most of us are problem finders. Change this mindset and cultivate a goal-oriented approach.

As Gandhiji said, "Find a purpose, the means will follow."

Always remember — pure strategy is a road map you create to reach your purpose. Tactics are how you handle the hurdles on that road.

46

Before you Attack

~⁀

There's an old saying in the army, "Your success in war depends on your preparation during peace." We are all preparing ourselves for some challenge that may crop up in the future — exams, interviews, presentations, meetings, and other such events.

But when it comes to a confrontation, we just cannot attack our enemy immediately. We have to carefully diagnose the opponent, and then decide about the attack. Sometimes, not attacking is actually the best attack!

Chankaya says,

"If there is equal advancement in peace or war, he should resort to peace." (7.2.1)

Yes, war is the last route a warrior should take. After all, it results in destruction and loss of life and assets. Even in a corporate scenario, if you are wondering whether to fight or not, evaluate the complete picture and then decide your move.

Unlike in the military, the corporate war may not result in actual bloodshed. But it does result in verbal arguments, an attack on the competitor's market, or may even end up in a courtroom and become a legal drama.

Chanakya tells us to hold on before taking such a decision. Peace is the first option. But how do we decide about an attack? Think through these lines:

• What Is The Loss?

One needs to ask oneself — what loss will I suffer if I take up the war? Apart from the monetary loss, there are other kinds of losses, such as losing time, energy, and the team's loss of morale. War is always a costly affair. As an army officer put it beautifully,

"What we build in over ten years, we can lose in one day of war!"

• What Is The Gain?

We also need to look at the possible gains we may get at the end of the fight — What are we fighting for? What are we going to win? Is the win really required for the benefit of one and all? Can I continue to grow without that particular gain? These deep questions need to be asked.

• The Timing

Finally, the decision to maintain peace, or to attack with all our power hinges on the right timing. This is a judgment call. The most well-equipped and trained group of people may not win the game if the timing is not right. And, on the other hand, even a small group of committed people can succeed if they make the right move at the right time.

Given this dilemma, the well-known serenity prayer could be modified, and then it would read like this — "God, grant me the ability to know when to stay quiet, the courage to attack when I must, and the wisdom to know the difference!"

47

Aspects of a Battlefield

In Book 2, Chapter 18 of *Arthashastra*, there is a detailed classification of the weapons used by an army. The Armoury-In-Charge is given instructions to take care of these weapons so that the soldiers are well-equipped for a battle. The knowledge of the weapons and the skills to use them are the keys to winning a war.

What are the weapons that leaders of an organisation should have before they step into a battle? Let us look at a few important aspects:

• Knowlege And Information

Today's economy is slowly becoming a knowledge economy. The more you know and are informed about, the better equipped you are to fight. If you study various industries, you will find that the companies at the top are those that have focused on knowledge utilisation, research, and development and have also made investments in knowledge assets. This will help you plan your battle well.

• Technology

In today's shrinking world, the effective use of technology is the solution to speeding up communications and transactions. Make your organisation techno-savvy. Spend time investigating and understanding the latest technology. Use them and you will find that you have a cutting-edge over your competitors. It also reduces overheads in a big way. Many small countries that have a small population but have powerful economies have used technology for higher productivity.

• People

The man behind the machine is more important that the machine. Yes, your people, your employees, comprise your army. Without a good strong and powerful army, you can't even think of stepping into the battlefield. Not only is the size of the army important — but even the quality of the army is important. The right person for the right job! Human Resource departments have been introduced in most organisations to fulfill this need.

• Inspiration

The most important weapon you need for fighting is inspiration. If your organisation is an inspired organisation with fire in its belly, there will be a transformation in the organisation's output. If you have this quality, the first three will follow. It is the 'human will' that creates change. Small organisations with tremendous will have changed the way business is done. This is also true for certain nations. A country like Singapore, hardly the size of Mumbai, is one of the most successful economies in the world today.

As a leader, when you are preparing for the external war, first try to win your internal war. All weapons are useless, if you are not inspired to fight.

As our former President A.P.J. Abdul Kalam puts it, "It is the wings of fire that gives you the ability to reach out to the skies."

48

Partnership among Equals

During the days when he was creating missiles, our former President A.P.J. Abdul Kalam was asked why he was creating weapons of destruction. He replied, "Only strength will respect strength."

This is true in every aspect of life. We can only partner with people who are equal to us. We do not see any 'value-add' in the time spent with people who are lower than us in stature or knowledge.

On the other hand, if a person is above us, then that person would not see any value in us. Thus, only like-minded people belonging to the same level can bond well together.

As the saying goes, 'birds of a feather flock together'. Chanakya gives a different angle to it. He says,

"An equal should over reach, or help an equal." (7.7.15)

The concept of an equal in *Arthashastra* is that of a *Mitra*, i.e., a friend. Thus, as quoted in the above verse, you should help your Mitra and reach out to him, even before he asks for help.

There are many benefits of forging a partnership among equals:

- Better Understanding

People at the same level have a better understanding of each other — their mindsets, their thinking patterns, their approach, etc. One company's general manager, who is in-charge of leading 400 people, will easily understand the problems of another firm's general manager who is also leading a group of 400 employees. Similarly, a Ph.D student will understand the constraints another Ph.D student is facing, even if they are from different universities. That is why even marital alliances are forged between those who have an equal way of thinking, economic status, and goals.

- Synergy In Thinking

When two people of equal status come together, they are beneficial for each other. One plus one is greater than two. Alternatives get created, approaches change, you get an insight about doing things in more ways than one. As an individual, you may be small. But two small people working together as a team can beat even a bigger enemy. Bigger battles are won by having more equals on your side.

- We Grow Together

It's in our human nature to grow. But of what use is growth that's meant only for you? A rich man had once said, "I was poor, yet happy with my childhood friends. Today, I am dying a rich man without any friends." Therefore, it is important that as we grow we include our equals as part of our growth.

Remember, human life is all about partnerships. But to be a good human being, look ahead with a vision, look around to face facts, and look back to pull others along.

These are also the leadership qualities that are required if you want to lead a community, society, or nation.

49

A Safe Retreat

≈୨

Emergencies happen. Fire-fighting situations could crop up any time. In our highly competitive corporate world, an enemy can attack you swiftly and suddenly. One needs to be prepared for all these eventualities.

Chanakya says,

"In the absence of help-mates, he should find shelter in a fort where the enemy, even with a large army, would not cut off his food, fodder, fuel and water, and would himself meet with losses and expenses." (7.15.9)

There are times when emergencies and crises force people to run away. At such times, one needs to go to a friend or an ally who will extend a helping hand.

But, when that is not possible, one still needs to retreat into a shelter.

Chanakya gives us tips for this:

• Finding A Fort

A fort is generally a well-protected place and not just some ordinary house, or shelter. A fort has guards protecting it and will house the king in the center.

In today's corporate world, a fort would denote those places where the heads of organisations usually operate from.

Therefore, it is suggested that a king (the chairman, director, or CEO) should maintain a good relationship with many other kings (his counterparts). So that in troubled times, he can seek shelter in their fort.

• Protection From The Enemy

The enemy could be someone who is not only after you, but can also reach you. And when he realises that you are under the shelter and protection of another king in his fort, he will think twice before attacking you.

After all, battles are won not only in the battlefields alone, but also in the minds of warriors. And when you have another king on your side, you automatically gain a psychological advantage.

• Inflicting Losses In Return

When you are attacked, you can be certain that the enemy has made this move after calculating all possible losses and expenses. These calculations were relevant when you were alone, and when it was easy to grab you.

Now, when you are in the shelter of another fort and protected by a friend, it will take more effort, energy and time for the enemy to get to you. He will be forced to plan a new strategy, and consider how many soldiers he may lose himself in the process. It is a very positive situation for you, you have upped your enemy's losses.

Chanakya, a very sharp military strategist, always planned an 'exit policy' before such a situation would actually arise. So should you. In the corporate boardroom, or in the market place, or even while signing any contract, it is very important to think about the situation from all aspects and include an exit option for yourself.

50

In the face of Competition

≈୨

A leader's position is an eternally challenging one. While he has to ensure that due credit is given to everyone during good times, he also has to play the role of a motivator through bad times.

Kautilya's Arthashastra exhorts a king (leader) to ensure that his people know how to tackle the challenges he will be giving them.

Chanakya said:

"The conqueror, desirous of capturing the enemy's fortified town, should fill his own side with enthusiasm." (13.1.1)

This couldn't be more applicable in today's corporate scenario.

While India Inc. is on a roll with various mergers and acquisitions, they still need to be vigilant as they are marching ahead like conquerors out to win over their competitors — just like in a war.

They have to be aware that, before they use their employees in their onward march, inspiring them is an essential step for success.

• Understand Uncertainty

When war is declared, soldiers start speculating about their king's next move. That's because all strategies cannot be openly communicated to everyone. This naturally festers doubt in the ranks.

It is typical human nature to think negatively, rather than focus on the benefits. As a leader, you have to understand this uncertainty and think of how to take your team into confidence.

• Communicate And Inspire

Once you have your plan ready and want to communicate your intentions to your team, do it calmly and clearly. Winning your team's confidence is very important. No external motivational speaker can inspire a team the way its own leader can.

Also, it's vital your team is acquainted with the firm's vision and targets that they move in the desired manner. The added advantage of this is that employees get more inspired when their doubts are cleared.

This is essential to have optimum productivity from your team members. They will ensure you are never alone as both you and your team will have a common purpose.

• Go Forth And Conquer

It's these vision and leadership initiatives that finally make the winning moves.

Size doesn't matter, planning does. Even Chanakya talks about how guerrilla warfare tactics can help the smallest but well-inspired team take over huge armies through careful moves.

Indeed, a carefully planned strategy, an inspired team and the right leadership attitude are not only essential but also the only factors needed to win any war. But remember to share the benefits of the success with the team which helped you to get there.

51

Acquiring a Company

Mergers and acquisitions (M&A) are key strategies for almost all top corporations today, especially our desi ones. Indeed, India Inc should be at the forefront of any M&A action, given that the concept was dealt with in great detail in our ancient texts.

Kautilya's Arthashastra even defines the ways of acquiring a firm:

"Acquisition is of three kinds — new, formerly possessed, and inherited." (13.5.2).

But Chanakya also made it clear that acquisition is not just mere killing and conquering. Rather, it's a well-thought out strategy which strives for the betterment of both the parties involved.

In addition to material benefits, M&As should look after the people too. If this is understood, all such processes will automatically be successful, whatever category they belong to.

• Taking Over A New Firm

In the olden days, kings used to win over new territories all the time. But they needed to do a lot of study and research since not enough was known about a strange new place.

Even today, the first step in acquiring a firm is to research it in detail. This study is usually the responsibility of a strategic planning team. Due diligence and meetings can follow only after an in-depth study.

• Taking Over An Existing Firm

More often than not, regions that were under a particular king's control are taken over by another region. This can be due to bad management, or lack of attention.

This happens in the corporate world too. When companies grow, they lose focus on their small businesses. By the time they become aware, they find that their ownership is under threat. So, the next type of acquisition is to conquer firms formerly possessed.

• Taking Over An Inheritance

A prince may have inherited a kingdom. But in due course of time, it may have been taken away from him, possibly by his own 'trusted' ministers. So when the prince matures and wants control of his inherited share, he may have to fight it out. This is acquisition of inherited property.

All those court cases you see for ownership of a small property or firm denotes this situation perfectly. Fighting back is the only way to get back what one had inherited, but lost.

Whatever the type of acquisition, having a strategic plan is a must. And more importantly than that is to provide for people on both sides of the negotiation table.

52

Where to Expand

∼⌒∽

While it's true that all companies need to expand, serious thought has to be given to where exactly they can invest. This holds true even for individuals, especially when it comes to investing in property.

Chanakya had advised:

"As between a small proximate land and a big land that is distant, the small proximate land is preferable. For, it is easy to obtain, to protect and to get rescue (oneself). The distant one is the opposite of this." (7.10.17-19)

The Tata Motors-Trinamool Congress of West Bengal state tussle over a piece of land in 2008 brings to my mind this particular verse from Chanakya's *Arthashastra*.

In the case of the Nano plant, the Mumbai-headquartered Tatas stood to lose Rs 500 crore as they dropped their project at Singur. According to Chanakya, an alternative site for the Rs 1 lakh car should be somewhere closer to headquarters, and where local leaders are open to discussions.

So, Maharashtra or Gujarat was the best option and finally Gujarat won. Let us see why:

• Proximity

The land located nearer is always more advantageous, even if it's smaller than the far off land. That's because it's easily accessible, which makes application of decisions a lot quicker. In the case of West Bengal, it's now becoming difficult to get the concerned leaders to even come to the discussion table.

With distance being a huge disadvantage, it's difficult to find a common ground easily. Moreover, local leaders will always have a bigger say compared to any well-wishing, but external investor.

* Obtaining And Protecting

One can understand the local laws and the demands of people residing nearby more easily. Thus, it's easy to acquire and obtain. It's also easy to protect it.

Even if there is a difference of opinion, the local people and their leaders can be approached easily and discussions can reach fruitful conclusions faster.

* Rescuing Oneself

In a worst-case scenario, it's always vital to rescue oneself and the team immediately. The prime duty of a leader is to protect the safety of his subjects. Imagine the costs involved if the Tatas were to airlift their 800-strong force from West Bengal to safeguard them from local attacks.

This would be more easier and cost-effective if they were closer to the head-office based in Mumbai.

Basically, a company has to look at all such dimensions before making an investment in a new place since, in the end, success can be achieved only through a win-win situation for all.

And of course, the leadership and the local government policies also matter the most. This is the advantage that Gujarat had.

53

Peace and War

≫⃝ℑ

Terrorism, bomb blasts, communal riots, political protests — have become a regular part of our lives. While this is not good for any country, or even its governance, is it in anyway linked to the business community and working-class people?

Of course! The concept of 'risk management' as related to business growth is becoming an interesting field of study. But what does Chanakya have to say about it?

"For, when the gain is equal there should be peace, when unequal war is considered desirable." (7.8.34)

This is a very interesting statement that Kautilya makes — if there is a win-win situation between two parties, we should consider peace. However, if we are only at the receiving end, war has to be considered.

Now, how do we decide if we still need peace talks, or if it's time to attack?

• Punishments Are Necessary

In addition to commerce, *Arthashastra* is also a book about law and order in society. Therefore, it is also known as *Dandaniti* (*Danda* — the rod, and *Niti* — the strategy) i.e. a book of punishments.

Only if the fear of punishments exists, will there be discipline and peace in society. No one really desires war. But, at times, it is unavoidable. 'War against terrorism' is what politicians are now talking about all around the world.

• But, Consider All Options

Chanakya's famous theory of *Sama, Dana, Danda, Bheda* comes into play here. First, try talks and discussions, not only with enemies, but also with your team members. Understand what the enemy really wants.

Also, have a dialogue with the leaders of our society — businessmen, academicians, artists, spiritual groups, media, etc. Get all of them involved and try to understand what we as a society think about it.

• Decide And Act

After all this analysis, it's important to decide the next course of action. There comes a time in every country's history when a firm decision must be taken and acted upon. Such a decision not only changes the course of history, but also decides the very survival of the nation.

During the British Raj, many believed that our colony was governed by a 'Divide and Rule' policy. Sardar Vallabhbhai Patel, our first Home Minister and Deputy Prime Minister, had a different opinion. He said, "We divide ourselves, and they rule!"

54

Tackling Terrorism

India attacked!

So, what's new? Ask any Indian how tired he is listening to this same news every year, it seems as if he is almost used to hearing about such terrible attacks. Most people have a fatalistic philosophy, *"Akhir ek din to marna hi hai* (after all, we all have to die one day)"*.

But there were also numerous disturbed readers, who sent me e-mails asking if Chanakya had suggested any solution for terrorism in the *Arthashastra*.

He had. Chanakya had said:

"Three Magistrates, all of them of rank of ministers, shall carry out suppression of criminals." (4.1.1)

This is the opening verse of Book 4 of *Kautilya's Arthashastra* on tackling ('suppression of') criminals.

• Make A Strong Policy

How many times have we observed that even the most deadly criminals manage to get away scot-free in this country? There is no fear of the law.

Therefore, the state has to adopt a much stronger law and order policy. Did you note how, after 9/11, America did not suffer from any more terrorist attacks? In our case, the attacks just grow bigger and deadlier with time.

Since 2004, we have faced as many as 16 major terrorist attacks. Why do we still need a reason to wake up? Why are we not ready to learn from our mistakes and rectify them? A strong stand against terrorism is the need of the hour.

• Study And Execute

Our ministers should study how America and other countries have tackled similar situations. They should learn from them and make an action plan. And, after doing this, it's important that they do not just sit back and do nothing.

Our ministers should learn to execute these plans. In the final showdown, the fate of the country is always in the hands of the leaders. They have to learn to be proactive.

• Get Senior Judges Together

Read what Chanakya said centuries ago — not one, but three judges should come together. Why? Because they will offer different viewpoints and perspectives. However, in the same sutra, Chanakya also advises that these 'Magistrates' should have the rank of ministers.

In the olden days, a minister was close to the king. The same situation can be replicated today by giving our law experts and judiciary more power, especially to those who have already proved the soundness of their executive powers.

As they say, "Let's work hard now so that we can sleep peacefully later."

People

55

Growing Under a Mentor

≈୨

We require the help of experienced people while undertaking various projects, or assignments. However, even though we want guidance from our seniors, we do not want them to decide how we should do our work. *Freedom* coupled with guidance is what every employee needs.

This guide can be a mentor. A mentor is an evolved leader. A leader commands, while a mentor directs. A leader is a part of the process; a mentor is a catalyst, who guides without being part of the action.

Each employee has to be nurtured with the help of a senior person who is experienced in that particular skill. This system of mentoring has taken strong roots in today's corporate training structure.

For instance, Narayan Murthy is now officially the Chief Mentor of the Infosys Group. We may have a good mentor around us. But we should know how to benefit from their company and experience. The *Arthashastra* gives us various tips on how to do this:

- Accept His Authority

  "Training and discipline are acquired by accepting the authoritativeness of the teachers in the respective fields." (1.5.6)

  The junior needs to have an attitude of surrender towards his mentor, his Guru. Initially, this may seem difficult for a novice brimming with ideas.

  However, accepting the mentor's authority helps build discipline. The person should be able to accept that the mentor understands the subject better than he does. At times it might be difficult to accept his decisions, but he still needs to follow them. The complete picture will become clearer in due course of time.

- Constant Association

  "He should have constant association with elders in learning for the sake of improving his training, since training has its root in that." (1.5.11)

  Trying to associate with the mentor's thoughts, ideas, and way of thinking is very essential. This helps develop the mindset required for the job.

  Being in the company of the mentor gives us a practical insight into the theories we have heard about management. The basics of any training is to improve oneself. This will happen in the presence of the mentor.

- Keep Learning And Applying

  "(From) Continuous study ensures a trained intellect, from intellect (comes) practical application, (and) from practical application (results) self-possession." (1.5.16)

Finally, one has to keep applying what he has learnt from the mentor.

Continuous study helps one develop the intellect. Then he has to test his intellectual understanding by applying the lessons in practical situations. Once he sees the results, he is convinced about his knowledge. Now he has mastered the field. In fact, with the help of his mentor, the theory and practice have become one.

56

Motivating Employees

Human Resource departments in modern corporations are focused on how to motivate the employees, or guide them to perform better and increase productivity. Chanakya uses motivational techniques in various departments of the State. Many of the methods can today be applied in the corporate world when it comes to handling employees.

Using his deep understanding of human nature, Chanakya developed a system of motivation which worked with the carrot, the stick, and many more other motivating factors. The application of his theory of motivation — *Sama, Dana, Danda,* and *Bheda* are unlimited.

• *Sama* Or Consultation

This is the first step that should be taken whenever it appears that an employee is not working properly — listen to him. Have a clear understanding of his side of the story. Senior managers get information from various sources. They will get the whole picture if they listen to the information directly from the person involved.

One can discuss and suggest various solutions for the particular problem. If it is a complex problem, external experts could help.

- *Dana* Or Reward

Employees work for wages and salaries. That is the key motivating factor that ensures they stay on in the organisation. The next thing is honour. Without these two kinds of encouragement, no employee will have any reason to continue working in that particular company.

Therefore, Chanakya suggests rewarding employees sufficiently in order to get work done. The reward could be in the form of incentives, paid vacations, bonuses, or promotions. Another reward would be awarding employees for their performance, such as the 'best employee award' or 'most productive person award' — a common practice in several companies today.

- *Danda* Or Punishments

Many employees may not show any signs of improvement in spite of constant prodding and various other efforts. Neither rewards nor incentives will bring them out of their lethargic state. This is a serious situation. If not corrected, a sense of complacency can spread through the whole organisation.

Therefore, Chanakya recommends a stronger step — punishments. A rap can be subtle or gross, depending on the person as well as the situation that warranted it. It can be a warning, a suspension, a cut in salary, or even a demotion.

- *Bheda* Or Split

Though this is not encouraged at all, it is the final step. When none of the other methods work, it is concluded that the organisation and the employee cannot work together any further. It is best to part ways for the benefit of both.

If it is a large organisation that can bear the financial expense of that particular employee, he can perhaps be transferred to a department where his productivity will not be a major issue. In smaller firms, or employee-productivity-oriented organisations, he must be asked to leave.

57

Bidding Goodbye to Employees

✌

The skilled manpower is increasing in our country, the competition for hiring better employees is growing at an unprecedented rate among companies, the attrition rate is going up, and the challenge of retaining your able force is increasing. This is the scenario in almost all sectors of the economy. Every entrepreneur is thinking about and forming strategies to tackle such incidents.

During such a phase in any industry, Chanakya, says,

"Masters may bear testimony for servants, priests and preceptors for disciples, and parents for sons." (3.11.32)

If your subordinate is leaving the organisation for better prospects and you are not able to provide them with the same benefits, it is the duty of a senior to offer his best wishes to the junior and say goodbye.

The above verse says that the master should also provide certificates (testimony) and reference. Let him prosper in his life — is what you should feel for that individual.

However, such parting of ways is not very easy to accept. How can we make such moves in life more positive and happy, for both parties?

Tips For Employees Leaving The Organisation:

• Give Advance Notice

Every company has a minimum notice period. Make it a point to fulfill that agreement and do not just run away. Speak to your boss and make him understand why you are leaving.

- Replace Yourself

  When you leave, the biggest question for a boss is — who is going to do your work? The best solution is to have an alternative ready. Even you can look for potential people and bring them to your boss's attention.

- Train Another New Person

  The best way to tackle this situation is to get a person trained to do your work before your last day.

  Tips For Employers:

- Accept Reality

  People will leave and you must accept this important fact. Do not expect that someone will be devoted to you all their life.

- Continuous Training

  Keep recruiting and training people on a regular basis. If you have a requirement of 50 people, train 75-100 people as ready backup.

- Multi-Tasking

  Teach all employees how to perform multiple processes. So, when someone leaves, you can immediately ask others to take up his task.

  Chanakya suggests that no employer should let his employee leave after a fight and with hard feelings. You never know when you will require the person again.

  In *Mahabharata* we find this pearl of wisdom — "Life is alike logs of wood flowing in a river, they flow together for some time and part, and meet again."

  So, you never know when time will bring your old acquaintances back in your life.

58

Managers into Leaders

～○

Human capital, intellectual capital, human resource — these are terms used to define the value of people in any organisation. These days, every organisation is focusing more and more on these aspects. Today, a company's ROI (Return on Investment), productivity, as well as profits in all areas, are based on the quality of people it has.

An organisation may have good manpower in terms of numbers. But, if these people are not fully productive, or not working to their optimum potential, the organisation is at a loss.

The first challenge for any organisation is to get good people. The next challenge is to train those good people into becoming good leaders.

On this Chanakya says,

"When he (prince) is ready for it (knowledge), experts should train him."
(1.17.27)

When the HR Department is recruiting people from business schools, or even from other companies, they are initially looking for good managers. But if the company has to scale up, the next challenge is to make them great leaders. Even in the above verse, Chanakya calls for the identification of potential leaders and then for providing them with leadership training. But how do we understand if a manager, or an employee, is a potential leader?

Here are some tips:

• Leadership Is A Mindset

Leadership is not a position or a designation. It is a way of thinking — a mindset. Therefore, a business leader has to keep an eye on the quality of the minds of his people. A leadership mind is a great mind. It is continuously learning. It does not get stuck when it sees a problem. It will seek alternatives and find different methods to get out of it. It challenges itself.

• Solution-Focused

A potential leader is solution-focused. Once, I was conducting a training programme which dealt with the topic, 'From good managers to great leaders'. A delegate asked me, "My boss is always the decision-maker. He usually brings the solution. Then why should I not just go to him with problems?"

I said, "Yes you are right. You have to present the problem to him. But go to him with two or three alternative solutions. Let the boss decide which solution is best for the organisation. But the thinking *also* has to be done by you, not only your boss!" *Think solutions* — is the mantra for success.

• Implementation

Most managers are good planners, but bad implementers. The difference between a manager and a leader is this implementation aspect. Just do it. At times, you do make mistakes, but learn from the mistake and move on in life.

59

Delegating Work

॰੭

Look at any organisation and you are bound to find a boss who is frustrated with his subordinates. While a junior can be blamed for non-productivity to some extent, most of the problems are caused by the leader himself, due to improper delegation of work.

In *Arthashastra*, Chanakya had included a chapter on the 'Training of elephants'. He said:

"In conformity with the appearance, he should give exercise to the gentle and the dull (elephant), and to the animal with mixed characteristics, in various types of work, or in accordance with the season." (2.31.18)

So, Chanakya calls for identifying potential candidates as per their (an elephant in this case) nature and even according to the different seasons, as it may affect the way they work.

In human terms, we can understand how much thought goes into choosing the 'right person for the right job'. After all, a mistake at this stage can result in real frustration in the long run.

But how does one do this?

• Evaluate People

This is the first step for effectively carrying out what is called man-management. Many bosses fail to do this. When an interview is conducted, a well-written CV or resume can impress everyone. Even the answers and opinions revealed during the interview will help you realise if the candidate is promising.

But, there is a big difference between promises and the actual delivery of work. Give yourself time before passing any kind of judgment on anyone. Always observe and study a person for a minimum of three months (that's what training periods are for).

Watch them closely and observe their strengths and weaknesses. You will get a better grasp of the person's nature, behaviour, and potential output.

• Different Situations

A person who is very successful in one venture may not be successful if asked to handle a different situation. Even the most successful salesman may fail when it comes to selling a different product, or in a different region.

So, understand that each person's output is not guaranteed forever. Different situations and circumstances can change a person's productivity and even performance. And you have to identify these traits.

• Different Timings

Next, you really need to understand how a person's output changes at different times. For example, students generally learn much better if they study during the early morning.

That's simply because the mind tends to become lazy later on in the day and hence, memorising information requires less effort in the morning.

Chanakya referred to this as 'seasons'. So find out what are the best productive times for your subordinates and allocate work "...in accordance with the season!"

All successful businessmen and leaders know the art of delegating work. If you want to be a successful man-manager too, then thinking, planning, studying, and experimenting with human psychology will become essential.

60

Protecting Old Employees

～૭

Look at any business organisation which is over 20 years old and you will find that it has two generations working there. Both these generations have different mindsets and attitudes.

While the younger generation has great opportunities and switches jobs very easily, the older generation is more committed and steady.

We see a similar dichotomy in today's urban-rural divide in India, wherein the urban residents are inherently restless and on-the-move, while the rural denizens are more sedate and satisfied with life.

Chanakya had a suggestion for employers who want to create appropriate policies for both:

"He (leader) should grant safety to the countryside as it may have been settled." (13.4.2)

In the olden days, kings had to think deeply before taking any decision that would have affected people residing in the villages. Providing safety and security was of paramount importance, as residents of those particular places did not want to shift easily. Similarly, the older generation in any organisation must also be taken care of.

They are committed and set in that one place (organisation). To the leader of such organisations, Chanakya suggests that instead of trying to alter their job profiles — provide them with safety.

But how do we deal with the older employees in an organisation?

• Benefit From Their Experience

Experienced people are valuable assets for any organisation as they have put in a lot of hard work to support and build it.

Never take them for granted as they prove to be useful in the most difficult of times. The best utilisation of senior employees in a company is to make them train the younger ones and the new entrants with their rich experience. This has the added advantage of creating mutual respect between the two generations within the organisation, and will also be in accordance with Chanakya's advice to a prince — "Meet elders and learn from them."

• Change Them, But Slowly

Change is a fact of life. And while the younger generation is quick and ready to change, the elders may resist it. So, even though it's important and a must, give the senior employees more time to change.

In addition to older employees, this patient approach will also benefit the overall company as the most successful organisations are the ones that understand that the path to success is led by the maturity of the seniors coupled with the dynamism of the youth.

To Avoid

61

What a Leader should Not Do — 1

≈つ

Arthashastra is not only a compilation of Chanakya's wisdom, but also contains practical insights into even more ancient lessons of management, politics, and strategy.

Arthashastra contains a wealth of wisdom on leadership, its development, and application. There is some valuable information about the challenges of leadership, something that today's corporate world is struggling to understand. Chanakya not only tells us what a leader should do, but also what he should 'not' do.

In Book 7, Chapter 5, from verse 19 to 26, Chanakya outlines 21 things that a leader should avoid doing. We will be studying these words of caution in the next ten chapters. These can be applied not only to business leaders, but also to heads of departments, project leaders, community leaders, politicians, and can even be applied by the head of a family, or any other institution, or organisation.

Chanakya had said,

"Reasons for dissatisfaction of subjects: discarding the good and favouring the wicked." (7.5.19-26)

Who are the subjects?

Well, they are the people who are reporting to you, or are dependent on you. They wait for your directions, which in itself has a direct effect on their lives. In the case of a company, it's the employees. In a department, they are your team members. In a family, they are your children and relatives. The first and foremost duty of a king (leader) is to keep his subjects happy.

Now, the first reason for subjects to become unhappy is when the king discards the good and favours the wicked. Subjects come to the leader for justice. When they do not find a solution to their problems among themselves, they seek the leader's advice, direction, and justice. If he favours the wrong and discards the right, this is a very serious problem.

Here are some tips on how to understand who is right:

* Listen To Both Together And Seperately

    It's very necessary to listen to both sides of a story. But after the two parties have expressed their views together, do not hurry with your decision. When both parties are facing each other, there are a lot of emotions and personal feelings expressed. Therefore, listen to them separately too. Get the facts. You will get a better idea of who was right. At times we are not able to come to any decision, this is called 'Dharmasankath'. In such conflicting situations take the help of books (scriptures) and masters learned in the particular field.

* Announce The Verdict Unemotionally

    After you have analysed the situation, announce your verdict. Also explain the 'reason' behind the conclusion you have reached.

Be just. But more than anything else, be unemotional. That's the most vital part.

The whole idea is not to hate the bad. As Gandhiji put it, "Remove the wickedness, not the wicked." Even while punishing the wrong, one should give them an opportunity to learn and improve.

62

What a Leader should Not Do — 2

Among the many things that a leader should avoid doing, Chanakya says,

"Reasons for dissatisfaction of subjects: By starting unrighteous injuries not current before, by indulgence in impiety and suppression of piety, by doing acts that ought not to be done." (7.5.19-26)

These three actions could alienate a leader from his subjects. First, if a leader starts harming others in a way that was not used before. Second, by indulging in wicked deeds and suppressing good deeds. Third, by performing actions that should be avoided.

How does the leader know if his behaviour and actions are right? Here are some tips:

• Do Not Start New Punishments

In every company or organisation, there are methods of punishing the wrongdoer. For example, warnings and memos are issued. At times, employees are even suspended. But note that these are within the laws of the company. Never ever try to do any serious injury that goes beyond the law. For example, never slap or hit an employee in front of others, even for a serious lapse, or bad behaviour. After all, this is not only a physical injury, but also an emotional injury. Punishments within the right limit are always respected and honoured.

- Be A Person Of Character

We find that many leaders are hypocrites. They show a very different face in front of their employees, while their private life is generally not very ideal. As it is said, "The character of a man is what he is in the dark." So a leader, even in his non-public life, should remain a man of great integrity. Be truthful to yourself.

- Differentiate Between 'Right' And 'Wrong'

This is the greatest quality that a leader can develop. While running an organisation or company, there are times when the leader comes across conflicting situations. Sensitive issues like money, people management, etc become his regular concerns. If he cannot differentiate between what to agree and what to disagree with, he will always be stuck. To master this art, learn from those who are far more experienced, or others whom we call 'men of wisdom'.

Always, remember that the well-known serenity prayer of Reinhold Niebuhr also applies to a leader when he walks into an office:

"God grant me the serenity to accept the things I cannot change; courage to change the things I can; and wisdom to know the difference!"

63

What a Leader should Not Do — 3

≈つ

A leader should be very alert and vigilant about his own actions. Chanakya points out,

"Reasons for dissatisfaction of subjects: By ruining rightful acts, by

not giving what ought to be given and securing what ought not to be given to him (the leader)." (7.5.19-26)

There are leaders who try to suppress the good deeds performed by others. For example, if there are any projects or ideas that have been worked upon by the subordinates, they should not be destroyed. Rather they should be preserved and considered as an asset to the organisation.

Next, what rightfully belongs to the subjects should be given to them — be it their salaries, incentives, or promotions. Even a pat on the back is a great reward for juniors.

Finally, the leader should not try to get for himself that which he does not deserve. He should only take his due share.

Here are some tips:

• Encourage New Ideas

Your employees are not just machines to be operated. They are human beings with a head on their shoulders. Each mind can create a different idea, and new ideas are the fuel of any organisation. As a leader, it is very important to keep note of these new ideas and experiment with them.

While doing this, involve the employee who came up with that particular idea. Also give credit to him/her.

• Honour And Respect Them

A psychologist once said, "Like food, shelter and clothing, *appreciation*, is a basic human need too." So learn to appreciate every person. A good word from the boss goes a long way in boosting employee morale.

And this should not be artificial. Show that you genuinely respect them. In many companies, there are 'employee of the month' awards and in some organisations, a photo of the most efficient employee is displayed at the reception.

• Never Misuse Your Power

Remember the famous dialogue from the movie *Spiderman* — Peter Parker receives sage advice from his uncle, "With great power comes great responsibilities!" A leader can misuse the power, if he is not a person of integrity. Especially if he is not answerable to anyone. However, he should make himself accountable to himself. Additionally, see to it that others get equal opportunities to become good leaders themselves. A good leader is the one who creates more leaders.

In the Navy, when the ship crosses the equator, a ceremony called 'Crossing the Line' is held. During this, a junior cadet is made the captain of the ship and all the senior officers have to follow his orders. Try this for a day in your organisation. While this may sound like fun, you will also learn a lot about what your juniors think about you.

64

What a Leader should Not Do — 4

Leadership is a very dynamic responsibility. It's not something to be learnt from books or lectures alone. Rather, it's about various factors that one needs to tackle in any given situation.

Continuing this series on Chanakya's tips for effective leadership, we find that he repeatedly emphasises the importance of leading by example. The next two points tell us what makes a bad leader:

> *"Reasons for dissatisfaction of subjects: By not punishing those deserving to be punished; by punishing those not deserving to be punished."* (7.5.19-26)

In the movie *Troy*, an officer tells the General, "Sir, the army is under fear that you may punish them." The General adds something very important, "Fear can be constructive if you can manage it well."

Men are managed by the fear of punishment. It is because of the fear of the police, that the crime rate is controlled. It is because of the fear of losing the job that employees become productive. It is only because of the fear of punishment that children are controlled by teachers and parents.

However, managing someone's fear is an art.

Here are some tips on managing fear:

• Be Fearless Yourself

It is easier said than done. Being fearless at all times is the highest human achievement. Only years of doing the right things can make one totally fearless. A warrior once said, "If I look directly into the eyes of the enemy for a few moments, my fear disappears." In other words, face the challenges of life directly without depending on anything or anyone.

• Never Misuse Fear

Leaders can misuse the fear of their subordinates. One naturally commands respect just because of being in a position of power. Still, respect cannot be demanded. One can force others to respect them through authority and the power wielded. But to earn respect, you have to win the head and the heart of the other person. If you want to check if you are a successful leader or not, try to understand if every one is comfortable and happy when you are around.

• Punish Fairly

At times, punishment is unavoidable. However, one can punish rightly and justly. If you punish too much, you will be seen as a terror. But if you are too soft, the work will not get done. It's a balancing act. So think twice before you pass your judgment — be firm, yet considerate.

A criminal was being sent to the gallows. He was asked what his last wish was. He replied to the shock of the jailor, "To kill my father because of whom I am going to the gallows..." he continued, "He never corrected me when I was wrong, nor did he punish me when I deserved it."

65

What a Leader should Not Do — 5

Controlling crime is an extremely vital function in any society. By not arresting criminals, the police not only gives support to existing criminals, but also encourages new criminals. On the other hand, if the police arrests someone who should not be arrested, a new criminal is created.

A leader should be aware of this truth, since such a situation can easily arise in any corporate.

Hence, Chanakya says,

"Reasons for dissatisfaction of subjects: By seizing those who ought not to be seized; by not arresting those who ought to be seized." (7.5.19-26)

The classic book by Victor Hugo, *Les Miserables,* brings this out in a very dramatic manner. A man gets arrested for stealing a loaf of bread under unavoidable circumstances and is put into prison for over twenty years, and from a noble man a criminal is born.

While taking any decision, the leader should carefully consider this aspect. But how will he wipe out crime and still be just? Here are some tips:

• Understand What Causes Crime

There are two reasons why a person becomes a criminal — one is need, and the other is greed. When a truly needy person cannot fulfill his basic needs, he takes the easy route of crime. Food, clothing, shelter, and financial security are basic needs. If these are not provided, there is a high risk that the person will take to theft and robbery. A leader should have the complete knowledge of his subordinate's basic requirements. He should even go that extra mile to make sure that even the employee's families are taken care of.

• Control Greed

The second reason for a person to take to a life of crime is greed. In spite of their high standard of living, many people from rich families turn to crime. In such cases, the leader has to enforce the fear of punishment. If not punished, they can take the law for granted. "Arrest them," says Chanakya. Once given a loose hand, it is difficult to control them later. When one such powerful person is punished, automatically the others come under control.

• Make And Apply A System

The only way to keep crime under control is to make systems that are beneficial to the law and order of any state or organisation. However, just making systems is not helpful — they need to be applied properly. The law should not stay in the books alone. Rather, it should be used to maintain social order.

Always remember that you cannot support a criminal even if he is someone known to you.

As a thinker once said, "If you share your friend's crime, you make it your own."

66

What a Leader should Not Do — 6

≈୨

A leader is a protector. He can be compared to a shield that saves the subjects from external enemies. But, what would happen if the protector himself became the destroyer?

Consider Chanakya's words seriously, or expect your subjects to feel insecure.

He says,

"Reasons for dissatisfaction of subjects: By doing harmful things and destroying beneficial things, by failing to protect from thieves and by robbing (them) himself." (7.5.19-26)

First and foremost, a leader should not do anything that will harm people or the organisation. Also, beneficial things should not be destroyed. For example, destroying respected religious symbols can lead to problems.

Secondly, a leader should protect the subjects from robbers or any other external factors that can erode the wealth of the people, the state, or the employees of an organisation. Most importantly, he should not rob them himself!

But how can a leader ensure such protection? Here are some tips:

- Be The Wall

The leader has to be like a wall — a protection as well as a barrier. When an outsider tries to attack your subordinates, step in front of them and face the challenge yourself. An employee may not know how to take care of himself. In such situations, the mighty leader is his/her only hope. So be there when they need you.

- Take Action Against Outsiders

"Any one who disturbs the happiness and the peace of my subjects will not be spared!" said a king. Similarly, as is indicated in the verse, Chanakya says that the king should protect the subjects from thieves. If a thief is caught, punish him immediately. If he is left free, the fear of the thief returning lingers in the minds of all. Strict actions will ensure the people's confidence in the leader.

- Don't Rob Your Own People

Robbing does not just mean stealing money and other physical objects. Honour, dignity, and gratitude can be stolen as well. If a

118

person truly deserves it, then give him rewards and awards. Your people are your greatest assets. Pay them well, pay them on time. Remember, only if your own army is strong will it fight for you.

A leader also has to be a good fighter. And when he has to fight for his people he needs to do his very best. As Faye Wattleton said so beautifully, "Whoever is providing leadership needs to be as fresh and thoughtful and as reflective as possible to make the very best fight."

67

What a Leader should Not Do — 7

High attrition rates are a major problem in the IT, ITeS, BPO, and other sectors. The reasons why people leave a job could be anything — the lack of incentives, or better offers from rival companies who are luring away the employees to deal with their own shortage of manpower.

But regardless of such external conditions that the current employers can hardly do anything about, the fact remains that employees are motivated or demotivated by the way their employers treat them.

There are three ways of getting work done from your subordinates — instigation, motivation, and inspiration. Instigation is the way terrorists are made to work. Motivation involves incentives and promotions, whereas inspiration comes from within the self, which is eternal and everlasting.

The real challenge for an employer is to take his employees from 'Motivation to Inspiration'.

Chanakya outlines the reasons that demoralise employees,

"Reasons for dissatisfaction of subjects: By ruining human exertions, by spoiling the excellence of work done." (7.5.19-26)

Employees work hard and exert themselves. If their efforts are not recognised and are destroyed instead, the first seed of attrition is sown. Secondly, when the employees create or produce something better for the company, he or she deserves rewards. So, how does one inspire one's employees?

• Money Is The Priority

Do employees work for money? Yes, they do. That is the first and the most important requirement. No organisation can keep a person inspired, if the salaries are not paid on time. Also offer options beyond their salaries — employee stock options, incentives, shares in profits, and other schemes can be worked out by the management to keep the employees financially secure.

• Work Hard, Rest Well

The employer has to believe that optimum productivity is achieved by giving space and peace of mind to the employee. In some developed countries, employees work very hard for ten months to take a two-month vacation. We may have a problem with this model, but the important fact is that the thought of a two-month vacation has made the employee work hard for ten months. The balance between work and rest has to be maintained for better results.

• A 'Higher Purpose'

Employees want something beyond money and that is respect and challenge. They also want a purpose for their lives. If the leader is able to find that 'purpose' for the employees then phenomenal success is guaranteed. This is a spiritual requirement. The Spiritual Quotient (SQ) of the employee has to be developed for this to happen.

A recruitment advertisement of a well known IT company carried a caption under an employee's photograph: 'I found a purpose to live for in this organisation'. A 'Best Employer' survey has also found 'higher purpose' to be essential for employees.

68

What a Leader should Not Do — 8

During one of my training programmes, while discussing the leadership qualities described by Chanakya, a participant observed, "It would have sounded more positive if the session was called 'What a leader *should do*'."

I explained that the title of the session which emphasised what leaders should *not do* was by design, rather than by fault. The human mind works in a certain pattern and studies reveal that we become more alert when we hear negative words.

Words such as 'danger', 'death' and 'destruction' have the power to move a person from lethargy to activity. So continuing this ten-part series, we now look at a few more things a leader should *not* do...

"Reasons for dissatisfaction of subjects: By doing harm to principal men and dishonouring those worthy of honour, by opposing the elders, by partiality and falsehood." (7.5.19-26)

In the above verses, the emphasis is on three key ideas — respect for elders, being impartial, and not engaging in falsehood.

• Respecting Elders And Principal Men

A society which does not respect elders and men of knowledge cannot survive for long. The Sanskrit word for elders is *'Vriddha'*. The word 'elder' here has two meanings: one, a person who is elder by age, and second, a person who is elder by wisdom. It is natural to respect any person who is elder to us by age. We find that, across Asian cultures, respecting elders has been considered a noble and high virtue. However, there are young people with a lot of knowledge or wisdom who also command respect. Even they are *Vriddhas*.

One of the reasons why young managers from top business

schools land high salaries and top positions is the knowledge they bring into the company. Such young, but senior, people should always be respected and never dishonoured. Do not oppose them. Listen to their views before taking any decision.

• Not Being Partial

In conflict management, the best thing to do is to do what is 'correct'. Do not favour those who are wrong even if they are the people closest to you. On the other hand, always support those who are right, even if they are not known to you. Partiality demoralises everyone in an organisation. So be even-minded, and take an objective view before making any move.

• Not Indulging In Falsehood

Satyameva Jayate, says the Indian national emblem. But almost everyone thinks this cannot be practised in today's world. This is not true. The reality is that we do not have patience to wait. All the top companies that practise good governance look for long-term benefits. Focusing on research and development, people, strategy over tactics, etc are key aspects of success for such organisations. Therefore, you should also not support falsehood.

69

What a Leader should Not Do — 9

A management student once asked me, "Do businessmen think only of money all the time?" I replied, "The answer to this is very subjective, however there are many other things that the businessman needs to think through, even for making money. Being financially successful — which is a basic requirement — is determined by other parameters like goodwill, service levels, and also commitment from your very own people."

Now, we will look at some more factors highlighted by Chanakya that a leader should be alert about:

"Reasons for dissatisfaction of subjects: By not requiting what is done, by not carrying out what is settled." (7.5.19-26)

In other words, a businessman also has to think about his subordinates who become unhappy when they are not paid for what they have done and, secondly, when their leader becomes complacent.

- Not Paying For What Is Done

The economic cycle of a business is dependent on cash flow from one person to other. The client pays for the service to the provider; they in turn pay their employees and suppliers. The suppliers will have to pay their suppliers. Even if one link in the chain breaks, there will be disharmony. Therefore, a leader needs to pay his dues to everyone *on time*. After completing a job, always pay the people involved.

- Not Being Complacent

An entrepreneur started a business and struggled a lot. Finally, his business became financially successful. He then went to his mentor and asked, "Sir, now my business is doing well. What should I do?" The mentor advised, "Go start another business."

This is where the real fun begins. The spirit of being industrious needs to be carried forward. After having learnt all about how to start and run a business, one should never become complacent.

In fact, use your know-how to start other businesses and projects. Till this point, you required a mentor. Now you can become a mentor to other struggling businessmen.

- Continuing What You Have Started

Starting another business does not mean that you must stop your first venture. From being a person who worked on the specific details of the first business, you can now move on to a supervisory level. You still need to drive the sales of the first business, but adopt a holistic approach. Your time will be spent between the first and the new business you have started. Manage both with equal commitment.

I was acting as a consultant for one of India's biggest conglomerates. As we were discussing strategies, the director told me, "For us, it is not about just running a business. We are in the business of running businesses!"

That is how great businessmen think!

70

What a Leader should Not Do — 10

An employee's happiness or unhappiness is purely in the hands of the leader. With this, we come to the last two notes of caution for leaders.

Chanakya continues,

"By the negligence and indolence of the king and because of the destruction of well-being (through these causes) decline, greed and disaffection are produced in the subjects." (7.5.19-26)

A leader should never be careless. Even a small issue should not go unnoticed. Secondly, the employee's prosperity and well-being should never be disturbed. If a leader ignores this advice, the downfall of the organisation begins.

The primary reason why leaders tend to be negligent and indolent is lethargy. Without vision, greed takes over. The organisation begins to break apart.

Throughout this series of ten chapters (Chps 61-70), the one clear message is — 'Be Alert'. Keep watch over others and also over yourself. Some tips on being alert:

- Be In Touch With The Last Man

The challenge for any government is to check if the last man in the last village is happy. Till that is achieved, a leader's work is not complete. At times, we find that what is reported is only the success of a few people. As a leader, never go by these reports. Be on the 'ground' yourself. Regularly track what even the peon or driver feels. Talk with them, understand what keeps them going, or makes them feel frustrated. Take corrective steps.

- Take Time Out Without A Reason

In the corporate world most of the work done is based on agendas, results and targets. It's important to open up your mind. It gives a fresh outlook to the organisation. There should be at least a small part of your day when you do nothing! The space that this creates in your mind will give a new insight into the work one does. With that insight apply new techniques.

- Keep Watch

Keep an eye over the people. Keep watch on what is happening in the industry. Keep a watch on changes in the surroundings and your society. All things in the world are interconnected. A small change in some other place will affect you soon, in some way or the other. Therefore, keep yourself updated and informed in all matters.

In this 10-part series we dealt with 21 points that a leader should avoid doing. A student once said to me, "Sir, this is very difficult to follow as I can't remember so many points."

Well, one does not have to remember them all. If you practise even one of these rules, the remaining will follow. They are interconnected. Just start. That is the only way to be sure if these techniques work.

Good luck on the journey to discover the leader in you...

PART II

Management

Employees

71

Safety and Security

The days of conventional wars, when kingdoms or nations fought with weapons like swords and later with sophisticated and more disastrous mass destruction weapons, are over. Now, wars are being fought between democracies with terrorism. The nature of these wars is more complex. This is the time when the importance of security cannot be undermined.

Terrorists target common people, the battlefields are public places and their aim is to disrupt economies. Corporate setups are soft targets and the only weapon we have is vigilance to prevent problems and the knowledge to fight back unanticipated disasters.

Chanakya says,

"For the guard not reporting to the city-superintendent an offence committed during the night whether by the animate or the inanimate, the punishment shall be in conformity with the offence, also in case of negligence." (2.36.42)

This means, an alert security person should be very alert. He has to report to his superiors every single offence that has been committed. He cannot take any seen or unseen movements for granted. If his superior also does not do this, even he shall be punished.

A special focus has to be given to corporate security personnel in the following manner:

• Extra Training

The guards, watchmen, and other security guards in your organisation have to be given extra training and information about the current scenario. They should be briefed about the threats faced by the country and the region specifically. You can also take the help of the local police, or intelligence agencies, to give them the latest updates about security measures suggested by the local, state, and union government.

• Support The Security Guards

All employees have to be made aware of the alarming situation we are in. They should cooperate with security officials. Being frisked and having your bags and personal belongings checked should not be taken as an act calculated to offend you. Do not feel insulted or ashamed. The security personnel is performing his duty. Be part of the system and help the system protect us.

• Work As A Team

It is important to note that it is not the duty of only the security guards to ensure security. Each employee has to play his/her role. Even security guards are human beings working round the clock to ensure safety. Understand their problems as well. Note that we have to work as a team.

Today, the nation, its economy, corporate houses, and our lives are under threat. And we have to rise and fight.

72

Selecting the Right Managers

~~♈~~

An executive manager plays a key role in the successful functioning of a company. His selection and appointment is very important for the growth of the organisation. Headhunters and placement agencies provide resources and services for hiring the right candidate. However, the parameters have to be set by the employer.

Kautilya, in his *Arthashastra,* gives us detailed guidelines to follow while selecting managers who are fresh management trainees, and also those who are experienced and need to be directly recruited for higher responsibilities.

A. Selection of Management Trainees:

Book one, Chapter five, points out the various qualities that must be tested by the Human Resource department when it hunts for management trainees during campus interviews.

Kautilya says that a 'trainable' person is one who has the following six qualities:

1. Desire To Learn: Should be open-minded. After learning all the theories of management, a trainee should be eager to learn the practical side of it from seniors.

2. Effective Listening Ability: Listening is hearing plus thinking. He should be able to understand what is expected from him.

3. Ability To Reflect: He should be able to analyse a situation from various perspectives. Both logical and creative thinking is required in the field of management.

4. Ability To Reject False Views: He should be able to reach his own conclusions. He should be able to understand various points of view.

5. Intent On Truth, Not On Person: This is the ability to separate the person from the problem. He should be able to stick to the 'truth' that he has reached after his own careful analysis.

B. Selection of Experienced Managers

The qualities that must be tested before recruiting a person from another organisation is given in Book one, Chapter nine of the *Arthashastra*.

1. Technical Competence: This must be tested with the help of those people more learned in that science.

2. Intelligence, Perseverance, And Dexterity: His experience should also be coupled with the intelligence to understand the 'crux' of any problem. He should also have the ability to progress inspite of various hindrances.

3. Eloquence, Boldness, And Presence Of Mind: He must have the ability to make quick decisions and a personality that reflects confidence. Eloquence also means to communicate words in a brief, yet effective manner.

4. Ability To Bear Troubles During Emergencies: The true test of a good manager comes during a crisis. He should be able to shoulder all responsibilities and execute an immediate action plan.

5. Uprightness, Friendliness, And Firmness Of Devotion While Dealing With Others: He should be a people's man. Management is the ability to get the work done from the right people.

6. Strength Of Character: Moral strength and ethical dealings have to be conveyed by action rather than just words.

73

Deciding Rank

❧

Degrees and certificates can never guarantee the results a manager can produce. Some of the best managers never completed their formal education. Neither Bill Gates, nor Henry Ford, needed an MBA before starting their respective companies.

A CEO has to focus on the results a person can bring about while recruiting his team of managers, not only their qualifications.

Kautilya says,

"From the capacity for doing work is the ability of the person judged. And in accordance with the ability, by suitably distributing rank among ministers and assigning place time and work to them he should appoint all the ministers." (1.8.28-29)

While the job responsibilities are being delegated to team members, Kautilya outlines five focus areas for a CEO.

• Capacity

The capacity for doing work is the key factor in understanding a person's ability. Only an able person can bring out the best results. In many organisations, managers are recruited based on influence. However, if the person is not capable, the professionalism of the company suffers. One may get the 'chair' based on influence but the 'chair' will not let you be there for long.

• Rank/Designation

Rank and designation should be given based on the candidate's ability. In the current corporate world, we find that ranks are distributed freely. Even freshers are given senior positions without examining their output. The distribution of designations should be done based on the results produced. This is the key to success, particularly for many family-managed businesses in India.

* Place

A person needs to be appointed at the right place. In most industries, if a new branch is being opened, a preference is given to the local candidate. This is because he will understand more about that particular region than others. In the tourism industry every traveller prefers a local guide to an outsider, as locals know more details.

* Time

Timing has to be assigned to the person. First, the time by when he must join the project. Then, the timeframe has to be agreed upon to finish the project. Time-bound targets have to be set in order to bring out the best in a person.

* Work

The work expected to be done by that particular manager has to be defined. Management By Objectives (MBO), a concept of Key Result Area (KRA) gives a definite focus to the manager. This should be followed by a proper and regular feedback system.

When the above areas have been taken into account, it saves a lot of future misunderstanding and complications. Clear communication and an agreement to achieve the defined results not only makes a person effective, but also makes the organisation productive.

74

Stopping Attrition

The biggest challenge faced by any company is that of attrition, i.e. when employees leave the organisation.

Tackling this is the most important task of any and every HR department. Strategies and policies are eternally formulated to solve this problem. After all, continuous training, promotions and hikes in salaries are not enough to stem attrition.

Kautilya suggests,

"He should favour those contented, with additional wealth and honour. He should propitiate with gifts and conciliation those, who are discontented, in order to make them contented." (1.13.16-17)

There are generally two types of employees — content and discontented. Kautilya gives us a tip about handling these two types.

According to him, ignoring the employees who seem content (those who do not ask for a promotion, or a pay rise) is a very bad HR strategy. Every person works in the organisation for his salary. Just because the employee seems content does not mean that he/she really is.

Such people just need a bigger offer from a competitor, and they will be gone like the wind. Hence, if you see a content employee, favour him with additional wealth, awards, and also increments. You will find that they will be more loyal to you. Why? Well, you understood their needs even before they expressed their feelings. After this, there would be no unions or strikes!

As for those who are very restless and discontent, give gifts and other notable benefits to them as well to retain them in the organisation.

There are a few more useful tips that can be followed to avoid attrition.

• Give Importance To HRD (Human Resource Department)

Most top managements consider the HR department to be very ordinary and merely the administrative part of their organisation. Its function is only to recruit, train employees, and maintain their records. In fact, each and every manager should consider the HR to be the top priority in their agenda. Work on your people. Only then will your people work for you.

• CEO Should Be A Mentor

A CEO should be a friend, philosopher and guide to all the employees. Running the business is only a small part of his job. His main job is to be a teacher and train people to become future leaders. He should use his years of experience in running a business to train others to do the same.

• Create Your Own Culture

Instead of copying from others, develop your own culture — an organisational culture that is unique. Others can copy your product and services, but never your culture. Such a culture should be friendly and open. Every employee should feel that he is part of a family.

Break all the rules. Get out of your cabin and spend more time with your staff. Let your organisition be the one where every one feels proud to work.

75

Changing Jobs

Let's face it. There comes a point in each and every person's career when he feels like running away from his routine, almost mundane, job. He feels like taking up a higher responsibility and earning more than what he is currently getting.

For such people Kautilya advises,

"One who is conversant with the ways of the world, should seek service with a king, endowed with personal excellences and the excellences of material constituents, through such as dear and beneficial (to the king)." (5.4.1)

Such an experienced person, who is equipped with the know-how of his work, should definitely seek higher responsibilities. If not, he will feel depressed, stressed, and underutilised.

He should approach the king (leaders of organisations) and after recounting or presenting a summary of his experience and results achieved in the past, should ask for a better job. Now, changing jobs does not mean changing organisations. You can change jobs even within the organisation.

However, while doing so, one should keep in mind the benefits that he can bring to the owner, not just to himself. It is very important to remember that while one is being interviewed for higher positions/responsibilities, the interviewer will always consider the benefits the recruiting firm can get. Hence, keep that foremost in mind.

Steps that will help you take up higher responsibilities:

• Gather Experience

Experience counts a lot when it comes to going up in life. Learn from everyone and everything possible. Update your knowledge and gather some good skills. The more experienced you are, the better your chances of going up in life.

• Prepare A Document

While approaching the people who could promote you, or give you new responsibilities, always carry documents which show your successful endeavours. CVs, portfolios, certificates, press cuttings, reports of the projects you have handled — all these could be helpful.

• Talk About 'Their' Benefits

During the interview, it is very important to discuss the benefits that you can give to your organisation. Talk in terms of definite numbers. Do a little bit of research as you prepare for the interview.

Whatever new assignment you take up, you have to leave your mark.

Bob Dole, a former American leader who ran for the US Presidency, once said, "When it's all over, it's not who you were. It's whether you made a difference."

76

The First Step

≈⟩

Most of us wait for the right opportunity to start looking for our dream job. We wait for a 'wanted' advertisement to appear in the newspaper before even thinking of making the next jump in our career. Even businessmen wait for information to get the 'dream' contract.

This is a big mistake!

Even if our dream job or project is currently not available in the market, we can create the opportunity. Chanakya was a great believer in making efforts ourselves rather than depending on fate or destiny to shape up situations. He says,

"One trusting in fate, being devoid of human endeavour, perishes, because he does not start undertakings, or his undertakings have miscarried (failed)." (7.11.34)

Obviously, if opportunities don't knock on our doors, we go to the opportunities and knock on their doors! Now how does one do that?

Here are a few tips:

• Know Your Strengths

Before you go around banging on doors, do a little bit of introspection. Know your strengths. Focus on what you are good at. Chanakya calls this a person's '*Swadharma*' (what one is naturally capable of doing). Create your dream work/project to which you can deliver better than others. Prepare your résumé or business plan, clearly highlighting your past experience and what makes you different from the others.

- Tap The Right Persons

A good résumé or business plan is not enough in itself. We have to market ourselves. For this, it is important to know who the right people are and which companies would like to use our services. Mail your proposal, call up, and ask for an appointment. Finally, turn up on time and have a word with the right people. A face-to-face meeting is an absolute must. Don't wait for someone to call you. There are many companies that have vacancies and projects to be executed, but do not advertise.

- Be Clear About The Financials

Let's be honest, there are no free lunches. Before you pitch yourself, also think about how much money you want to make from this new initiative. During meetings, you must speak and work on the financials and economics involved. A win-win situation can happen only when our roles, goals, and more importantly, the financials are clear.

Remember that when you finally get your dream job or project, it is not enough. In fact, it's just the beginning. Then you must deliver what you have promised.

Show your capability, not just by words but by result-oriented actions too. And learn to work with others, for that's the secret for succeeding in any project.

77

Death on Duty

≈⌢

Life is very precious and the death of a person brings great sorrow to his near and dear ones. However, if he dies while he is on duty, then the death also becomes the responsibility of the employer.

Despite the best safety measures and policies made to avoid accidents, there is a possibility that an employee may lose his life during work.

Kautilya's advice for such unforeseen circumstances is:

"Of those dying while on duty, the sons and wives shall receive the food and wages. And their minor children, old and sick persons should be helped. And he should grant them money and do honour on occasions of death, illness, and birth ceremonials." (5.3.28-30)

For organisations like the defence forces, the government has worked out the compensation in such cases. But, what needs to be noted here is that Kautilya wants the employer to not just give the family financial compensation but, in fact, take on bigger responsibilities.

He suggests that the employer should consider the family of the deceased employee as his own family.

He should not only look after their basic needs like food and financial assistance but also consider the needs of the children like education, mentoring, and guidance. 'Honour on occasions' — to use the exact words.

Once an accident took place in a highly respected Indian company, and 60 employees lost their lives. The media asked the head of the corporate giant, "How much money are you planning to give their families?"

His answer was typical of the company's employer-friendly policies, "It will depend on each family's need."

Unlike our politicians, who announce a fixed sum of compensation for all families, the top company official had decided to understand the need of each family.

If some family required more money, it was given. Similarly, if someone required assistance in rehabilitation, it was provided, if a child needed education, it was taken care of. That approach shows concern.

Here are some tips for facing such situations in today's scenario:

- Insurance

Make sure that each of your employees has a life insurance. Have your HR department ensure that each employee has at least one policy in effect.

- Understand Each Employee

Each person in your organisation has different family needs. Keep a record of their family members — how many people in the family, what they do, and so on. Organise family meets to ensure a good family-worklife balance.

- Be There

When an employee loses his life, meet the family. Do not just send a manager with a cheque. Be present with the family and share their pain.

As someone has said beautifully, "After the death of a near one, I often wished for a few words of love, rather than the tears of thousands of people."

78

Taking care of Employees

Now this is more for your boss than you! Still, read on, as the ever-booming economy may someday help you establish a business and employ people yourself. And when you do that, you will soon realise that good, talented, and skilled people are really rare.

Ask anyone in the HR department. Not only do they have to

recruit and train people, but they have to also retain people within the organisation. In the end, it must be realised that it is not the brand nor even the salary that can retain people — it's the human touch the organisation is capable of giving.

For this, Chanakya suggests that the management needs to be totally aware of what the employees think — if they don't, they are playing with danger,

"Not being rooted among the subjects, he becomes easy to uproot."
(8.2.18)

Here are a few steps to do this:

• Take Time Out For Your Your Employees

It is important to spend time with all your subordinates, individually. There is just no substitute for this. Set aside half an hour every day for this purpose. This will help you understand the way each employee thinks and can help resolve problems as they first start to appear.

• Get Out Of Your Cabin

Do not sit in your cabin and give orders over the phone. Now and then, get out of our cabin and walk to the employees' desk and work stations. There are many benefits in doing this — one, this acts as a surprise check. Secondly, you will directly know what is happening in the office.

• Plan An Outing

There are limits in an office. An outing with your team, a celebration of major events at a different venue, a party or picnic, will not only reduce the stress levels but also help everyone emotionally relate to each other. Many talents are discovered during informal celebrations and gatherings.

• Keep Records

Now, this is the most important part. Maintain a different file for each employee with the help of the HR department. It should document the details of each employee. Record keeping is not enough; the management should look at it from time to time and make effective use of the employees by looking up their inherent strengths.

A recent survey to find out the best employer among the corporates indicated that employees who feel 'wanted and challenged' in a work place have better chances of staying committed to the company for a longer period of time.

This is better reflected in what the American industrialist Charles Erwin Wilson once said, "A good boss makes his men realise they have more ability than they think they have, so that they consistently do better work than they thought they could."

79

Security above Salary

I have once again decided to deal with the topic of attrition. Many are still surprised at the gigantic proportions this problem has taken. ALL the organisations face attrition today. Consultants are being appointed, research is being conducted and new methods and strategies are being sought out to understand why people leave organisations!

The first reason that people think of is that employees leave due to higher salaries offered by other companies. However, it is clearly seen that money or higher salaries alone cannot reduce the attrition rate.

Chanakya gives us food for thought,

"Even for a very large sum of money, no one would desire the loss of his life." (8.3.35)

So what is it that makes people shift jobs, or change companies? The answer is multifold.

- The Immediate Boss

There is a popular saying, 'People don't leave companies, they leave their bosses!' Your immediate boss is a reflection of the whole organisation. The Chairman may be the best leader in the industry, but he may not be able to reach the last man in the organisation. The heads of department, the middle managers, the line managers, all of them become a source of inspiration for the people working immediately below them. If this person is a good leader, people will be inspired to work. If he is not, even those in blue chip companies will quit their jobs.

- Salary

Yes, this is important. You cannot keep your employees dedicated and faithful to the company on an empty stomach. People need to earn good money and also receive a hike once in a while. Note that the 'high' salary an employee demands is not automatically the 'right' salary. The environment also plays a major role in the expenses of the individual. The cost of living in a particular place, the number of people who are dependent on his income, his lifestyle — all have an impact on determining the salary expectations of the individual.

- Security

This factor is the topmost on any employee's mind. How does one define security? It has many aspects. Financial security, mental security, and also a feeling of being at the right place at the right time. The definition of security will also change from person to person and even from generation to generation.

I was conversing with a top management professional from a multinational company who has spent over 25 years in the same firm, despite better offers. When I tried to find out why, he explained, "Ours is a human company. More than the salary, it was the fact that we always felt at home." Try to achieve this 'family-feeling' in your organisation.

80

Command Promotion

≈୨

Getting promoted should not be demanded, it should be commanded. Promotion from one position to the next is directly related to the results produced.

Regarding promotions, Chanakya tells the leaders,

"He (king) should make those his ministers who, when appointed to tasks, the income from which is calculated (beforehand), would bring in the income as directed or more, since (thus) their qualities are proved." (1.8.13)

The quality of a person is proved by his output. But here, Kautilya becomes more specific emphasising the productivity of the employee by saying that promotion is to be considered according to the income the employee brings to the organisation. Such a person should be made a minister (at a senior managerial position).

During a job interview, the employer talks about the pay package in terms of CTC (Cost to Company). At this point in time, the employer calculates the expenses he would incur for the candidate, if he were to recruit him. The employer will also look into the probable revenue generated by the candidate and accordingly, decide upon the package.

If given a particular assignment or project, the manager has a fixed budget within which he has to operate. There is also a particular profit expected from the project. If at the end of the project the expected profits (or more profits) are made, or even budgeted expenses are reduced, such a person should be considered for promotion.

So what can an employee learn from the above *sutra*?

• Make A Financial Contribution

Every employee irrespective of the department he belongs to

should make a financial contribution justifying the remuneration paid by his organisation.

Dr Makrand Tare, an Human Resource Management (HRD) specialist was addressing a group of HR managers. He said, "Even if you are in HR, you should contribute to your company in terms of financial gains, either by bringing down costs or by increasing the productivity of your employees."

• Show Your Result In Numbers

Just because you have made a financial contribution, do not just sit back. Show your results to your seniors by presenting them with numbers. Make a report, make a graph and tell your bosses how you, being a part of the project, have made a significant contribution. Learn to sell yourself at every stage of your career.

• Think Like An Employer

Give more than you take. Do not expect a promotion or an increment at the end of each year. Ask yourself, what your boss wants from you. Work in that direction. Produce more wealth for your organisation than what you consume.

An MBA student during his campus interview was asked, "What is your salary expectation?" His answer was, "Sir, that is for you to decide at this stage. At the end of six months let us review my performance. Then I will tell you what my expectation is." He was immediately recruited.

81

Make People Accountable

⋙⤳

While it's difficult to get the right people for the right job, it's even more difficult to make the people currently working with you be productive and efficient.

Chanakya has a solution for this — if employees are not productive, then impose a fine on them!

Chanakya provides an example:

"He (the leader) should wait for one month, if the (accounts officer) has not brought in the day-to-day accounts, after one month, the (officer) shall pay a fine of two hundred panas increased (by that amount) for each succeeding month." (2.7.26)

However, this system is to be implemented one step at a time, according to Chanakya who lists the tactics called *Sama, Dana, Bheda,* and *Danda.*

But how do we follow this system? Here are some tips:

• Define What Is Expected

This is the first step. Clearly spell out what is expected from the employee. Most problems start when we do not communicate our expectations clearly. A well-defined job profile and job description will help a person understand his role. One way of doing this is to document these roles and expectations. The best way is to make the person himself write it, lest he forgets.

• Regular Supervision

Keep an eye on the person who is doing the work. Regular supervision, and asking the right questions will help if the employee is about to lose direction. This does not mean that you need to be 'bossy' or restrict a person. You must allow the employee freedom to carry out the task in his or her style. You need not define 'how' but you will have to define 'what' and 'why'. It's important that the person maintains his focus on his productivity.

• Reminders And Following-Up

When you do this for the first time, it will take some time for the person to understand. However, with patience and practice, incorporate this into a system which runs the show, rather than doing this yourself! Of course, if you keep issuing reminders and the work still doesn't get done, then it is time to take some serious action.

- The Fine

Chanakya suggested that the unproductive employee must be fined! Just announcing this, or making this part of the company policy will not help. One has to implement it from time to time. This will get rid of lethargy and the employee will act quickly to protect himself. It will also send out the message that you are serious about your business and no one can take his work for granted.

If each person in an organisation works with optimum productivity as per the goals defined, the business world itself would be different!

82

Safety in any Deal-Making

In any leader's life, there comes a moment when he has to take some critical decisions while striking a big deal. At times, he has to consider the deal's financial impact, the impact on the morale (of the employees) and also any future impact it may have on the market position he currently holds.

During such difficult times, when he has do decide between the present and the future, Chanakya suggests that the leader consider the safety angle first.

Chanakya says,

"He should not follow that policy by resorting to which he were to see the ruin of his own undertakings, not of (those of) the other party." (7.1.24)

So, while going in for that big deal, always consider these aspects:

- The Financial Aspect

Business is about wealth creation, wealth management and wealth expansion. As a leader, one should not ignore this critical angle. Secure the wealth that you have created, manage the existing wealth and focus on the wealth that can be created in the future. Be non-emotional while dealing with this aspect. However, emotions cannot be left out all the time. This is where the next aspect comes in...

- The Human Aspect

The key asset in any organisation is the human one — those who created it, and run it. You not only have to take care of their well-being and development, you also have to consider the impact on their morale.

A huge team without any enthusiasm is nothing when compared to a smaller group with an 'enthusiastic' drive to change and excel. It's this enthusiasm which makes the difference in a war.

- The Social Aspect

This is very important. Even if the previous two aspects are taken care of while concluding a deal, never miss out on the social impact it may have. The deal may make a lot of money for the employees and also the shareholders, but if it causes problems in the environment, ecology, or nature, you need to think twice about the deal.

In the movie *Sarkar*, which was inspired by *The Godfather*, there is a similar negotiation scene. A drug-dealer comes to the Don and offers him a big deal for getting the necessary sanctions for a drug-shipment meant for the new-found market.

The money offered for clearing the consignment was huge, but the Don refused it since he found that even if he or his team made the money, it would cause a great problem for youngsters and the future generations.

It's not easy, but it's important to negotiate. The 'thought' that is put into the deal-making process, the 'study' and research all have an impact on the final outcome.

So sharpen your intellect, broaden your heart and, with maturity, strike the deal.

83

Welcoming back Ex-Workers

༄

Changing jobs frequently is a very common occurrence in today's corporate world. Gone are the days when a person retired from the same organisation which gave him his first salary cheque.

The reasons why people quit are many, but the most important reason is that they do not find growth possibilities, or that their immediate boss is not effective enough to retain or inspire them further.

But, there is one more scenario. What if someone who quit the organisation wants to come back? Now this is a dilemma for the decision-maker.

Chanakya guides us on what to do:

"One deserting because of the master's fault and returning because of his virtue, (or) deserting because of the enemy's virtue and returning because of his fault, is one deserting and returning on good grounds, fit to be made peace with." (7.6.24)

So you need to get a complete perspective — Why did the person quit? Why has this person come back? And what are the benefits or loss that it can lead to?

Let's look at these parameters in detail:

• Why Did The Person Quit?

Be honest — was it your fault as a leader that he left? In that

150

case, he is worthy of returning if you have learnt your lesson and are already working on improving your leadership skills.

Was it in a fit of anger that you fired the person? Or was it some miscommunication? Did the person quit because he found something good in the new employer? In that case also, it is a fault with the leadership, because you did not have that 'quality' which your competitor has.

In both cases, the person should be welcomed back.

- Was The Person Right?

There are issues and situations that were not under the control of the person quitting. For example, at that time, he required a pay scale (as a necessity) which you could not provide.

Or, did the person realise that it was his mistake to quit as your organisation was really better and genuinely wants to come back and work productively? In this case too he could be welcomed back.

- The Person's Virtues

The final check point! What is the value-addition the person brings? Probably, the person has a skill or art that only he possesses, and is already in demand in the industry as he is really 'good' at the work he does. Even in this case, the person can be welcomed back.

Whether you do all these calculations or not, it's finally your gut feeling that matters. You have to take a decision and look ahead. Looking back at the past is good, but moving ahead is more important.

84

Tackling Attrition

≈⁙

Big brands can attract employees, but they cannot retain them. A recent study revealed that it's the biggest brands that face the highest level of attrition. Surprisingly, smaller companies — some without a proper HR department — enjoy a near-zero attrition rate. Now, this is worthy of research.

In larger organisations, work is totally dependent on key people. Yet, as stated above, there is no guarantee that they will stay in the company forever. Now, how can one ensure that the required work is done despite attrition?

Chanakya suggests:

"He should establish (each) department with many heads and without permanency (of tenure of office)." (2.9.31)

People may run organisations. However, good organisations are run by good systems along with good people.

Therefore, one of the strategies that Chanakya suggests is to make a system that takes attrition into account right from day one.

In the above verse, he suggests some key strategic points for the job-profiling of senior people:

• 'Many Heads'

The head of any particular project or department is a key person. The dependency of an organisation on this person is very high. Chanakya suggests reversing this dependency — split the responsibility.

When he uses the phrase 'many heads' he means that if you require one head, have three heads instead. The reason? If one person leaves, there are still two more to look after things. The work continues without a break as the others take over.

So prepare all three heads with equal training and trust.

A company once had a vacancy for a President's post. But it appointed three Vice-Presidents instead and split the job. Amazing results were achieved. In the long run, they ended up with two highly productive Presidents.

* 'Without Permanency'

No one is permanent in this world, including the founder himself. What remains permanent are the vision and the goodwill created because of the work one has done. Therefore, with people too, do not expect permanency.

When you work with this attitude, you will give your best. The best way to make yourself permanent is to make more duplicates like you. Even if one duplicate is close to what you are, you have done your job. Let them take over and continue from where you have stopped.

* 'Establish'

The only way of ensuring non-dependency on people is continuous training. Now this is not just a formal process, rather, it's the very 'lifeline' of any organisation, the very breath that keeps it alive.

If we study organisations that have lasted for generations, we will find that they have put in place good systems along with continuous training. Adapt these and see the positive changes that it will lead to.

85

Quality Control

There are two kinds of players in any sector — those who offer high quality at a high price, and those who offer low quality for a low price. A customer chooses between the two depending on his priority.

However, no one can compromise on quality when it comes to critical items like food, beverages, and medicines. Otherwise, it could prove fatal for the consumer.

Chanakya not only emphasised the importance of quality checks, but also set up government control methods in his day to ensure that quality of products did not suffer.

"For perishable goods, a retraction may be allowed with the restriction: 'It shall not be sold elsewhere'. In case of transgression of that, the fine is twenty-four panas or one-tenth of the goods." (3.15.7-8)

In the above verse, we see that only for perishable commodities Chanakya sets a policy that it has to be consumed within a particular region. He even defines the punishment if this is not followed.

How does one ensure high quality products and services in one's own organisation? Here are some tips:

• Understand The Meaning Of Quality

The meaning of quality changes from person to person and also from market to market. It differs completely from one segment to another. For example, a person who always used to wear torn clothes will consider even a second-hand but decent shirt as 'high quality'.

A person who is privileged to wear clean and good clothes will consider only a branded shirt or designer wear to be 'high quality'. So understand this mindset and your customer's requirements to define what quality means. Another example would be the exporters who send second-hand Indian clothes to poorer nations as against the domestic textile industry.

• Set Up Parameters

It is important to set up parameters to ensure quality before sending, or marketing, the produced goods and services. All well-known brands have quality control departments which monitor processes in their factories at each and every level, rather than just at the final stage.

No wonder then that these departments are called quality 'assurance' instead of quality 'control'. Each person at every stage of production is therefore responsible for guaranteeing the quality.

* Improving Continuously

The demand in the market is growing, the needs of the customers are changing. Hence, the definition of quality also changes from time to time. Understand this and improve accordingly.

In a shrinking world, it's better to pitch ahead and make products that reach global standards. Therefore, it pays to apply concepts like Total Quality Management (TQM), ISO certifications, etc, in your processes and systems. Above all, learn from your mistakes, accept customer feedback and adopt the same in the next level of improvement of your quality standards.

86

Selecting the Right Person

Now this is a challenge that the HR departments face the most. But, today, almost every section chief has to take on the role of an HR person not only to keep his team intact, but to also strengthen it further.

That's because companies now fight more for people than for market share. Still, you can't recruit every other person. You have to carefully select the right candidates from all the applicants, and an interview is the most critical entry point as it determines the future of the new recruit as well as of the company.

Apart from salary, post, and job profile, Chanakya suggests that it is important to know the 'thinking', 'mind-set', and 'psychology' of the candidate:

"On finding out, he should keep him in accordance with his intentions." (7.6.29)

But which questions should one ask during interviews? Here are some examples:

• 'Who Is Your Role Model?'

Interviews usually start with the interviewer asking, "Tell me something about yourself." The very next query should be, "Who is your role model?" This is a very different, yet powerful question.

The answer will tell you about the candidate's thinking pattern, because a role model is a person one usually thinks about, relates to, and even tries to copy.

If a person says Bill Gates, you will know that there is a businessman or an IT professional inside him who is seeking an opportunity. If it's Gandhiji or any spiritual guru, it means that the person values noble ideals and gives importance to 'ethics' in life.

• 'Whom Do You Spend Time With?'

It's important to know the interests and lifestyle of the person beyond office hours. If the answer is 'family', you know he is a family man.

If the person's free time is mostly spent in libraries or with friends, you know he is seeking education and knowledge, or just companionship, respectively.

As the old saying goes, "Company makes the man."

• 'Suppose You Were Asked To....?'

It would help to give the person a cultural shock by forecasting a change in job profile. For example, if you are interviewing a Chartered Accountant for a senior financial post, ask him, "What if we ask you to head the marketing department in a year's time?"

The answer will tell you his ability for 'change management'. The more a person is adaptable to change, the more the benefit for both the parties.

Make the interview fun and mentally challenging, rather than just a mundane recruitment process.

If you interview a job candidate in this manner, you will understand the human mind better, and even accurately predict if the candidate will have a successful career in your firm.

87

Don't Beat Around the Bush

≈୬

Does this situation ring a bell? You desperately want to discuss something important with your boss. When you finally work up the nerve to enter his cabin, you start off by talking about everything, except what you really want to tell him.

Slowly, you see your boss getting irritated. In a worst-case scenario, your boss screams, "Please come to the point...fast!" By then, he's surely prejudiced against you.

You have to understand that people who reach the top are inherently sharp and can understand the 'core issue' very quickly. So when you are with them, do not beat around the bush.

Now after understanding this point, look at the same situation from the point of view of the leader. Our seniors always like to work with people who are sharp and can understand things immediately.

Even Chanakya had some very practical advice for leaders when it comes to choosing their subordinates. He said,

"The demand is to be made only once, not twice." (5.2.30)

In other words, a leader should be surrounded by workers who need to be told anything just *once*. And if you ensure you are good enough to be part of this crack team, your career is made:

• Be Among The Right People

All great leaders invariably have great teams, which were formed by ensuring that the right people were selected. Remember, we are talking not of the whole team but the core 'strategic' team. This will be the think-tank of the organisation. It requires mature, sharp, and brilliant people. If you work hard enough to get into this team, your most important work is done.

• Gain The Vision

Even though you may be sharp, you still need training to gain the same vision that your seniors have for the organisation. This has to be done in the right manner.

If you are really good, just one logical explanation with facts and figures will be enough. You and your team will then be a part of the senior's dream and the journey itself will be smooth.

• Stay In Touch

Hurdles are bound to exist and they come back in some form or the other. So you have to stay in touch with the leader as you need to make sure that you and your team are not drifting from the plan.

Keep yourself focused towards your objective and make sure that the entire team is doing this too.

Always remember that gaining leadership yourself is not just about strategies, but also about being part of a strategic team. Once your team is ready, any demand you make will surely be made only once, not twice.

88

Reward Productive People

≈୭

All of us are surrounded by people who believe that it's just not worth making extra efforts at the job if the salary is fixed. This is where the theory of productivity and incentives kicks in — the more you work, the more rewards you will get.

But the onus is on the boss and the firm's owners to identify the productive people in their organisations and not only reward them, but also make them stay.

Chanakya had a strategy in place for this:

"In case more work is done than agreed upon, he shall not make the effort vain." (3.14.11)

In addition to this being a rule for paying out bonuses, the above verse can also be used as a yardstick to check if employees are good — just check if they have done far more than what they were expected to do.

If the answer is yes, then the management has to ensure that their 'extra' efforts are rewarded. But how can a boss keep track of his employees' productivity?

* Keep Notes

It's important that the director, CEO, or even the head of a department keep notes of people who are productive. People who are sincere, dedicated, and committed are essential in every company. Such people are the pillars of any organisation. While it's good to keep mental notes of the staff's performance, it would be best if these could be written down for future reference.

* Look For New Opportunities

A leader should keep looking not only for new business

opportunities but also for opportunities that can be given to productive people. The basic thought should be that an employee who has been very productive and dedicated to the company needs to be part of any new and wonderful assignment which offers better rewards.

• Promote When Required

When seniors in an organisation find that certain people are good, they should not hesitate to promote them. Promotion means far more than just giving a higher designation. It can mean salary hikes, a share in profits, or even an opportunity to head a new venture. Thus, the person also feels empowered and recognised within the company.

They say, "People do not leave organisations, they leave their bosses." But, according to me, "People should not leave their organisations due to lack of identification of their skill by their bosses!"

89

Take the Initiative

≈9

A good leader inspires every follower and makes him productive — be it community leaders, spiritual leaders, or corporate leaders. In the presence of the master, everyone feels safe and secure. But the real challenge is when the big boss is not around.

There are two situations which may force a boss to not come in to work. Either it was planned and others were informed about his or her absence, or the boss has to deal with some emergency.

In either case, the subordinates are supposed to take charge. Chanakya says:

"The minister should take steps in case of calamity of the king." (5.6.1)

So, if the king is not around, the minister should take charge. If the Director or CEO is not present, the managers — or if the boss is not around, the subordinates — should take charge.

But, how does one go about this?

- Observe The Boss

So many of us follow a leader, yet forget to understand the leader. Following the leader is good, but understanding the leader is much more important. This is a skill that every person has to develop.

Whenever you are around the boss, observe him. Ask yourself, why does he do this? What does he really want?

Try to read between the lines and listen to the unsaid words. As the great Jesuit priest and psychotherapist Anthony de Mello said, "The words of a master seem ordinary, but have foreign meaning."

- Start Taking Small Decisions

Good leaders expect their team to take the right decisions in the overall interest of the company or country. However, if you do not have this habit, start taking small decisions yourself even when the boss is around. Taking small decisions will give you the confidence needed to take big decisions.

- Take Charge

Finally, when the boss is not around, the followers have to take charge. There should not be a vacuum just because the leader is absent. The show must go on. Each person should think like the boss and be a good boss himself.

Once, the leader of a successful organisation was asked how the company managed to maintain its good performance even after the Founder had passed away. He replied, "The master is gone, but he left behind masterpieces!"

90

Want to be a Good Boss?

≈⋺

Surveys have repeatedly proved that one of the biggest reasons why people leave an organisation is because they cannot work under their boss. To be an ideal leader, or a good boss, is an eternal challenge.

A good boss is not produced in B-schools, nor with the help of management lectures and seminars.

But Chanakya gives us a hint:

"And, in all cases, he should favour the stricken (subjects) like a father." *(4.3.43)*

In our own homes, the role of a father has been well-defined. He is full of love and concern. At the same time, he is also a strict disciplinarian. But whatever the case, a father will never abandon his children.

Here are some tips for you to adopt with your subordinates to become a good boss:

• Understand Them

Always remember that an employee is not just a money-generating machine. They have a life outside the office. They have a family, a friend circle, and also various interests and hobbies. It is important to understand their total personality. Once you understand their expectations, it will be easy to manage those expectations. Only then will you be able to tune into your employees.

• Give Time To Educate Them

No good parent will ever expect the child to work and make money for them from Day One. Similarly, your employees have to

162

be educated, instructed, and prepared before they meet bigger challenges. Even you have to be part of their training and development. No doubt they will make mistakes and just like children fall when they try to walk, so will employees stumble in the course of their duty. But with support and self confidence, they will one day run faster than you.

- Discipline With Love

The greatest challenge for any parent is to know the balance between discipline and love. The solution is love with discipline and discipline with love. An area has to be demarcated — a framework has to indicated — beyond which there is dangerous territory. Subordinates, like children, are full of energy and enthusiasm. It is important to encourage their creativity. But it is equally important to give direction to their work. Discipline, coupled with love, is the answer.

Finally, whatever you do, remember that no classroom lectures can achieve what one learns from direct experience. Therefore, in your own maturity, understand that in spite of your best efforts, the employee may still make the same mistakes that you did. Accept it with love and grace.

There is a beautiful phrase I am reminded of, "A man learns that his father was right, when his son tells him that he is wrong!" Maybe we will need to remember this while dealing with our employees.

Finance

91

Net Profit Counts!

I once met a successful French businessman who had started his business from scratch. It was while he was sharing his success stories with me that I got an insight into how beginners in the business field misunderstand 'profits'.

He said, "First-level businessmen always feel income is profit. Once they mature in running a business, they realise that real profit is what comes after calculating the expenses and taxes."

Now, this French businessman was merely echoing words that were first written by Chanakya two thousand years ago,

"When assigned work, he should show income cleared of expenses."
(5.5.1)

This is a simple, yet most important basic, lesson for the head of a business unit or profit centre. Such people, when they report to their head or board of directors, always show numbers, which is the top line (incoming). Now it's nice to have a good turnover, but sales are *not* profits.

But how do we understand this difference? Let us take it step-by-step:

- Top-line

The sales numbers (what is sold and orders that have been confirmed) is generally called the 'Top-Line'. These numbers are what people look at. "We reached a 100 crore figure this year." This statement would generally mean that the sales that particular year have touched a figure of 100 crore. Sales are the revenue for any organisation. It is also called 'ITB' (In The Box), the sales pipeline that have been converted into confirmed orders.

- Expenses

Sales bring money into an organisation. This incoming is the cash flow of the organisation. A regular and strong cash flow is the backbone of any business. After this, expenses take place. Salaries to the staff, investment in infrastructure like office, technology, and information systems are calculated. Next, we have other overheads like travel, marketing cost, training etc. All this put together are the total expenses of the company. As the company grows its top-line, its expenses also grow accordingly.

- Bottom Line

What is left from sales minus the expenses are your profits — the Bottom line. This is what differentiates successful businesses from sick businesses. There are companies that have great top lines but small bottom lines. Yes, now there are other factors as well — like taxes, total assets and their valuation etc. However, what the shareholders will generally look at is the dividend which is now called the real bottom line.

Adi Godrej, Chairman of the Godrej group of companies had summarised it briefly, "Sales is Vanity, Profit is Sanity, Cash is

Reality!" Understand this basic principle and you will understand how to make your company more profitable.

92

Take Care of the Treasury in Difficult Times

≈⃝৩

The king (leader) plays a very important role in any organisation. He has to take care of all his subjects (employees). The only way to do this is if the king has financial stability and security. So, keeping his treasury full should be the leader's prime concern.

Therefore, Chanakya advises us:

"The (king) without a treasury should collect a treasury, when difficulties concerning money have arisen." (5.2.1)

There will always be difficult times, when money does not come into a treasury. Even during these times, a king has to carry on with collecting revenues and keep the business going.

This is a major challenge for any organisation's leader. But the following tips will help make the organisation financially stable:

• Budget

Money may keep flowing into an organisation, but it also goes out at double the speed it comes in! Controlling this outflow is possible only if one plans in advance. You should have a system similar to the dam on a river which helps in storing water so that it can be used as per our convenience.

• Learn About Finance

One very important aspect of financial management is to continuously learn financial skills. As your company grows, the financial challenges grow too.

It starts from the capital requirement stage, and then comes the short-term 'running capital' requirement, and, if not tracked well, there could even be a debt-stage which can prove fatal for the organisation. So, keep learning new financial skills about investments, tax structuring, etc.

• Network

This suggestion may not seem to be related to financial planning, but it is very important. It's our friend circle and the network of goodwill that we have created which will help us during financial crises.

Yes, in spite of all our planning, there are times when things can go terribly wrong. Then how will you fill up your treasury? It will be this network which will prove helpful at that time.

Be proactive in creating a good friend circle. As they say, "The best time to make friends is before you need them." Friends make you richer not only in monetary terms but also in the help you get while facing challenges in life.

As Swami Chinmayanandaji said, "To have a friend, you need to be a friend first."

93

Wages

∼◌

For Chanakya, the subjects and their welfare was more important than kingship. Every idea in the *Arthashastra* is directed towards this end. Thus every CEO has to take into consideration the welfare of his employees first, which will ultimately benefit him. The *Arthashastra* clearly shows that Kautilya envisioned the welfare of society,

"In the happiness of the subjects lies the benefit of the king and in what is beneficial to the subjects is his own benefit." (1.19.34)

Arthashastra evolved a wage structure, which provides the protection of workers against exploitation, or unduly low wages, and also facilitated justice and fairness for the sound relationship between the employer and the employee.

- Consideration For Employees

What had been visualised by Kautilya in 3 B.C. found its way in the Minimum Wages Act of 1948. It recognises that wages cannot be determined by market forces of supply and demand alone. Workers also were allowed to choose their work and enter into a contract before starting any work.

If the employee gets sick he is also given due consideration,

"If he is incapable due to ill health or due to a calamity, he shall get an extension." (3.14.2)

Whatever salary was fixed for labourers, the master was obliged to pay it, and in case the rule was violated, he had to undergo punishment,

"In case of non-payment of the wage, the fine is twelve panas or five times the wage." (3.13.34)

- Consideration Of The Employers

However, the wage structure was not one-sided. The employer's efforts were also safeguarded. Productivity of the workers was taken into consideration while paying wages,

"A wage is for work done, not for what is not done." (3.14.8)

According to Kautilya, if the labourer after receiving the wages, did not complete his work he was fined,

"An employee not doing the work after receiving the wage, the fine is twelve panas, and detention till it is done." (3.14.1)

If the employee did not return to his work, the master was at liberty to engage another worker,

"In case the employee misses the time (or completion) or does the work in a wrong manner, he may complete the work through another." (3.14.10-14)

• Deciding A Fair Wage

But how do we decide what is the correct wage? For this, we will have to meet the current industry standards and also consider the time and effort that is put in a job,

"The payment of the wages was decided on the basis of work done, time spent in doing it, at the rate prevailing at the time." (3.13.27)

This concept has been adopted by the committee of Fair Wages, Government of India, set up in 1949 which prescribed,

"The prevailing rates of wages in the same or similar occupations in the same or neighbouring localities." (Report of the Committee of Fair Wages, Delhi, 1954).

94

Budgeting

≈୨

The term 'budget' signifies estimation and organisation of revenue and expenditure of an organisation or state. A strong financial foundation is necessary for an organisation or state to be sound and stable. Good budgeting is the basis of a strong financial architecture. Hence, financial management plays a prominent role in the development of any organisation or country.

"All undertakings are dependent first on the treasury. Therefore, he (the leader) should look to the treasury first." (2.8.1)

The CEO of an organisation is advised to focus on increasing the revenue and cash flow into the treasury. He is also recommended a good management system to take care of budgeting. Forecasting the details of financial management constitute the exercise of budgeting.

Kautilya emphasises that the officer-in-charge of finance (the

CFO in today's corporate world) should concentrate all his efforts on increasing income and reducing expenditure.

The details of each financial activity, including record keeping, types of income and control of expenditure and taxation is given in Book two, Chapter seven of *Arthashastra*.

• Accounting Systems

"He (leader) should check the accounts for each day, group of five days, fortnight, month, four months and a year." (2.7.30)

The leader is expected to maintain a system of daily, weekly, monthly, and yearly accounting systems to regularly check the income and expenditure. Thus, he can make required corrections and control expenditure.

• Record Keeping

"He should check the income and expenditure with reference to the period, place, time, head of income/expenditure, source, bringing forward, quantity, the payer/ paid, the person causing payments to be made, the recorder and the receiver." (2.7.31-32)

Kautilya has recommended maintaining the records of financial transactions in minute detail. He has suggested limiting withdrawals from the treasury. In short, the state should regulate its finance in such a way that it can easily manage through calamitous times.

As an economist, Kautilya balanced his budgets well and always preferred surplus budgets to deficit budgets.

• Taxation

However, while filling up the treasury he was conscious of the economic structure of the people. Several sections of society such as old people, crippled persons, and widows were exempted from taxation.

Kautilya took several steps to ensure that a king got taxes from people like a person picked up ripe fruits from a tree. The king should not anger the people by over-burdening them with taxes, just as one should not pluck unripe fruits as it affects the growth of the tree.

95

Internal Accounting Systems

∼の

The treasury is the heart of an organisation. It is always based on the financial performance of the company that is evaluated by its investors, shareholders, and promoters.

Both the CEO (Chief Executive Officer) and the CFO (Chief Financial Officer) ensure that the organisation is in good financial condition. It is important for them to not only build a good internal accounting system, but to also ensure that there are no unwanted expenses. Thus, they ensure that the employees are not corrupt.

In order to achieve this, Kautilya says that a good financial reporting system has to be developed in an organisation. He offers some advice regarding a good accounting system within an organisation:

In addition to reporting in detail as well as in aggregate, there is also an individual accountability for the revenues and the expenditures." (2.7.24)

Revenues and expenditures are part of the continuous cycle in any economy. A regular record of both has to be maintained. A detailed account of each of the heads of revenues and expenses is to be recorded by the accounts department. The *Arthashastra* deals with this topic, covering this subject from various angles.

Mostly, revenue is received via a single department, but expenditures are made by different departments. Therefore, a detailed as well as collective report of the revenue and expenditures has to be maintained. Expenses have to be recorded not only as heads, but also note the individuals who are responsible for it. In this manner, it is easy to track the outgoing in an organisation, and who is causing it.

"He (leader) should check the accounts for each day, group of five days, fortnight, month, four months (quarterly) and a year." (2.7.30)

Not only do proper records have to be maintained, it is important for the leader to check these on a regular basis. Kautilya lists the periods when these accounts should be checked. He says that the check should be carried out daily, weekly, every 15 days, monthly, quarterly, and yearly.

This system started by Kautilya 2400 years ago has already been widely practised by organisations across the globe. Not only has this principle been applied in the accounting systems, it can be applied in various departments to ensure productivity.

For example, if a sales target, or the deadline for completing a project is set, the leader has to keep checking the progress on a daily, weekly, monthly, quarterly, and yearly basis. This will keep the employees on their toes and the leader alert and active.

Jack Welch, the former head of GE, once said, "Regular reporting and inspections are required in order to get focused and refocused on our goals."

96

Paying Taxes on Time

≈୬

March signals the end of the financial year when people start paying their taxes. Nearly every one is busy filing their returns and/or making investments that offer tax benefits. But should we manipulate our accounts so much that we do not pay taxes at all?

Kautilya says it is the duty of the citizen to pay taxes and that of the leaders to use the taxes for nation building:

"Those who do not pay fines and taxes take on themselves the sins of those (kings) and the kings who do not bring about well-being and security (take on themselves the sins) of the subjects." (1.13.8)

The concept of direct and indirect taxes and also fines was formally introduced and made systematic by Kautilya 2400 years ago! The income of the whole government machinery depends on taxes and fines. The money thus collected is used for national security, maintenance, and development.

Therefore, according to Kautilya, not paying taxes brings on our heads the sins of their leaders and the nation. On the other hand, the kings (politicians and government officials) who misuse the money collected will have to suffer for the sins of the people.

While filing your returns remember these tips:

• Do Not Wait For March

A recent survey showed that over 70 percent employees pay their entire salary for March as taxes. This is only because they postponed the essential. Plan your investments and tax payments in advance. A tax planner once said, "I invest a lakh in the beginning of the financial year, i.e. in April."

• Have A Tax Consultant

Lots of changes related to taxes, constantly take place in the corporate world. Even two years after implementing the Value Added Tax (VAT) and Fringe Benefit Tax (FBT), most company owners do not understand what it entails. Engage an expert tax consultant who can help you understand these concepts.

• Do Not Be Afraid

Do not be afraid of inspections by the government. If you have paid your taxes and discharged your duty towards the nation, why should you be afraid of inspections, or routine checks? Fear of government servants leads to corruption.

Let us take an oath to fight corruption. Fighting corruption will not be necessary if one only follows the rules laid down by the Anti-Corruption Bureau. Corrupt people will be caught and punished only when each citizen awakens to the commitment of nation-building. Being fearless is the only way to proceed.

97

Profit Margin

∽◦୨

It is taken for granted that a good business venture, or a well-to-do person, has to have a good financial plan. Even Chanakya, centuries ago, believed that a good 'treasury' is one of the strong pillars that supports successful businesses.

He had suggested,

"He should secure an undertaking requiring little expenditure and yielding large profit and get a special advantage." (7.12.31)

In other words — control the expenses and keep an eye on the net profit or savings.

But how can one become financially successful? Well, these tips will certainly help you:

• Spend Time Budgeting

It is worth spending time on calculations. A businessman would need to calculate the time required for a project and the number of people required. A salaried person would be concerned with his goals and the money to fund it. But, both need to keep an eye on possible miscellaneous expenses. Finally, don't forget to keep some extra money aside as buffer. If you are new to such an exercise then take the help of your seniors, or people who have such experience.

• Keep A Daily Check On Accounts

The discipline of maintaining daily accounts has to be introduced, especially in the face of deadlines and routine activities. It may seem difficult at the start. But, a daily check ensures that one is in control of one's finances. Successful companies and people know exactly how much income has been received daily, how much expense has been made, as well as the balance in the 'treasury'.

- Special Advantage

Earn from your experience. If you are a 'niche' player or a talented professional, make it a point to take advantage of this and charge extra. Experts have the advantage of being rare in the market and receive a lot of offers. This advantage has to be used! With less time in hand and more to deliver, it is better to charge 'extra' and mark up the profits. We see celebrities doing that. So can you.

- Cash Flow

This is the bottom line — the most important factor. In any business or house, a regular cash flow is required. But the pipeline alone is not important, the conversion is. We have salaries/bills to pay, suppliers to be taken care of, and regular maintenance to be carried out. So be sure of your plan/path and build a model where the cash flow is regular and sustainable.

When financial stability is thus secured, you can take bigger risks, invest in new ventures and gamble a little in unknown areas. For Chanakya this was how a country became prosperous.

98

Proper Accounts

≈୨

Chanakya's *Arthashastra* is an ancient book that explains financial procedures and systems in detail. Some of the accounting models used by Chanakya are still a wonder to modern finance wizards.

Chanakya emphasised the importance of maintaining regular and daily accounts. For those who mismanage the treasury, the punishments were outlined:

"If the (officer) does not deliver the income that has accrued (or) does not pay the expenses put down in writing (or) denies the balance received, that is misappropriation." (2.8.18)

But how do we maintain regular accounts in our day-to-day life? Well, here are some tips:

• Learn To Write It Down

Money management is about discipline. And only a disciplined man can keep control over his accounts. People withdraw money from ATMs and spend it without having any clue about where it went. If you also do this, you'd better make it a habit to write down your accounts — daily! This should include how much money you had at the start of the day, where you spent it, how much balance was left at the end of the day. Start this exercise — now!

• Analyse It

Just writing down your expenses is not enough. From time to time, look back and take stock. A man who had no clue about where all his money was disappearing did the above exercise. At the end of one month he realised that he was spending nearly 60 percent of his salary on restaurant bills. He understood where his expenses could be cut. He was more aware about each rupee he spent.

• Differentiate Between Need And Greed

This is the biggest challenge! While buying things, ask yourself, "Is it my need or greed?" If you want to buy a good pair of shoes — buy it. But if you are buying three pairs because of a discount, that is greed. These days, every consumer faces this challenge frequently. In Gandhiji's beautiful words, "There is enough for everyone's need, but not for one man's greed."

- Be Careful With The Credit Card

A leading financial expert said, "The credit card is the most dangerous invention of mankind!" Truly, the 'Buy now, spend later' philosophy it encourages can be dangerous, unless you pay your bills in time. Else, God save you! Warren Buffet, one of the richest men in the world, has never taken a credit card.

99

Advance Money

Every organisation incurs fixed expenses to fund day-to-day operations. Their budgets factor in costs incurred on travelling, stationery, office maintenance, power consumption, salaries, etc.

In addition to this, certain people have to be assigned advance money to handle these transactions and make payments. If this is not done, even the most well-established business could trip over minor issues.

At the end of every month, the firm produces an expense statement to show how much of the advance money — known as 'imprest' money in the modern accounting world — has been spent. It's definitely a good idea to pay attention to the smallest detail as it better equips a businessman to analyse costs (for his firm) and even the end price (for customers). This is not a new concept. Even Chanakya referred to it in the ancient accounting system in *Arthashastra* nearly 2400 years ago.

He said,

"The horse attendant shall receive from the treasury and the magazine a month's allowance (for the horse) and carefully look after it." (2.30.3)

The above sutra gives us an insight into how, even two millennia ago, a horse attendant was given enough food and advance money so that the horse under his supervision enjoyed good health and the person in-charge did not suffer.

But how do we adopt this system today? Here are a few tips:

• Factor In Everything

If you set up a new firm using this exercise, you would actually be creating a new system too. So, you need to plan in detail, factoring in all possible expenses including those that are likely to happen in the future. Also, take into account inflation and other price hikes.

• Ask An Expert

Never hesitate to take advice from an expert, like a chartered accountant who has the requisite skills and knowledge. Accept the fact that you may know many things about your business, but the expert knows many businesses like yours. He can suggest more additions.

His insight will help you not repeat mistakes made by others.

• Audit Regularly

Making a system is not enough — using the system is! Therefore, after creating a system, train your employees to use it regularly. Audit it from time to time to ensure that things are in place. This also helps you monitor and direct work in a better manner. You can engage internal auditors and external auditors.

Do remember that any system you employ has to be useful, user-friendly, and able to generate the report you want at the click of a button.

100

Paying Your Taxes

∾୨

Come February in India and the entire business community waits for the presentation of the Union Budget. Everyone looks forward to news about any new tax rules or, better still, reforms.

Taxes are an extremely important tool for nation building. It's one of the major revenue streams for any government. The money collected is used for infrastructure, education, health, defence, and other similarly vital sectors.

But, while it's imperative that the government sets tax slabs judiciously, it's also important that all citizens pay their due taxes honestly and punctually.

Even Chanakya had said:

"All experts shall fix revocation in such a way that neither the donor nor the receiver is harmed." (3.16.5)

In the above verse, we find one of the most beautiful words of advice given by Chanakya — the best way of collecting revenue. He stressed that this part of governance should not adversely affect the giver, or the receiver. The giver should be happy to give and the receiver should be able to meet his target.

But why should the giver happily pay his taxes?

• The Nation Needs You

There are people who are better placed financially than others — individuals and companies whose basic requirements are fulfilled. They need to step up and contribute to nation building, making the maximum contribution.

Chanakya has not forgotten the payers' needs too. He had said, "Taxes should be collected the way a honeybee collects honey from the flower." The flower is willing to give up its sweetness, but the bee also takes care that only a little is taken without hurting the flower.

- Why Some Are Not Taxed...

I am sure that, at some point or the other, you may have felt you are being taxed far more than others. But understand that these 'others' are those who have been left behind by society.

These are the financially insecure people who are still struggling to buy such basic needs as food, clothing, shelter, and need a semblance of financial security. Naturally, not only will they require tax exemptions, but also other privileges.

You have to understand that these people, with your tax support, will eventually come up to the first level of paying taxes themselves.

- For Total Development

This is the government's responsibility. While funds need to be allocated taking the human happiness index into account, it should be distributed in such a manner that it helps the total development of the society.

Even arts, sports, literature, and research needs to be supported financially. And if you pay your taxes, you would, basically, be financing them too. It's like the Lebanese-American author Khalil Gibran wrote in The Prophet, " ...and if there come the singers and the dancers and the flute players, buy of their gifts also."

Thus, one can support the artists directly, and also indirectly, by paying taxes.

101

Making Timely Payments

≈✑

Business is not about creating only goodwill. Rather, it's about creating real brand value in the hearts of customers, suppliers, and even the employees. One way of doing this is by making timely payments to all vendors and employees.

Chanakya also emphasised the importance of paying wages on time. He even suggested penalising those who didn't:

"In the case of non-payment of the wage, the fine is one-tenth or six panas. In case of denial, the fine is twelve panas or one-fifth." (3.13.33)

This verse highlights the sanctity of an agreement.

Even in today's world, if a person rescinds on making a promised payment after the required work is done, he can be punished under the law of the land.

But, in addition to adhering to the law, a leader has to also understand the benefits one gets by giving people their dues on time:

• A Promise Is A Promise

When a company's chairman, or the head of any department or strategic business unit promises something, he represents his entire team. It becomes his responsibility to fulfill the promise.

While defining leadership qualities in the *Arthashastra*, Chanakya had said that one should never 'over-promise' something and then 'under-deliver'. Instead, he said, it's better to 'under-promise' and 'over-deliver'! Of course, the best thing would be to never promise anything, if you are not sure about its execution.

- Be Clear In Financial Dealings

The first rule of business is to look at all financial matters before committing to anything. In fact, you should also apply this rule in your personal life — it will prove to be very beneficial.

If you need a new television, you should first determine what your budget is. For example, if you have only Rs 10,000, then buy a TV that costs that much. It's no use wasting time in showrooms looking at an LCD for Rs 50,000, or breaking your head over consumer loans and EMI schemes. In other words, always work out your financials first, and then accept the deal.

- Have A Clear Conscience

A man of wisdom once said, "The softest pillow is a clear conscience." If you keep your word even in the smallest of deals, you will be able to sleep well.

Of course, there's always a chance of some miscommunication, or minor irritation. However, it's important to discuss and solve these issues in order to restore a good working relationship.

Remember, the real goodwill is the brand you create, and nothing should be allowed to tarnish it.

102

Dirty Money

≈୨

Narendra Modi, Chief Minister of Gujarat State, was addressing a gathering of businessmen in Mumbai. While he was encouraging investments in Gujarat, Modi said that 'dirty money' was a big danger to the entire economic recession.

Now, dirty money is not the same as 'black money'. The word 'dirty' is used to describe money that is used by such extreme antisocial elements as terrorists and even the Mafia. If we allow its use in the mainstream economy, there will be very bad consequences. Therefore, one of the prime objectives in today's world is to make sure this kind of suspect finance, and the people behind it, are not supported.

Chanakya had said:

"For one calling another, who is not a thief, the punishment shall be that for a thief, also for one hiding a thief." (4.8.6)

Now this verse highlights something important — never ever support wrong-doers. If that happens ("one calling another..."), the situation will become uncontrollable. Hence, the punishment for such people will be the same as that given to the wrong-doers themselves.

There are some simple things that you can do to avoid such a scenario:

• Deal With The Right People

Regarding business and the work place, it's important to choose the right organisation. Half the battle is won when we work in a good environment and with good people. If you work with suppliers, choose those who display good ethics and right practices. If you are a housewife and are trying to choose a product from two different companies — choose that company which is trustworthy.

• Think Long-Term

This is the biggest solution to most problems. Working with the right people may not give us immediate benefits. But, in the long-term, the returns will be very high.

I know of many people who started working in the right companies and received small roles and salaries. Today, they are well-respected directors. So, choose wisely the company you want to keep and the career you want to build. Do it while keeping the long-term benefits in mind.

• Oppose What Is Wrong

If you find out about some wrong practices, stop it. Chanakya made it clear that keeping quiet is a big crime. I know someone who used to file a complaint for every wrong practice he noticed — whether it was a corrupt traffic policeman, or an autorickshaw driver with an extra-fast meter. Today, he is feared by politicians and is an inspiration to the younger generation that is passionate about fighting corruption.

103

Money for Wealth Creation

Chanakya has two famous works to his credit, the elaborate *Kautilya's Arthashastra* with nearly 6000 verses and *Chankaya Niti*, a key to *Arthashastra* with just 330 one-line verses. Various verses in both the books deal with the principles of creation and the management of wealth.

Kautilya says that money is not wealth. It is just a tool. Wealth is ever present in the universe. Like energy, wealth is constant; it only changes its names and forms. The secret of wealth creation is to understand the movement of wealth from one person to another, from one nation to another, from one generation to another.

Wealth is not only what is 'with' you but also what is 'in' you.

Arthashastra says that the qualities of a person, character, and knowledge are prime requirements for wealth-creation.

It is largely misunderstood that wealth is what is around you. Your car, your house, and other possessions do not constitute real wealth. In fact, they are byproducts of your inner wealth.

The inner wealth of knowledge, experience, and wisdom are your true wealth. Without them, you cannot create external wealth. Only continuous empowerment with knowledge helps wealth flow to you. "A knowledgeable man can create wealth anywhere anytime."

"Be ever active in the management of the economy because the root of wealth is economic activity; inactivity brings material distress. Without an active policy, both current prosperity and future gains are destroyed." (1.19.35-36)

Chanakya says that activity is the root of wealth. An organisation without active strategies, constant information flows, and regular reports cannot sustain itself. A lazy organisation will plunge into distress. Wealth creation is impossible without an active policy. Without an active economic and financial policy, the present hard-earned wealth will be destroyed and there will be no hope for future profits.

Targets, deadlines, and a focused approach are just pointers to keep employees on their toes. A good profitable organisation requires continuous activity, without which wealth will never be attracted towards it. Also, individuals who are lazy will not be able to create wealth.

104

Money for More Money

"The objective of any king (leader) or state (organisation) is to create, expand, protect and enjoy wealth." (Book 1, Chapter 1)

The role of a CEO is very clearly defined by Kautilya at the very start of the *Arthashastra*. It is to create wealth for all the stakeholders of the organisation, the employees, and for himself to enjoy.

He should not be satisfied with what he has got. He should constantly think about how to expand his territories and reach new markets.

"Just as elephants are needed to catch elephants, so does one need wealth to capture more wealth." (9.4.27)

This is an old, but very important aspect, of wealth creation—*paisa lagaye bina paisa nahin aata* (there is no business that can create wealth without any investment). The example Kautilya gives here is that of a hunter who catches elephants.

Elephants always move around in groups. To catch an elephant, a hunter needs to use another elephant. Only then will the targeted one be lured away and caught.

Having produced wealth, the king should know how to protect it. If, for instance, we have a vessel with a hole at the bottom, we may keep pouring more and more water into it. However, no water will stay in it unless it is protected from the leak.

How does one do this?

"He (leader) should constantly hold an inspection of their works, men being inconstant in their minds." (2.9.2-3)

The employees are primarily concerned with their salaries. An attitude of complacency can crop up if a regular and vigilant check is not kept on them. The reason is quite obvious. The human mind is very unpredictable. No organisation can reach its goal without a continuous push and pull system.

"All state activities depend first on the Treasury. Therefore, a king (leader) shall devote the best attention to it." (2.8.1-2)

In Book One of the *Arthashastra* titled *The Topic of Training*, the teacher proposes a daily time table for the king. He says that during the first part of the day, he should check the accounts of income and expenditures of the state. It is only after doing this that he is advised to look into the affairs of the citizens.

Do not get carried away by the regular problems faced by your subordinates once you enter your office. Relax! Just take control of the financial status by monitoring the financial reports first.

105

Road to Wealth

～❧

Go rural, is the theme of every big corporation today. While FMCG companies eagerly wait for the post-monsoon rural demand to boost their sales, banks, which now sell myriad financial products, are gradually realising the potential of rural areas. Several corporations are re-orienting their growth strategies — ITC's e-choupal and Hindustan Lever's Project Shakti for example — to bring villages into the centre of their plans.

Kautilya was inspired by this principle when managing his treasury.

"Wealth and power comes from the countryside, which is the source of all activities." (7.14.19)

Going rural has two benefits. First, the countryside is the place where raw material is available in plenty. Minerals, food crops, labour all find their sources in the countryside. Second, it is also a ready market for high-volume business. Even today, India lives in the villages. Be it the soft drinks, the mobile phones, or the insurance industry, all have already tried to penetrate the rural sector.

In the Book 2 of the *Arthashastra*, Chapter 8, Verse 3, Kautilya points out various elements which contribute to the increase in the treasury:

• Increase In Commerce And Trade

Commercial activities recycle the wealth of a nation. It helps the wealth flow from one sector to the other, from one geographical area to another. Trading helps in wealth being circulated from one nation to another. Exports and imports are the lifeline of any economically developing nation.

- Arresting Perpetrators Of Crime

Monitoring and controlling theft is essential. A system of checks and counter checks are necessary to protect the treasury. Theft can be an inside job, or can be influenced by external elements.

- Reduction In Establishment

Expenses can be controlled by reducing the size of the organisation. This is done by keeping the minimum required employees, as well as reducing the number of liabilities. Outsourcing is one of the best ways of controlling the overheads of a company.

- Plenty Of Crops

Even today, India is an agriculture-based economy. A lot depends on the monsoons. Investment in R&D in this sector to increase crop yields, better warehousing of agricultural produce, and food processing, could add significantly to the growth of the economy.

- Plenty Of Marketable Goods

Sales and marketing should be supplied with enough products. Availability of stocks at the right time, sales order processing, logistics and distribution have to be in place to ensure the achievement of any sales target.

- Freedom From Calamities

A lot of unseen and unknown factors affect the economy of a nation, organisation, and also individuals. The board of directors should consider all these aspects, under the 'Risk Management Plan' of an organisation. Insurance, savings, and good investment plans are the steps taken to ensure freedom from calamities.

Team Work

106

Security and Monitoring Systems

Everyone knows how important security is. Still, most people do not maintain a proper monitoring and vigilance system, although it can avoid, or at least immensely contain and confine, leaks. Without a proper security system, processes will get out of control one day and this could be fatal for the organisation.

Chanakya has devised systems for the security and protection of goods in an organisation. He says,

"Every object should go out of, or come into (the palace), after it is examined and its arrival or departure is recorded." (1.20.23)

In an office there many transactions taking place daily. People

191

come in and go out, goods are delivered, some are sent out. Such exchanges are more common in manufacturing sectors, like factories, and other production units.

Chanakya has clearly noted the importance of good strict security procedures systems and documentation of all goods-related transactions in the organisation. He also suggests that, before they are recorded, the information should be examined to ensure that what is recorded is correct and genuine.

How do we follow this advice in today's corporate scenario? Here are some suggestions:

• Use Technology

We now have various gadgets and equipments that easily record and document all transactions. Cameras perched on top of gates for surveillance, bar-coding for tracking goods and other such systems/processes can make things easy and save a lot of time. Technology also has the added advantage of reducing human errors.

• Make Your System Unique

Even though there are various readymade software packages available in the market for security purposes, make sure that you pick the one that records all the things that are important and useful to *you*. If need be, get a tailor-made system in order to get the required reports as quick as possible.

• Monitor The System

Just setting up a working system will not ensure its smooth functioning. Make sure that you, as a manager, keep checking the system at regular intervals. In this way, the security personnel — and even the general staff will always be on their toes.

• Conduct Surprise Inspections

This is the most effective way to keep security under your control. Keep a close (and unannounced) watch on the people who handle your security systems. Subject them to surprise checks. At times, it is also important to transfer security personnel without giving them any notice.

Finally, do remember that security is not just about having technology in place. Rather, security is about you being alert and vigilant all the time, for all the required processes. After all, like a leading consultancy once noted to its dismay, "It just doesn't work if you check all the visitors and their bags on the way in, but hardly ever when they are going out!"

107

Right Business Partner

~∾

In today's corporate world, getting funds is not really a problem. The Indian market is flooded with money for anyone who comes up with good ideas.

Of course, in the initial stages while struggling, a new businessman may think his idea is not good. However, if he strongly believes in his own idea and continues to put in efforts, the situation will change eventually. He will even find many people who are ready to finance his company. This is when he gets opportunities for finding a new and financially stronger partner. However, when such offers come flooding in, the challenge is to choose the right partner.

Chanakya advises,

"If situated between two stronger kings, he should seek shelter with one capable of protecting him." (7.2.13)

So, when multiple potential partners arrive with a lot of money and experience, you should be very alert and cool-headed. After all, a wrong choice can ruin the business that you have created from scratch.

To make the correct choice, one should be able to evaluate

each potential partner's strengths and only then tie up with the one who is strongest. Here are a few tips to determine who will be the right partner.

• Consider Your Values

Business is about the values you follow. Each person invests his feelings, hopes, and emotions into the organisation. When a new partner enters the picture, it is important to consider if your values and his values match. Both parties should have the same wavelength.

• The Long-Term Approach

At times, one may impulsively accept funds when it's readily available. But consider all possibilities, and devise a long-term strategy before you tie up with anyone. Else, the situation will resemble that of a person who has been looking for a spouse for a long time, and as soon as anyone says 'yes', the person will get married, only to realise later that this was the greatest blunder in his/her life! So check your partner's credentials with known sources before the partnership becomes legal. It may take some time, but you will be the winner in the long run.

• It's Not Just Money

Partnerships are not just about money. It is not just plain give-and-take. In fact, it is about a life-long relationship that needs to be worked upon. As Stephen Covey says in his book, *Seven Habits of Highly Effective People*, "....you need to develop an emotional bank account." You will have to spend time with your partners regularly. It is necessary to communicate with them so that the relationship strengthens beyond just business transactions.

Remember, every business story is the story of building the right team to work with and being able to work together. No wonder then that choosing the right team members is highly important to win the game.

108

Effective Meetings

Meetings, meetings, and more meetings! As you climb higher up the corporate ladder, and your business grows, meetings will become an inevitable part of your life.

Meetings are like a double-edged sword — they are either a waste of your time, or you can scale up your business. It all depends on how effective you are in conducting meetings.

Chanakya gives us some tips on this issue:

"He should declare without loss of time what is in the king's interest." *(5.4.11)*

The following are also some tips that can help you in meetings:

• Have An Agenda

Most meetings are a big drain on one's time, because there is no clear agenda. The purpose of the meeting has to be clear. The best meetings are those that take into consideration the vision of the company, or what is of interest to the seniors.

Preparing an agenda gives a sense of direction to the meeting. If you have called for the meeting, then ensure that the agenda is clearly communicated to others. Also, ensure maximum attendance and least confusion by telling the participants in advance about the day, time, and venue of the meeting.

As Bill Gates wrote it in his book, *Business at the Speed of Thought*, "Those meetings that are planned well in advance are the most effective ones."

• Give Direction

You can be open for a brainstorming session, or a discussion.

But that should not allow the meeting to go astray. As a chairperson, you need to give the meeting a sense of direction.

You have to be like a good televison talk-show anchor — when the answers to any question are going off-track, or if the person being questioned is talking too much, you cut him off diplomatically, and move to the next question.

* Come To The Point, ASAP!

This is very critical. Meetings need to be started off like any other session. Be casual — ask the team about the status of the project, find out if there are any issues, offer tea, start the discussion, etc.

However, as the meeting proceeds, it is very necessary to come to the point as soon as possible, ASAP! We have to monitor our time.

Therefore, the success of any meeting lies in having only a few and important points in the agenda. Most importantly, as the meetings come to the end, make an action plan. Take decisions and execute them. Otherwise it will be like the old office joke, "When our boss has nothing to do, he calls for a meeting!"

109

Planning a Business Trip

≈୭

Travelling is a very important part of business development. It helps you approach new clients, try new markets, and get feedback on new products and services that your firm may be experimenting with.

In today's globalised corporate world, travelling across the country, or even across continents, is an essential part of any business. Exploring new business development opportunities, reaching new investors or seeking Joint Ventures (JV) are common and important tasks even in small-sized companies.

But planning for your business travel is an equally important task. Chanakya gives us a hint:

"He should start after making proper arrangements for vehicles, draught-animals and retinue of servants." (1.16.5)

Here are some additional tips to be kept in mind while planning for your business trip:

• Have A Clear Travel Plan

It is important to make a clear travel plan — complete with an itinerary for the number of days you will be in the new region. Take into consideration the requirement of time, money, and various other factors. Use local contacts to make your plan clear and precise. Leave some extra time to explore any unexpected opportunities.

• Your Travelling Team

Who are the people travelling with you? How many? What are their roles? These are some important questions that need to be answered. A team also adds strength to your mission. That is why government officials always travel with a delegation.

• Study Potential Prospective Targets Well

Even before you leave, study the prospective target. Most of the basic information will be available on the internet. Verify the information through trusted sources. When face-to-face with them, ask them specific questions to make sure all the information is correct. After all, if you are looking at a long-term association you need to make sure you are signing a deal with the right partner.

• Do *Not* Close Deals Immediately

At times, it is very exciting to close deals in the very first meeting. Resist this temptation. All that glitters is not gold. The first impression need not necessarily be the lasting impression.

197

Come back home. Then, with a cool mind, restudy all the important areas and, with the help of experts, take the next step.

Remember, while every new opportunity is a possibility, it is important to do a little bit of thinking so that you can handle future events better. You should aim to be like the successful businessman who was once offered a billion dollars as investment in his company. Quick came his reply, "Thanks for the offer, will get back to you soon!"

110

Public Relations

⨯⨍

Peter Drucker, the well-known management guru, had once remarked that one of the top priorities of a business leader is to network, socialise, and maintain great PR (Public Relations). "It's all about great relationships that you maintain with your clients, suppliers, shareholders, employees, and every other person you come in contact with!"

Even our own ancient guru and probably the first management thinker, Chanakya, brought out the same idea in his book of advice for kings and other leaders,

"He should establish contacts with forest chieftains, frontier-chiefs, and chief officials in the cities and the countryside." (1.16.7)

But, how to build a network and maintain contacts is an art every leader has to develop. Here are some tips:

• Attend Meetings

For a CEO, not a single day should go by without meeting at least one new person. He must attend business conferences, training programmes or even one-to-one meetings with important people. In addition to making contacts, he should even start learning from the experiences of others.

• Keep In Touch

Collecting contact details may not be enough. Most of us return from various conferences with a pile of visiting cards and do nothing about it. Hence, a follow-up with each important person is a must. Think of the business possibilities with each person you met and work out a proposal.

• Two-Way Approach

Most businessmen go wrong by thinking only of the benefits that he will get from the new contact! Rather, think about how you will be able to help them. At times, you can offer a tip or suggestion that will scale up their business. Help them, and probably, they will help you when you need them.

• Long-Term Approach

In human relationships, time is important and in business 'timing' is important. But to know the right timing, you have to spend enough time. Never spoil any potential business relationship just because it may not appear to be immediately beneficial. One has to always think about the long-term. Take it slow, but sure. You never know. A person who seems small today may become a giant tomorrow, while a giant today may be out on the streets later.

Always remember that while leadership is an art, business is a far more superior art. It requires the understanding of people, understanding their minds, and also understanding the various factors that fulfill each person. Thus, in business, PR cannot be done by just outsourcing it to an agency. You may have a PR agency if required, and your personal involvement, your time, and effort must be invested wisely.

111

Honour Men with Qualities

~⸙⁹

A sharp person knows how to differentiate between ordinary men and great men. And if a leader can successfully inculcate this quality, he can easily become victorious in all walks of life. Just like a jeweler does, one should have the knack of differentiating between rare gems and ordinary stones.

According to Chanakya, the greatest resource a business has, is the workforce. In fact, people are the source of all great achievements, all of which are performed by men who have great qualities.

And it's these qualities that have to be recognised and honoured. Chanakya, while defining these qualities, had said,

"Men are to be honoured on account of excellence in learning, intellect, valour, noble birth, and deeds." (3.20.23)

In other words, men of each type have to be honoured in any organisation. Let us look at each type separately:

• Men Of Learning

Men of learning are the most respected people in every society. Other than academic and scholarly learning, this description also relates to men having the wisdom of experience.

In India, especially, we have always held men of learning in very high esteem. A sociologist had once said, "A society that does not respect men of learning is bound to collapse."

• Valour

The brave. The fighters. They have that extra quality in them to 'go on', in spite of problems. They are even ready to face death, if required. Such people are called Kshatriyas. They are the soldiers and guards who protect us. As the armies say, "We keep awake in the nights so that all of you can sleep peacefully."

- Noble Birth

Persons born in noble families are automatically respected. Now this is not being caste-biased or racist. However, we find that certain qualities are genetic. The family background also influences the personality of a person.

- Deeds

Finally, your actions speak louder than your words. What you achieve will automatically command respect. Therefore, men who have done great and noble deeds need to be respected too.

When you identify such persons, you can associate with them and learn from them. You will then find that the benefits you get can be plotted on an upward sloping curve.

This is especially true in the world of business. It is said that J.R.D. Tata was able to identify 'quality men'. He made them part of his team, and the Tatas have been succeeding for generations.

112

A Good Meeting

Bill Gates had said in his book, *Business At The Speed Of Thought*, "The most effective meetings are the ones in which the participants come well-prepared."

This is true, and Chanakya had made this a rule a long time ago in our country. He wanted people to not only be punctual for meetings, but also be well-prepared with reports.

If they turned up without reports, they were actually fined, or even punished.

He said,

"For (managers) not coming at the proper time, or coming without the account books and balances, the fine shall be one-tenth of the amount due." (2.7.21)

Disciplined behaviour during meetings is very important. Chanakya also listed other important aspects of a well-prepared meeting.

* Why Have a Meeting?

A meeting is an event where two or more people meet to discuss certain ideas. In a company, most meetings have an agenda. For example, a sales review meeting. This will require the sales team to get together and discuss the targets achieved, upcoming strategies to meet the next targets and also the plans for moving ahead.

A meeting is also held to exchange ideas, it is an opportunity to network, understand the working styles of others as well as to share, or seek, information.

* The Benefits Of A Good Meeting

A good meeting is one that has a clear agenda. The timing for such meetings is worked out well in advance and communicated to all. It starts on time and also ends on time. People feel good after such a productive meeting, rather than feel frustrated at having to sit through one meeting flowing into another without any progress being made.

In today's scenario especially, when time is a precious commodity, one should not call for a meeting without a clear agenda. Every second has to be productive.

* Preparing For A Good Meeting

The first thing one must prepare is what needs to be communicated. This is the role of the organiser. Remember, you have to communicate four things to the relevant participants way before they even get together — where, when, who, and what.

Where is the meeting going to be held (venue). When (the time, both start and end times), who (the chairperson, or speaker, for the session), and what (the agenda and the topic for the meeting).

In any event, if you are a participant in the meeting, you must always come prepared with relevant reports and required papers.

When asked for any particular information, no time should be wasted. A quick and prompt response will help the decision-making process.

Additionally, try to understand the importance of a meeting. Be a good organiser, conductor, and participant. Also, never hesitate to teach others the importance of effective meetings.

113

Finish What You Have Started

I have a friend who seems destined to end each and every project he takes up with nothing but success. I once asked him to share his secret with me.

He said, "Before taking on any new project, I always complete the previous work I have undertaken. That ensures that I single-mindedly, and successfully, finish every project I take up!"

These words immediately reminded me of a verse by Chanakya:

'Activity is that which brings about the accomplishment of works undertaken.' (6.2.2)

Very few people are good at completing the work they have already started. Indeed, almost all of us keep on taking new projects, accept new orders and even pick up new books to read without asking ourselves, "Shouldn't I first complete the existing one?"

No wonder we land up with various problems like stress, atrocious time-management, and a pathetic work-life balance. Why don't we first complete the work we already have at hand?

Chanakya says that this happens because we are not 'active'. We have to 'act' to complete all existing work. There's simply no alternative to this.

And you only need to remember a few steps:

- List All Pending Work

If you want to see why your life is in a mess, try this simple exercise — list the number of activities that you have started, but not completed, or finished, till date.

It could be finishing a report, calling up and thanking the organisers of an event, or simply completing that book you picked up. If you're honest, you will be shocked at the size of your list!

- Plan It, And Do It

Now, list the time required for completing each unfinished work. For example, it may take a half hour to finish that report. Or about 5-10 minutes to call and thank the organisers of that party. Or the book that you started reading and left mid-way may take about three hours more to finish.

Keep some time aside, say about an hour daily, to complete these unfinished tasks. More importantly, you must actually do it! Don't just think about doing it.

- Make It A Habit

This exercise may look difficult initially. After all, we all do get into the dirty habit of procrastinating. But if we really discipline ourselves by completing all unfinished tasks, our self-confidence will grow and we will even yearn for bigger challenges.

The chairman of a multinational firm once revealed to me that he spends his Saturdays just completing any work that may have been left unfinished. This shows how important it is to be a good 'finisher' rather than just being a good 'starter'.

114

Want to Succeed?

≈⌒)

Kautilya's *Arthashastra* comprises fifteen books. Of these, the sixth book has only two chapters. Yet, it's very important as it explains how a king can run his kingdom successfully. It also lists the three ways to succeed and how we can do it.

Chanakya had said:

"Success is threefold — that attainable by the power of counsel is success by counsel, that attainable by the power of might is success by might, that attainable by the power of energy is success by energy." (6.2.30)

While it takes a lifetime full of valuable experience to understand the meaning of these words, we can at least understand its essence:

• Succeed By Counsel

There are many people who try and keep trying, and still don't succeed. Frustrated, they believe it's not in their destiny to succeed. But they might have just not got the right advice from the right person.

I remember a foreigner who was trying to set up a business here and could not get started for nearly two years. He finally approached a legal advisor who gave him just a few tips, and he was off!

This accurately portrays the first kind of success which, according to Chanakya, is achieved by listening to, and learning from, the right experts.

- Succeed By Might

  When we fight our battles alone, the chances of winning are less. "Together we grow," a spiritual master had once rightly said. Therefore, the second method is to succeed by might — i.e., by the power of association.

  I have a friend who is into politics. He always rues the fact that he had to spend a lot of time trying to understand just how politics worked.

  "I wish I had a Godfather who would guide me," he once confessed. That's as close to the truth as you will get in today's highly competitive world. In life, if we get to associate with a powerful person, success is virtually guaranteed.

- Succeed By Energy

  There are quite a few people who, even if they cannot achieve success via the first two methods, still succeed driven purely by their energy and dynamism. Their enthusiasm is very contagious too. They have a 'never give up' spirit. For them, life is not about how many times one fails. Rather, it's about the feeling — "Success is just a step away!"

  They learn from their mistakes, from books, from every person they meet and from every event in their life. Life is a journey for them, and never a destination.

  Remember, success is an attitude a person develops. So never give up till you achieve your goal. Chanakya had said, "Even after a hundred trials, an enthusiastic man will surely succeed."

115

Working Together

≈ 9

In the 1970s and 80s, many Indian companies were gearing up to landmark events. Globalisation had not yet begun. Computers were just being introduced, and mobile phones and the Internet were still ideas. Those were the days when the biggest challenge Indian industries faced were labour problems. Misunderstandings between the various labour unions and the company management occurred all the time.

Obviously, not all negotiations produced positive results. Many companies succumbed to those tense situations, eventually shutting down, with entire industries suffering. Only a few organisations emerged as winners.

A key question often asked then was — is it possible to have complete co-operation between unions and managements?

Well, even the experts weren't sure of an answer. However, Chanakya had a solution.

He had said:

"And without informing the employer, the union shall not remove anyone or bring in anyone." (3.14.15)

So, in Chanakya's time, while a union had to be completely in line with the wishes of the management, they also consulted each other before taking decisions.

So what are the lessons our generation can learn from this?

• Unions Will Exist

Today, many management thinkers feel that the 'days of the union' are over. This is not true. Only the name and form changes. What is a union? It's a group of people coming together on a common platform. They discuss their issues together and put forward their proposals to their seniors.

This exists even today. Look at the various committees and groups in any company. As any seasoned corporate official will admit, things flow smoothly only after such problems and issues are sorted out early.

• Need For A Common Vision

Whichever corporate office or industry we work in, we have to realise that we are not fighting against each other, but against the bigger enemies. Therefore, it's important for the top leaders to communicate, to the whole organisation, the company's objectives and goals. This will help everyone in the company — including not just the seniors but also the juniors — share a common vision.

• Regular Communication

One's responsibility doesn't end with just informing the workforce about policies and developments once in a blue moon. As with any relationship, the strength lies in regular and effective communication.

Even though there could be hierarchies and different levels in an organisation, it's important to meet everyone from time to time and discuss issues and problems.

This becomes the firm's strength. No outsider is required to solve a problem if people inside the house are completely in tune with each other.

In the end, remember that it's not 'I' that should win, but that 'we all' should win with the right methods and for the right purpose.

116

Get Everyone Involved

❧

Problems are always cropping up in any organisation. The moment a problem crops up, all the employees need to think about how it can be solved, rather than just sit and worry about it. They should never expect that the solution will always come from a particular person, department, or group of people.

Chanakya had a suggestion for this:

"He should fight with the mobilisation of all troops." (12.1.3)

In other words, the entire office team has to come together when fighting a problem. For example, if your company's sales figures are affected, don't expect only the sales and marketing department to look into the issue. Call key persons from all departments and brainstorm the issue together. You will then see a different, possibly better, approach to the problem.

Here's a step-by-step process for solving problems together:

- Identify The Problem

Before solving a problem, identify, and understand it thoroughly. It's just like a medical diagnosis which is necessary to identify the root cause of an ailment and find the required medicine.

Thus, if challenged with problems as varied as attrition, financial issues, sales targets or any other, first identify where the problem started.

- Think From Different Perspectives

Do not assume that your first diagnosis is correct. Take a second opinion. It would be even better if you called for a meeting of all senior people. For example, if the manufactured goods are not up to the mark, do not just blame the production team. Instead, call all the department heads — like purchase, R&D, and even sales — and ask them for their opinion on how the issue can be solved. This will help you attack the problem from different perspectives.

- Create A Task Force

Now, after analysing the problem, it's important to fight it till it goes away completely. You have to create a team, or a task force for this as a lone person can get demotivated tackling it alone.

Another advantage of a team is that any of its members can

take a break, or rest, for some time, while the others continue brainstorming, this will help maintain morale.

Remember, the whole dynamics of a battle changes when the entire army is focused on winning the battle, no matter who is crowned the 'best warrior'. The secret of team work that guarantees success is that each individual has to surrender to the higher goal.

117

Power of Communication

∼❂

A business school conducted a survey of its former students' careers, grading them 20 years after they completed the course. Surprisingly, the successful ones were not the toppers, but those who knew how to work in teams and, more importantly, had good communication skills.

Chanakya knew the power of communicating well. In fact, he highlighted how it's even easy to use words as a weapon, and how to avoid this from happening:

"Defamation, vilification, and threat constitute verbal injury." (3.18.1)

When you get down to it, you realise that every person requires 'appreciation'. If you cannot appreciate others, you certainly cannot indulge in the opposite:

• Defamation

It means to defame or insult a person. This is used often as a tool by people to get public support. Politicians, celebrities and well-known people always use and abuse 'defamation'. Any top-level official in an organisation also becomes a soft target for defamation. Basically, it questions the credibility and goodwill of the person. You should never defame anyone, unless and until you have your facts right.

- Vilification

This means backbiting. But you should remember this rule, "If you want to appreciate someone — do it in front of others; if you want to tell him about his wrongdoings, do it when he is alone."

Backbiting does not solve any problem. In fact, it's a sign of a weak person. If you feel there is something wrong, go and explain this directly to the person concerned and also tell them why you feel the situation needs to be corrected.

You see, backbiting creates a lot of negative energy which is harmful not only to the person targeted, but also to the one who does it, as well as those who listen to it. This has to be avoided.

- 'Threat'

This means warning a person and trying to infuse fear into him. While phrases like, 'Do this, or else...' are commonly used by competing youngsters, in the adult world it is considered a crime to threaten anyone.

Never try to infuse fear into a person. The reason is that not only does this constitute a crime in the eyes of the law, but for you in the long-term you never know when the person will find the strength to hit back.

The best way to communicate is in a soft, yet firm, manner. Chanakya had once said, "When you communicate, it should be *Satyam* and *Priyam*, i.e. being truthful in a nice manner."

Develop these qualities to succeed in life.

118

Stopping Fights

⊷⁹

The human mind is very unpredictable. At times, it gets attached to certain ideas and becomes obstinate about it. Then, when someone else comes along with a conflicting idea, it leads to some kind of friction, and may even result in a fight.

Such behaviour can be very destructive if not controlled at the initial stages. Interpersonal rivalries, corporate battles, wars between countries — all rarely leave even the most neutral party untouched.

Hence, fights have to be stopped, especially group conflicts, and this can be done only with the help of group psychology.

Chanakya, a master psychologist, had a solution:

"Strife among subjects can be averted by winning over the leaders among the subjects, or by removal of the cause of strife." (8.4.18)

Let us take this advice step-by-step:

• Identify The Problem

When a fight occurs, it immediately distorts the region's peace and a lot of time and energy is wasted.

As a strategist, it's important to end the fight and move on in life. However, to do this, it's essential to deeply analyse the situation from all angles and find the root cause of the problem. You need to plan a tentative solution, if not a permanent solution, to end the present fight.

• Talk To Group Leaders

Ask any police officer how they try to calm things down during riots and they will tell you that the first step is to get the warring factions talking.

But it may not be easy to tackle a group of hundred people, if all of them are marching towards you on the streets.

The solution is to identify who the group leaders and influencers are. Call them out separately and talk to them. If the leader is convinced, the whole group comes under control.

It's like shutting down a machine in an emergency — instead of switching off hundreds of buttons, it's better to put off the main switch to deactivate the entire set.

• Solve The Problem

Do not spend all your energy on just discussions and debates — peace has to be achieved. So the aim should not be forgotten — solve the main problem and end the fight.

In the *Arthashastra*, Chanakya talks about the theories of *Sama* (discussions), *Dana* (offering of rewards), *Danda* (punishments) and *Bheda* (creating a split). You can use these methods alternatively, as the situation demands it, to achieve your goal.

119

Team Work

The most successful companies, organisations and groups have one thing in common — the ability to ignore individual differences and work as a 'team'. Team work is the most essential ingredient that helps groups achieve various goals in spite of various ups and downs.

The leader may be talented and capable as an individual, but he cannot achieve his goals without the help of an efficient team. As one goes up the management ladder, the leader realises that, the most important role of the captain is to 'lead' a good team. He needs to delegate and share his responsibilities with other efficient team members. Apart from his own performance, he needs to play the role of a strategist.

Kautilya warns leaders, who think they can manage on their own without the help of others, about their folly:

"Rulership can be successfully carried out (only) with the help of associates. One wheel alone does not turn. Therefore, he should appoint ministers and listen to their opinion." (1.7.9)

Good generals have good lieutenants. Good CEOs have good managers. They complement each other. As the vehicle cannot run on one wheel, similarly a CEO cannot perform without good managers.

There are a lot of hidden benefits of good team work:

* No One Is Indispensable

Too much dependency on one person is very dangerous. However, if we have a good team, his absence is made up by another talented or skilled person. It not only eliminates dependency but also keeps everyone on their toes performing well.

* Individual Weaknesses Are Covered Up

Everyone makes mistakes. But these must be seen as lessons. Other team members perform their best to cover up the loss. In the end, the total result matters, not the individual achievements.

* Individual Strengths Become 'Total' Strength

Each person has his own strengths. Now, these individual strengths collectively become more powerful. Remember the concept of synergy? One plus one is greater than two. One always performs better as a team rather than as individuals.

* You Think Along With Others

Each person has a different understanding of the same situation. Take the opinion of the team members with the help of a little brainstorming. Thus, one thinks about a solution with the help of another person's mind.

As Stephen Covey says, "Strength lies in differences, not in similarities."

Thus, one thinks of a solution to a problem with the help of another person's mind. Therefore, it is important for a leader to appoint the right managers, listen to their opinions and proceed with a certain strategic plan.

Theodore Roosevelt, the 26th president of the United States was once asked about team work, "The best executive is the one who has sense enough to pick good men to do what he wants done, and self-restraint enough to keep from meddling with them while they do it," he said.

This also takes a lot of pressure off, and unwanted expectations from, the leader.

120

Brainstorming

Many management words and jargon currently used in the modern corporate world define actions that were practised in India ages ago. One of them is the concept of 'brainstorming'.

Kautilya in the *Arthashastra* gives us a step-by-step formula on how to conduct a brainstorming session. Brainstorming can be used not only for crisis management, but also for the creation of new ideas and innovative thinking. Kautilya's tips can also be followed by project managers who want to effectively use the skills of their team members.

He says,

"In an urgent matter, he should call together the councillors as well as the council of ministers and ask them what the majority among them declare or

what is conducive to the success of the work, that he (leader) should do."
(1.15.58-59)

- Call For A Meeting

Whenever there is any important or urgent matter to be resolved, the first step is to call for a meeting of the team members and advisors. One can involve not only the managers, but also the non-managerial staff, as well as external experts in the discussion.

- Ask Them

The leader should be very clear about the 'particular issue' that he is seeking a solution for. If the important issue is not brought into 'focus' properly, it will be like a blind person leading the blind. One finds that without direction it does not matter how many meetings are planned, they will all end up as a waste of time. Therefore 'ask' everyone the right questions.

- Take The Input Of The Majority

What the maximum people in the group consider to be the ideal solution should be taken into consideration. The leader should also take note of the smallest suggestion, even if it may not be applicable in the current situation. May be these small suggestions will be useful to solve some other problem.

- Decide If The Majority Is Right

Just because the majority has a particular opinion it may not necessarily be right. Therefore, Kautilya says the final decision of what should be the next step, should be decided only by the leader. While creating an action plan, he should consider what is conducive to the success of the work. Finally everything is dependent on the 'results' not just on the generation of ideas.

Akio Morita, the founder of Sony wanted to create the first ever VHS video tape. For months he brainstormed with his team what the 'size' of such a video tape should be. This led to no clear solution.

One day, out of frustration, he threw a book on the center of the table. "I want the tape to be of this size. I don't care how you do it". In a few months, the first VHS tape was out in the market — the size of that book!

121

Teaming Up to Succeed

୨ର

Working in a team is better than working alone — this is the key to success when it comes to working on a project. Chanakya puts the same thought in the following verse,

"Let us two build a fort." (7.12.1)

Man is a social animal and requires the help of others to survive. From a 'competitive mindset' one should move to a 'compatibility mindset'. Leaders should develop the ability to work in teams and also inspire their teams to work together. And this applies to all the facets of life, at the workplace, in a competitive market and even while managing home affairs.

- Discuss The Project Before You Start

    Better to involve, than just inform. If you are going to take up a new assignment, call your people and tell them about it. "What do you feel? Is there a better way to do it?" The suggestions and opinions will help you look at the project from different angles. Sometimes the best ideas come from the bottom, even a child's simple ideas can be highly beneficial.

- Show The Direction, But Let Them Walk

    As a team leader this is your most important role. Tell them where to go and when to reach there. Let them decide which route to take. Give them the freedom to complete the work their way. Most leaders have a major problem in this regard. 'When I did it the last time, I did it this way, and you also should do it this way!' the leaders think. There are better ways of doing things. Try to adapt to change.

• Do Not Lose Focus

Just by giving them the direction and freedom is not enough. As a leader, one should closely watch developments. Be around when the team requires you. Be focused and help them get refocused. A team should take regular stock of the situation and realise whether it is doing the right things, or not. If the leader does not do this, he will regret later because, he might have started to head north and reached the south. Keep looking at your compass.

• Enjoy Together

The journey itself is the destination. Remember, happiness is not in 'then and there' but lies in the 'now and here'. Do not forget to enjoy the journey. Have fun while working together. Share the team's joys and sorrows. Stress is the result of not taking breaks and sharing burdens.

When you succeed — celebrate! In case you lose, get up again, and move ahead. As it goes, "In happiness and sorrow, in illness and health, in good moments and sad — *together* we shall be."

122

Common Purpose

≈૭

Life is all about partnerships — be it between spouses, friends, or even business associates. Many relationships work, and many don't. So what is it that differentiates a successful partnership from unsuccessful ones?

Chanakya gives a very clear idea about the same. He says it's the 'common purpose':

"Being not restricted as to place and time and because of having a common purpose, allied troops are better than alien troops." (9.2.17)

Look into your own life, and you will find the above verse to be very true. Whenever you get a partnership offer, always think about the possibilities of failure before you strike a deal. Have an open discussion to identify what is possible and what is not possible.

Now, without much experience, how does one decide whether a particular partnership will work well or not? Here are some thoughts you can dwell on before tying the 'knot':

- Define Your Purpose

First things first — what do you want in life? What are your core values, your purpose, your goals and objectives, your vision, your life's mission? All these are very important parameters within which an individual operates. If, as an individual, you are not clear about your purpose, then you are only confusing yourself and you will end up confusing even those you work with. So define these areas well and create a road-map to achieve the targets. If you have never done this exercise, take a pen and write down your purpose in life now. It will give you a tremendous focus.

- Have An Open Discussion

Once you are clear about what you want, it becomes easy to discuss your goals and objectives with another person. Have a very open discussion. As you are selling your ideas, also listen to the ideas of the person you are discussing with. Keep looking at the common objectives at a strategic level. If you find that there are areas that are common between the two of you, then there's scope for further discussion.

- Give Time To Each Other

Before you sign the MoU (Memorandum of Understanding), give yourself some time. Think things through. Look at all the things that can possibly go wrong, as well as all those things that can go right. Be realistic. Have a long-term view.

Now, before you finally take things forward, comes the most important part. If at the end of all this you still feel that the deal is not workable, be unemotional, and be ready to walk out. An initial uncomfortable feeling is better than suffering all life long.

In leadership and management, the most important thing is what you do *not* do, rather than what you do. So strike the right chord and have a wonderful partnership.

Strategy

123

Requirement of Information

Due to the rapid growth in the Information Technology (IT) industry, any information is now available in a split second. Online search engines, mobile phones, radio, television, and newspapers also add to the ready availability of information at the speed of thought.

However, one wonders if all kinds of information are really useful, or is it just junk that is being dumped on us. Some careful thought will help us 'use' all this information productively.

Kautilya in the *Arthashastra* says it is very important for a person to be well-informed, but the important question is, why is this information required?

"Coming to know what is known, definite strengthening of what has become known, removal of doubt in case of two possible alternatives, finding out the rest in a matter that is partly known — this can be achieved with the help of ministers." (1.15.20-21)

Let us look at each aspect of 'information' separately:

• Realising What Is Known

Some information we get, is already known to us. India's win in the cricket match could be direct information that you might have received while watching a live telecast. The same information may be repeated in the next day's newspapers. This information has very less value addition.

• Definite Strengthening Of What Has Become Known

At times the information provided is half-baked. We are not sure if it is correct. An additional information resource will help one understand if what is hearsay is correct, or not. We come to know that the director of a particular company has quit — this may not be correct information. It has to be cross-checked with the person who is directly working in that company.

• Removal Of Doubt In Case Of Two Possible Alternatives

Let us consider a situation where a hotel has been publicised as a 5-star property by its marketing team while the news is that it falls only in the 4-star category. There is a conflict of information. In that case, the right information, maybe from the hoteliers' association or from the tourism board's reports — will help one make the correct assessment.

• Finding Out The Rest In A Matter Partly Known

Most of the information floating around is not necessarily correct. They could be just gossips, rumours, and personal viewpoints. Therefore, it is essential to verify the facts and conduct research before we rush to make judgments. This is done by going to the primary source of the information rather than relying only upon secondary sources.

Most important — all information is really not required. One should be focused on what one wants. As Philip Kotler the marketing guru says, "Marketing research and market intelligence should give the information that *you* require, not what others want you to know."

124

Principles of Management

All management theories and concepts are based on certain principles. These essentials are the foundations with which we evaluate if the manager has been efficient, the organisation productive, and the objectives achieved. Today, management is not just a subject, but is also considered a science and an art.

But what exactly is management? How does one define management? Various voluminous books are available to answer this question. However, Kautilya has given the most refined view of management in a single verse, as short as five pointers in verse 42 of Chapter 15, of Book one of the *Arthashastra*.

Chanakya says, the basic elements of management are:

• The Means Of Starting Undertakings (Assignments/Projects)

When we say we have to manage, the question is what to manage? We need some project or assignment, in order to start acting upon it. Without a project, or an assignment, one cannot be called a manager. However, the best manager is the one who not only takes up a project given by his boss but instead 'creates' projects on his own. Stephen Covey in his book, *The Seven Habits of Highly Effective People*, describes this as 'proactiveness' — the highest quality of a good leader.

- The Excellence Of Men And Materials

A manager has some resources, which can be used, according to his discretion, to accomplish his tasks. They are the men who work under his direction and the tools that are used by him and these men. Hence, the other quality of a good manager is to make his men highly productive and ensure the optimum utilisation of materials like machinery, space, budgets etc given to them in order to reach the objectives.

- Deciding The Suitable Place And Time

Management is all about deciding the right place and right time to make our moves. Like in warfare, the timing is very crucial. When the enemy must be attacked, is not a question to be answered quickly. It requires careful planning, analysis, and also patience. This sense of the right 'timing' comes from one's own experience, knowledge, and also guidance from other sources.

- Provision Against Failure

Every move has to be carefully planned, taking into consideration two alternatives — the best case scenario (success) and the worst situation (total failure). Therefore, some kind of backup is required for every move. One needs to have alternative solutions ready in case of failure.

A businessman was once asked the secret of his success, for which he replied, "I take into consideration maximum failures at each stage. I plan the alternative moves even before I start the venture." It's like having Plan A, Plan B, and Plan C in place.

- Accomplishment Of Work

Finally, management is all about getting 'results'. All said and done, at the end of the day, the achievement of results is what finally counts. It is very important to set a parameter to check if we have actually achieved what we set out for. That takes us to the first aspect of management — starting a project. Every project is started with a certain objective in mind. The process gets evolved and refined. But finally, the target has to be achieved even if the route taken to get there is different.

125

Keep an Open Mind

∾

The mind is like a parachute — it works only when it is open. Some of the best business ideas come from listening to others.

Chanakya emphasises the importance of this point for various leaders,

"He should despise none, (but) should listen to the opinion of every one. A wise man should make use of the sensible words of even a child." (1.15.22)

A father was once watching his daughter play. She went to her mother and asked, "Mummy when will I get my new doll?", the mother replied, "It will take a few days, we will have to go to the shop which means we will have to travel for at least two hours."

Her father, who was thinking of a new business venture, realised the lack of a toy shop in their area. After a little bit of market research, he understood that, like them, all the parents in the area had to travel a long way to buy a toy for their children. He started a toy shop in the area and became a successful businessman.

One never knows where the next biggest idea will come from. The art of effective listening is very important in business. Even the most unexpected person could give you the key information and direction that you might have been waiting for, for years.

The following are some keys of effective listening.

• Despise None

One should be able to listen to every one without any preconceived notions. Politicians use this as their most effective tool to gather information at both, the top and the grassroots level. At one moment, they could be listening to investment proposals made by business tycoons, while the next moment they might be listening to the complaints of a local resident. Taking the total picture into consideration, they plan their next move.

Even a child's viewpoint is to be considered, as Kautilya said.

• Never React

At times, while listening to the opinion of others, it is tempting to say, "Oh, I already know that. I know it will not work." However, one should know how to control oneself. Cutting off a person while he is talking, is not just an insult to him, but will also end the possibilities of understanding the central message he is trying to convey.

Remember this, "The most important thing in communication is to hear what hasn't been said."

• Make Use Of The Ideas

You may have the best ideas, but what is the use if you do not benefit from these ideas? Information is useless, unless it is applied for an effective purpose. Hence, we need to experiment with whatever we have understood. Successful businessmen are not those who just sit around and only think. They are men of dynamic action who are ready to take calculated risks and give their best to make an idea and plan work.

If you do not use your ideas, someone else surely will!

126

Managing Multiple Projects

≈

Every leader, manager, and executive has to handle multiple tasks at any given point of time. This is unavoidable. He may have been appointed for a particular work; however, with time, he will naturally get more and more responsibilities.

Management guru, Peter Drucker, in his book *On the Profession of Management,* is compassionate while describing the role of manager. He says, "The role of today's manager is very difficult. In any given situation, he has to handle multiple projects and assignments. He is always under pressure."

Kautilya, advises us on how to manage multiple projects and make more profits for the company;

"And (they) should bring about the commencement of what is not done, the carrying out of what is commenced, the improvement of what is being carried out and the excellence of (the execution of) orders, in the case of works." (1.15.51)

He looks at four types of works that an executive has to carry out:

• Commencement Of What Is Not Done

There are many things that need to be done. Good managers are those who start work on their own, rather than wait for the bosses to tell them what to do. Each person has to be proactive. He needs to build his own pipeline. New work has to be started. New experiments have to be tried. New techniques have to be applied.

• Carrying Out What Has Been Commenced

A project manager said it well, "It is not important how many projects I started, but how many I have completed." Everyone knows about pressure getting built up, simply because we are not able to complete the jobs we started. Procrastination is the worst disease. Once you pick up this bad habit, decisions are not taken on time, papers get piled up, and people lose focus. The best solution is the old adage, "What you ought to do tomorrow, do today, what you want to do today, do it now!"

• Improvement Of What Is Being Carried Out

One needs to ensure that the work started should end with high quality output. We should continuously strive for excellence.

The core idea of the Japanese theory called Kaizen is that there is scope for continuous improvement in each task a person can do. Excellence then becomes a habit.

• Excellence In Execution Of Orders

This means effective delegation. A manager, like all the other employees, has limited time and resources. Thus, in order to perform multiple tasking, he has to delegate some tasks to either his team members, or he must outsource some activities. Learning this art of effective delegation is very essential if one wants to climb up the corporate ladder. Management is not about only doing work on your own, but getting work done from others.

Once, a successful CEO who always seemed relaxed, was asked the secret of his cool temperament. He said, "Immediate decisions, faith in people whom I have given the work to, and spending more time in activities which will give us more money."

127

Politics and Politicians

≈⃝

'Politics is dirty business — it's not for me...'. Most of us run away from the very word. After all, politicians are commonly perceived to be selfish, corrupt, and totally manipulative.

This may be true to a great extent. But don't generalise. You can benefit a lot from 'good politicians', more than from management books. Leaders of various organisations, especially from the corporate world, can learn a lot from politicians about how to run an organisation.

Kautilya declares that a king who has not learnt politics is an unfit king,

"A king who has not learnt the teaching of the science of politics is unfit to listen to counsel." (1.15.61)

It means that such a leader will not be able to benefit from the advice and suggestions given to him.

For most people, reading this statement may come as a shock. However, it is by learning politics that Chanakya himself became a mastermind. A master strategist, a great visionary, a kingmaker, Kautilya was also an expert in the science of politics, which made him an unparalleled statesman.

- Why Should A Corporate Leader Learn Politics?

Well, when you learn the science of politics, you will understand the way a politician thinks. A politician is one of the most powerful persons in society. If you want to understand power, understand politics.

- How Can We Learn Politics?

Know your local politicians. Not many people are even aware of the names of their corporator, MLA, or MP. When problems arise, they blame the system. But if you know your local politicians, then you can take the initiative by making a telephone call, filing a complaint, or even asking for a meeting with them.

- Keep An Open Mind

When meeting politicians, keep an open mind. You will learn more than you expected.

Politicians are wonderful resource managers, crowd-pullers, and team leaders. Since they move around a lot and deal with various levels of people in society, they are more aware of the problems faced by others, than a person sitting in the office knows.

- Learn Both Theory And Practice

One should also start reading the rules of political science from books. Such theories can be learnt from experts who have learnt 'academic politics', while the practical knowledge can be learnt from those occupying the all-powerful chair.

There is hardly any difference between the corporate world

229

and the political world. It's all about power and authority. It's about dealing with the people. It's about how you can sail your ship in rough weather.

128

Constantly Educate Yourself

෨෴

All of us must have, at some time or the other, heard people complaining about not getting 'deserved' promotions, or the boss not noticing their 'hard work'.

However, few realise that it is not the boss who is responsible for your growth in life, but the knowledge and the experience that *you* acquire. We need to continuously learn in order to grow. Only then will external benefits like increments, promotions, and higher responsibilities come to us.

Now, most believe that they do not get time to learn as they are fully occupied with work. So how will such 'busy' people learn new things?

This is where Kautilya advises us:

"During the remaining parts of the day and the night, he should learn new things and familiarise himself with those already learnt, and listen repeatedly to things not learnt." (1.5.15)

It is a very simple principle of time management. Utilise your evening and night hours to learn new things, instead of spending them on most unproductive things like partying, or other activities which are really meaningless.

Even in an office, the peak business hours are generally in the morning. The latter half of the day could, and should, be used meaningfully and effectively.

You may even use this time to ask questions and learn from

seniors about processes that you have not fully understood.

Here are some tips on how you can use the second part of the day more effectively:

• Join A Class/Course

Today, there are various courses and classes conducted during post-office hours. Even MBA courses are offered for those who can attend evening classes. If you enroll for any such course, you will automatically leave the office on time.

• Read Books

Get into the habit of reading good books. Especially in a city like ours, you can effectively use your commuting time to do this. Choose the right books for learning new things. Do not just open any newspaper or magazine for the sake of passing time. You should read with a purpose.

• Meet The Right People

You should make it a point to meet at least two new people every week. They should be experts in their own field who know much more than you. Go to them with humility and learn the secret of their success.

All of this would, no doubt, make you a better man. After all, you would be following the old adage, "The only time well spent is the time spent learning new things!"

129

Disaster Management

≈Ɔ

Why do disasters, or calamities, happen? Well, who better to answer this question than the world's first management guru —

Chanakya — who says,

"A calamity of a constituent, of a divine or human origin, springs from ill luck or wrong policy." (8.1.2)

So, whether we look at a state government, or a corporate entity, a calamity in any place or department always happens due to two reasons — ill luck, or wrong policy.

Ill luck is when a natural calamity occurs and is not in our control. Earthquakes, floods, forest fires, etc, might be predicted, but they certainly cannot be controlled, or avoided, fully.

However, the second type of calamity is man-made and happens due to mismanagement. Now, while these types of 'calamities' cannot be avoided, they can definitely be managed well.

But before we get into that, we need to ask ourselves why do human beings mismanage? Chanakya gives us the answer:

"Inversion of excellences, absence, a great defect, addiction, or affliction, constitutes a calamity." (8.1.3)

Let us look at each of them in detail:

• Inversion Of Excellence

Simply put, it means 'not being excellent'. This happens when a manager is not proficient in his work. To avoid this, he has to be up-to-date with the latest developments in his own field. He should know both theory and practice, including the latest technical advances.

• Absence

If a person is absent on a regular and continuous basis, he will lose touch with what is happening at office. It is very necessary to take breaks from the work life. But, it is equally essential to get back into action once you are back to work. Every person should know how to switch off after a break and get back to work immediately.

- A Great Defect

Sometimes, a bad management team is the cause of calamities. People who are not qualified are placed at the helm. Or a bad decision-maker is made a leader due to the influence of his power. There could also be some personal defect in the leader which one may not be aware of. During high-pressure situations, such persons can't do anything. Worse, they run, blaming others if things go wrong.

- Addiction

Wine, women, wealth, and wielding power! Addictions to anything and everything will always ruin a leader's clarity of thinking. Therefore, throughout the *Arthashastra*, Chanakya emphasises that the king control his senses, only after controlling oneself can a leader control others.

- Affliction

It means causing pain and suffering to others. There are people who create unwanted and unnecessary problems to others. When in a position of power, a person should know how to use it for the benefit of others — not misuse it.

Therefore, it goes without saying that the first step towards effective disaster management is to select the right people, free from the above negative qualities.

130

Timing it Right

There is a time for everything and everything has a time. Chankaya makes us understand this golden age-old rule by using a metaphor,

"The time of catching (elephants) is in the summer." (2.31.12)

This rule has to be understood by all those who run a business. Many businesses are seasonal and are dependent on various factors, for instance, tourism peaks during the vacation, and insurance and tax consultancy get more business during the months when returns are filed.

As we mature in our understanding of business, we get a better understanding of such cycles. Then the game becomes very easy to play. But how do we identify the 'right timing' in business? Here are some tips:

- Play The Game

When you do start a business, it is very hard initially to get a grip of all possible situations. Even if you are still unable to understand the rules of the game fully, please hit the ground running and play the game with the right spirit. You will mature with every fall.

Your mindset will change. You will get an insight into the way the industry works and will, eventually, end up at a much better place than where you started off from.

- Learn From Seniors

Every industry has businessmen who have played the game for longer than you have, and who know the cycles much better than you do. Seek shelter from them. Listen to their advice.

Try to have a godfather, a mentor or a guru who will not only guide you, but also allow you to make some mistakes. Having a guru means you are virtually safe with your experiments. He will never allow you to be a failure. Trust him. Your aim should be to become like him. As a senior corporate giant stated, "The best time of my life is when I sat at the feet of great masters and observed how they ran their businesses."

- Time Every Move

After the initial learning stages, you are prepared for the big war. In war, and in life, timing is the most critical element. No mistakes are allowed since you are now responsible not only for yourself, but also for the whole organisation.

Strategise, prioritise, plan and time every move — be it for marketing, or for launching a new product. As a leader, you have to be involved in the process — planning, executing and monitoring moves at every stage.

Business is all about preparing ourselves for the right time and opportunity. But remember — when the right time comes knocking at the door, we should not be sleeping inside.

131

Corporate Social Responsibility

The concept of Corporate Social Responsibility (CSR) is well-known throughout the business world today. It not only speaks of contributions made towards the benefit of the less privileged, but also calls for making oneself accountable to society.

Many think that CSR is a new concept. However, in our country, kings have been practising CSR for thousands of years. Even Kautilya's *Arthashastra* speaks about this.

He makes it clear, that, while it is the government's basic duty to maintain a society's well-being, even companies cannot stay away from this responsibility.

Referring to this issue, Chanakya had written,

"And those who are without relations have to be necessarily maintained." *(1.12.1)*

But how do businessmen practise these ideas? Here are a few tips:

• Take Responsibility

Dr. M.B. Atreya, a well-known management guru, had once

said that we have to rise from CSR to PSR (Personal Social Responsibility). Each person has to personally commit to make his little contribution to improve the world around him. There are many things you can do — educate someone, plant a tree, support an artist, clean up the locality, etc

- Contribute Money

  Fund an already existing NGO project, or a spiritual organisation, this is the best way to start. You can even pool in the money. Collect a fund from the people interested. Then, every month, contribute the money collected to a project that you feel strongly about. There are many social projects that require funds. Find out about them on the Internet, but do not forget to check their authenticity, and only then make a contribution.

- Take Time Out

  You just have to make time. Most of us always say that we do not have time, or that we are too busy. But it is important to shake off this mindset. Take time out once a week to do something for others.

- Don't Discourage Others

  Under no circumstances should you underestimate this endeavour. Leaders are created when they see the problems of others. It's only then that they work towards solutions. In fact, the most important thing is that one should never discourage anyone who is performing some good deeds for the benefit of others.

  The Chairman of a company had once decided to donate millions of dollars for handicapped children. During the board meeting, he was asked whether it was really worth donating such a huge amount for these children. He answered, "Yes it is, if one of them turns out to be your own child!"

132

A Stable Organisation

≈☉

Everyone aims for the growth of their organisation — getting more projects and sales orders, increasing turnovers, and employing more people — are always the top priorities for business heads.

But, before we all begin to take the big leaps, we have to make sure that our foundation is strong and that we are stable within ourselves.

Chanakya says,

"The policy, following which he were to see neither the advancement nor the decline of his own undertakings, constitutes stable condition." (7.1.28)

What has been achieved, should not be lost. Even companies are now realising that, as they march ahead, their support system should be in place to conquer bigger markets. That's because it's important to keep your house in shape before you invite guests, or alliances.

• Financial Stability

Ensure that the cash flow into the organisation is regular and long-term. Outstandings have to be reduced. Collections from customers should be in time. A good banking and accounting system should be in place. Monitor finance reports regularly to keep an eye on these.

• People Stability

A company may be getting more orders, but what's the use if existing employees are shifting jobs? Stability of people has to be ensured. It's a major challenge to all HR heads that, before they recruit new people, their existing ones should not leave. It's a case of ensuring that the bucket you are filling with water has no hole in the bottom.

• Learning Stability

It's the world of knowledge-workers now. It's important for everyone to maintain a steady search for knowledge. Continuous innovation and upgrading is the secret of success of all great companies. The decline starts when one thinks he knows it all. Learn from others and your own experiences.

• Vision Stability

To fulfill the above requirements, a stable vision is very important. Before anyone starts an organisation, it's important to have a clear vision and a mission. If the company's sole motive is only to earn profits, the future is going to be dark. It is also important to impart the vision of the leader to every single employee to inspire them to work hard. Only when the 'inspiration' is maintained will the organisation grow.

You have to always remember to think about the long-term, instead of the short-term. Our Indian scriptures use two words to indicate this. *Shreyas* — the path of the good, which is initially difficult, but the person who selects it emerges as a winner at the end. *Preyas* — the path of the wrong, which initially seems comforting, but ruins us in the future. So, just take a deep breath, choose the right path and keep walking...

133

Working in new Regions

The need for expansion and growth is universal. Like humans, even corporations want to grow. Companies want to introduce new products, explore new markets, and grow in their turnover. But when a company wants to expand into new territory, it has to send people into the region first.

For such people who are sent out to make new discoveries, Chanakya suggests that the company take full responsibility of them in the unexplored region:

"He should provide one making a new settlement with grains, cattle, money, and other things." (5.2.4)

When a company sets its sights on a new region, it has to send one of its trusted seniors to go there and settle down for some time. The cost of this and their safety, has to be ensured. How does the leader do that?

• Do Your Research Well

Whenever a company wants to expand — whether for a new market, for acquiring another firm, or even making a strategic alliance — a lot of research has to be done. Reading, getting the information from industrial reports and consultants, etc is essential. Also, talk to a local person to give you further insights. This is the basic foundation for expansion.

• Send A Pilot Team

Based on the information gathered, send one or more members from your senior management to that region. Cross-verification of the facts gathered is essential. Meet lots of people — from various backgrounds — to understand the region, and its culture, better. Your 'eyes' and 'ears' are the basic tools for this. Document your study and, after you get back, present it to the parent company.

• Plan Your Move In Phases

If the venture seems profitable, move in phases. Have you ever observed how the various multinationals make their entry into India? Usually, a single person will move in first and stay in the region for about a year or two. During this phase, Chanakya advises that the firm handle the entire costs of living and security of the person. Some firms even move entire families of their representatives here, taking care of their children's education, vacations, and entertainment.

• Become Fully Operational

After gaining a year or two of experience, one will get a grip of the new region. Then move into full-operation mode and succeed in it. Note that it is not about conquering a new territory — a company also has to be socially responsible. Make sure you also 'contribute' to the new place instead of just making profits and taking it away from there.

Swami Ishwaranandaji of Chinmaya Mission put it best when he said, "Conquering does not mean killing. It means taking a place in the hearts of the newly acquired region."

134

Intelligence Management

Since our ancient Indian and traditional management books are based on sound principles, they have always had a lot of depth. This is the reason they have survived the test of time. Even today, readers write in with queries on the relation these age-old books have with today's world.

Well, they are in august company.

Being in the field of corporate training and strategic management consulting, I have also been asked by various directors, CEOs, and chairmen — "What's so special about Chanakya (or Kautilya) and his book *Arthashastra* that makes it so relevant even in the modern business world?"

Now, this is a very interesting question for all those who want to study and practise the pearls of wisdom gleaned from the *Arthashastra*.

Here are two very strong reasons that make *Kautilya's*

Arthashastra an eternal masterpiece, and Chanakya himself an unforgettable legend:

- A Subject Called 'Aanveekshikee'

One of the most striking features of the *Arthashastra* is that it is a very logical book. Before studying this book, kings had to go through a foundation course to prepare them for the higher knowledge of politics. In *Arthashastra* itself, Chanakya suggests that a student who wants to master this book should first study a subject called Aanveekshikee. This Sanskrit terminology is very hard to translate, but the nearest word in English could be 'Logic'. So Chanakya calls for a student's ability in logical thinking to be developed first and foremost.

Aanveekshikee is a very interesting subject, but hardly known to our generation. It is a mixture of logical, lateral, alternative, analytical, and out-of-the-box thinking. In short, we can call it 'the science of thinking'. It helps a person develop his IQ and converts him into a strategist.

Therefore, *Arthashastra* can be said to be a book on 'Intelligence Management'. Once this ability sharpens your intelligence, you will be able to handle higher responsibilities.

- A Foundation In Spirituality

The second strong factor in favour of the *Arthashastra* is that it tells leaders to inculcate an in-depth spirituality.

Why? Because, in the end, leaders have to deal with power and powerful persons. Power can corrupt, and absolute power can corrupt absolutely.

Therefore, to prevent the misuse of power, Chanakya suggests a study of the Vedas and other philosophical books. Thus, he attempts to create persons who will become value-based leaders. After all, a man is what he does in the dark when no one is watching him. Only a selfless leader can serve others properly.

Always remember that everyone is gifted with some intelligence. But hardly anyone is taught to 'manage' their intellect. And everyone may seem to be spiritual, but rarely do leaders of

241

position take spiritual-based decisions coupled with logical insight.

Now, the *Arthashastra* guarantees both and is, therefore, an eternal book of management.

135

Organisational Planning

~9

The invention of the calendar is a very important landmark in the history and development of mankind. It helps us track time and document the various events of the past. It tells us our present conditions and also helps forecast, predict, and plan for the future.

Can you ever spend a single day without knowing the date, or even the time? We would not only get confused ourselves, but also end up confusing all those around us.

Therefore, time-keeping instruments like the calendar are very important tools of reference in our lives.

Chanakya also used the calendar as a basis for time-management:

"The royal year, the month, the paksha, the day, the dawn (vyushta), the third and seventh pakshas of (the seasons such as) the rainy season, the winter season, and the summer short of their days, the rest complete, and a separate intercalary month are (the divisions of time)." (2.6.12)

In the above verse, one is able to see the periods factored in for planning. Some of these are still good for organisational planning today:

• Annual Planning

Here, the goals for the year are set and the road-maps are prepared too. Strategies and polices are factored in to achieve the same. Usually, Annual General Meetings (AGM) are organised to inform all members of a team about these targets.

If need be, new teams are formed and new job profiles are defined to meet the set objectives. AGMs also help one take stock of the previous year's performance.

- Seasonal Planning

Everything has a season and there is a season for everything — this is nature's law. Once we understand this, it's easy to look at the ups and downs of any plan.

After all, you will never find a farmer expecting his fruits to be produced the same day he has planted the seeds. He knows he has to wait patiently for the right season after carrying out the required duties.

Even in business, there are trends and seasons. Mature businessmen factor them into their long-term planning. For example, in India, maximum purchases occur during festival seasons.

Consider the recent Diwali season — every single person knows that the last festive week must have resulted in the bloated sales of every product in the market.

- Planning For Rest

One may work throughout the year, but it's important to rest from time to time so that we can work more effectively. Chanakya suggests the need to plan for rest too, in any organisation. I know of companies where, during the beginning of the year itself, all the employees plan their annual leave and apply for it.

In most European companies, it's compulsory to take a one-month annual leave for rest and for re-energising oneself.

A good organisational plan consists of a mix of long-term planning (five-year, ten-year, or even twenty five-year plans) and short-term planning (monthly, weekly, and daily plans).

The top management focuses on the broad framework while others focus on the nuts and bolts of the business. Together, their combined and time-managed work would ultimately better the future of the firm itself.

136

The Best and the Better

A great thinker once said, "If I were to create something new, I would study all that is best and make my product even better." About 2,400 years ago, Chanakya himself applied this law.

The very first verse of *Kautilya's Arthashastra* says:

"This single treatise (Kautilya's Arthashastra) on the science of politics has been prepared mostly by bringing together the teachings of as many treatises on the science of politics as have been composed by ancient teachers for the acquisition and protection of the earth." (1.1.1)

Did you know that there were at least fourteen other *Arthashastras* prior to the one written by Chanakya?

The masters of the past were not afraid to accept that innovation and creativity started by learning from others, and even gave credit where it was due, like in Chanakya's case in the above verse.

But there are certain steps for doing this:

• What Do You Want To Achieve?

First, our destination has to be clear. Define this and half the battle is won. When Ratan Tata first announced that he will bring out a Rs 1-lakh car, it showed clarity of purpose. The rest followed. If you are a businessman, think about the product, or service, you want to offer. If you are an artist, what will you create? If you are a player, where and which medal do you want to win? Remember Gandhiji's words — "Find a purpose, the means will follow."

• How Will You Do It?

You have to start the journey immediately after setting a goal. How? Well, Chanakya had said we should learn from the best that is already available. Do some research, read books by an expert in your field, study or join a course. Be sure about why you want to re-invent the wheel! And the key word is 'improve'. So learn from the best. If you are a swimmer, and aim to win an Olympic medal, you'd better get trained by the world's best swimmers. This will help you achieve the goal faster.

• When Will You Finish?

Now that you are ready to learn from the best, set a deadline for yourself — the time by when you will reach your goal, converting your study and training into success. This deadline will help you move with extra speed. When the American President first announced that a man would land on the moon and safely return to earth within a decade, it was a definite deadline. And the scientists achieved it! Chanakya followed the above steps too. That's the reason his *Arthashastra* has become an immortal book.

Now it's your turn to create something immortal too.

137

Time Management

All of us are living in an extremely fast world now, with a dire need for effective time-management. But one can always learn from Chanakya's centuries-old *Arthashastra*. According to him, being mindful of what we have to do is the biggest tip for managing time well.

Chanakya had said:

"Thus, he (superintendent of cattle) should be cognizant of the number of animals." (2.29.15)

Cognizant means being aware or mindful of one's responsibilities, and being in control of them. Hence, in this line, Chanakya says that, at any given point of time, the head of the cattle department should know the exact number of cattle his people are handling.

We can also use this verse to guide us in our daily activities:

- Understand Your Goals

The first step in time-management is to know where you want to reach, and by when. Most of us are running without an agenda, or clarity of purpose. Always question yourself — Why am I doing this? Am I supposed to do this? What results am I going to get by doing this activity?

Many of us do not know our job profiles properly. If you are not sure, ask your boss, and be clear about his expectations. Make a list of the roles that you play — department head, team leader, project in-charge, parent, child, etc. Then, under each role, write your responsibilities and prioritise them.

- Note Everything

When you are in the midst of your regular work, there can be various interruptions. Some are external disturbances, while others created by your own mind. Phone calls, a new idea, a bill that you had forgotten to pay — all these are common distractions. Such events disturb our current work flow.

At such times, note your thoughts down immediately on a sheet of paper, or even on your mobile, or computer. Then you will not forget it. Your mind will be at peace. Then, after making the note, continue doing your current work at hand, if that is your priority.

- Check Your List Regularly

When you are free, look at the list you have made and act on each item. A busy manager once said, "I look at my to-do list at least a dozen times each day. It constantly reminds me of what I have to do, and I accordingly make time for it in

246

my busy schedule."

The moment you have finished some work, make a note in a relevant file or folder. This can be useful when you prepare your reports. It's all about being "...cognizant of the number of animals."

Just keep in mind that all this advice can be useful only if one is self-disciplined. No amount of 'book knowledge', or time-management courses will help if you get carried away by the urgent matters 'others' bring.

138

Ensuring Growth

Being an expert in the field of *Rajniti* (statesmanship), Chanakya could communicate exactly what a leader (king) is expected to do to ensure the growth of his kingdom.

He had said:

"There is no country without people, and no kingdom without a country." (13.4.5)

Here, 'country' stands for the rural villages, or the 'countryside'. In other words, Chanakya stresses on the inter-dependence of people, villages, and the kingdom they form together, and the attention each needs for overall growth. The same law can be applied to any institution, or organisation, as well:

• People: Customers And Clients

Can any company survive without its clients or customers? Their needs have to be fulfilled by the company's products and services. So these have to be improved. But remember that the word 'people' here also applies to the employees and the managers who run the organisation. They also have to be taken care of, or there will be a disaster as no one would be ready to cater to the clients.

- Country: The Market

A large number of clients and customers grouped together in a particular region are called a market. Understanding the demand and supply ratio of any market is of prime importance. The company has to focus on this aspect of business.

Additionally, with all markets being dynamic and ever-changing, a company's sales and marketing department will have to stay on top of, as well as predict, these changes to stay ahead of competitors.

- Kingdom: The Company

People and the country come together to form the kingdom, or a company in today's corporate world. Remove either of the two and the company will disappear. If a company has to grow, it has to expand its current markets. This is what growth planning is.

Any person who wants to build a good marketing strategy should understand this rule. Study individual customers to understand market issues. Based on that, refine your products and services. Then understand the need of different markets and customise your products accordingly.

In this manner, the firm's leader will be able to keep his customers happy and, in turn, increase market capitalisation and make the company grow faster into a truly globalised organisation.

139

Land as an Alternative Asset

Owning property has become a key investment for many people.

In rural areas, land translates into the very existence of a person. Indeed, property is eternally named in that age-old formulation of the prime requirements for survival — *Roti, Kapda,* aur *Makaan.*

But here, the onus is on food, clothing, and, property, rather than shelter. Chanakya had stressed this centuries ago in the *Arthashastra:*

"Of the excellence of land, affording shelter is best." (7.11.22)

He had even listed many ideas on how to select land, or property, based on its qualities — conducive to agriculture, having a perennial source of water, rich in minerals, etc.

However, as in the verse above, he preferred that land which gives us shelter during tough times. Now, how do people like us, who stay in cities, apply this?

• Purchase Land In Smaller Places

Having a property in Mumbai is a dream. It's one of the costliest cities in the world. If you are among the lucky ones who already have a house in Mumbai, or in another similarly big city, do not stop there.

Purchase a small property in a smaller place as an additional shelter and investment. Why? Simple — if you can build one home in a metro city, it shows you have the capability for creating more, and you should do exactly that as an alternative to your residence.

• Build And Use It

Now do not just purchase a piece of land and let it lie waste. Build a house on it. Use it from time to time. There are many whom I know who own houses in their villages and small towns, but never use it. Someone else does.

It's important you stay there at least twice a year. Thus, you will get used to a different place. God forbid, in case you have to leave your current city, it will be an easy migration for you.

• It's Security

We never know what the future has in store for us. However, we can at least have a back-up plan for shelter and survival. If a natural calamity hits our city, at least we can fall back on a reverse migration of sorts. In spite of problems that may crop up, we can say — "At least I have a house for shelter. Let me start again."

This would especially help in times of economic crises, such as the recession that affected the world in 2008-09.

Chanakya's strategy was always to "...predict the unpredicted, and prepare an alternative." Your additional land or property can be this alternative.

140

Crime Planners

∽୨

After the terror attacks in Mumbai on 26/11, every citizen was angry. The international community also took these attacks seriously and lent its support. So now that Qasab, the sole surviving terrorist, has been sentenced to death, it is important for Pakistan to arrest some of the biggest masterminds behind such attacks. How do we punish the criminals after they have been caught?

Chanakya gave us his view in *Arthashastra*:

"He who causes another to commit an act of force saying, 'I shall accept responsibility', shall be punished double." (3.17.11)

In other words, according to Chanakya, those who force (or brainwash) others into committing a crime are more responsible for the consequences. Their punishment should be double of what is faced by those actually executing the crime.

Young boys like Qasab and the other terrorists who executed

their masters' plans were just a small part of the deadly show. Now that we are being led to the bigger planners, we have to tackle them:

- At The Top Level

A strong initiative must be taken by our government, as well the international community and the United Nations, so that this issue is dealt with far more seriously. This top level initiative should continue. The fight is till the finish.

So all the powerful — and responsible — authorities have to ensure that the results of their endeavours are much more better and fruitful than ever before. Timely execution of their plans is more important than mere academic analysis.

- At The Corporate Level

The attacks showed how even business organisations are now on the terror radar. Corporates like the Tatas and the Oberoi group were directly impacted. So the events of November 26, 2008, should always remind us that avoiding terrorism is not just the government's responsibility.

Companies have to take care of their employees — both need each other in equal manner in such times. The corporate leaders especially should communicate their concerns and issues to their employees and solve all security problems together.

- At The Individual Level

As I said already, one has to appreciate the way the fire is still in the hearts of our citizens. No individual should ever forget these incidents.

If you cannot participate, at least keep the momentum going by signing petitions, forwarding mails and voicing your opinion in some way.

PART III

Training

Trainees

141

Training Children

≈⌒

Many family-run businesses do not last beyond the third generation. To reach the top is easy, but to stay there is the most difficult thing to do.

The biggest challenge for a successful businessman is to ensure the maintenance of his wealth after he is dead and gone.

Children born with a silver spoon in their mouth would hardly understand the effort, pains, and hard work their parents put in to become rich. How are such people supposed to train their children?

Kautilya advises,

"For, like the piece of wood eaten by worms, the royal family, with its princes undisciplined, would break the moment it is attacked." (1.17.23)

Disciplining one's children is a must for every successful person. A certain level of control and direction has to be given to them. If not, they will become like a piece of wood, eaten by worms and white ants, that looks strong from the outside but is very hollow within. The moment some minimum pressure is applied, it breaks.

There are a few steps that will help discipline the child of a businessman.

• Give Challenges

Challenge them. Challenge their thoughts and ideas. Initially, it may seem difficult, but that is the only way to help them mature. Only when one's beliefs and ideologies are challenged, does one come out of the comfort zone. Secondly, let them face challenges on their own. It is very tempting for parents to go out and help their children when they are in trouble. But hold on! It is only by struggling to break the shell of the egg that the baby bird emerges.

• Learn To Say 'No'

It is important to love. But it is more important to teach the children to listen to the word 'No'. Born in luxury, one may take things for granted. However, when blocks are in the way, one understands that everything in life is not easy.

• Involve Them

It is important to give children on-the-job training. Many successful businessmen practise this. Even when children are in their teens they are involved in board meetings, asked to work on the shop floor, and also travel back home using public transport like regular employees.

Kumar Mangala Birla, one of the youngest business leaders who took charge of the Birla Group at an early age, attributes his success to the training provided by his father.

Let me share an anecdote with you.

A multi-millionaire was driving in a deserted region with his wife and son. As they stopped at a petrol pump the young son was asked to get off the car. The father gave the hotel address to the son and said, "Get here. We are going." The boy did not have any money, nor any sense of direction.

However, later, when he was a successful businessman himself, the boy recollected this experience as one of the best business lessons he had ever learnt — to find your own path.

142

Catch them Young

≈୨

A child psychologist was once asked by a father, "My son is eight years old. When should I start teaching him the values of life?" The reply was, "Start right now! You are already eight years late!"

Management training is somewhat similar. Leaders usually wonder when they should start training their juniors and subordinates for taking up higher responsibilities at the management level.

Kautilya advises teachers and students to begin management education as early as possible.

He says:

"For, a fresh object absorbs whatever it is smeared with. Similarly, this prince, immature in intellect, understands as the teaching of the science whatever it is told. Therefore, he should instruct him in what conduces to spiritual and material good, not in what is spiritually and materially harmful." (1.17.31-33)

It is important for the various B-schools and corporate trainers to understand that management is not just an activity or position, but a 'mindset' that needs to be developed as early as possible. Training people by giving various instructions, case studies, and also live examples, will attune the mind of young people to handle management responsibilities in a better manner.

Why should one start early?

• They Are Fresh

Young persons have an open mind. Since they are not yet exposed to pressures of targets, financial burdens and other major responsibilities in an organisation, they can learn very well — like water takes the shape of the vessel it is poured into.

• Understand Better

The younger you are, the faster your learning capacity is. A young person has a strong memory, which means he, or she, can understand and imbibe knowledge quickly. Moreover, anything told to them is permanently etched on their mind.

However, Kautilya warns us about the kind of inputs that need to be given.

• Right Instructions

One should teach the young and aspiring managers moral standards right from the start.

There is no point in telling them to be 'ethical' after practising corruption and bribery for a long time. They need to be taught such values even before they enter the corporate world.

In fact, not only do they need to be given instructions on moral standards, but these have to be practised by the persons teaching them. Leaders of various companies have to evolve as good teachers rather than just being executives running organisations. Teaching and mentoring the young ones personally has to be the top agenda of every CEO. Leaders should share all their valuable experiences with aspiring youngsters.

In an interview, Aditya Birla Management Corporation's Director, Santrupt Mishra, said, "I'm always teaching. Sometimes it's in a classroom, and sometimes during face-to-face meetings."

143

Do not Corrupt

≈

"The corporate world is bad! It's all dirty politics!" That's an impression many people have about the senior management in any organisation. Many companies may indulge in a lot of dirty games to achieve and/or retain power. They could also resort to such tactics in order to kill competition, to gain more profits, or to be in the limelight — all achieved by manipulation.

Obviously, it's good to hear about ethics and moral values in the classroom and during your management course. However, when it comes to practice — it is only said, than done.

We may write this off in a ubiquitous statement — *Kaliyug hai* (This is the end of civilisation). However, there is hope. Despite all the corruption, there are still a few organisations where values are maintained and principles are adhered to. But if all organisations want to be as ethical, then today's businessmen have to take a very positive step.

Kautilya advises,

"He should not effect the corruption of the uncorrupted as of water by poison; for, it may well happen that a cure may not be found for one corrupted." (1.10.18)

This thought has to be inculcated right at the start — the day the young managers/trainees join the companies with hope in their hearts.

Do not corrupt the uncorrupted young minds for they follow what you teach them. Just like children, even people working under you will naturally watch you and copy your actions.

We have to be positive role models, persons who practise what we preach. Just like professors are akin to God for college students, so too immediate superiors are like God for any employee.

A senior person should follow the following tips to create a beautiful, uncorrupted organisation:

- Be A Mentor, Not A Boss

The era of the 'Boss' is over. If you boss over your employees, they will run away the moment they get a better opportunity. In fact, there's a modern saying in the corporate world — people do not leave organisations; they leave their bosses. So be a mentor who guides them.

- Introduce Spirituality

It is the latest trend in the corporate world and disciplines like Yoga and meditation have gained a lot of popularity. Go a step beyond this. Invite spiritual people to give talks in your organisation. And just like you have various consultants in your organisation, you can even approach some noble person to be your organisation's 'spiritual guide'.

Moid Siddiqui, who is a leading personality in the area of 'spirituality at the work place', wrote in his book *Soul Inc* that "...some of the best lessons I learnt about values was by watching saint-like seniors."

So set a new trend with your own thoughts and actions.

Always remember, another world is possible...

144

Degrees alone are not Enough...

≈૭

A friend of mine who heads the HR department at a leading retail company once said, "I am frustrated with the quality of students that come to us!"

For me — as a person who believes in the potential of management students — this came as a surprise. But on further questioning, I found myself supporting this statement!

Most students from B-Schools also have MBA degrees. But few of them have any practical idea of the corporate world.

Chanakya had said,

"One conversant with the science, but not experienced in practical affairs, would come to grief in carrying out undertakings." (1.8.25)

With over a thousand management institutes across India, the 'quantity' of management graduates is increasing. But management gurus and thinkers are not convinced of the 'quality'. The theory of the science of management is good, but all that we learn has to be effectively applied as well.

This situation can be tackled by targeting the different levels of education and vocation. Here are some tips for the same:

• For Management Students

Management students, or those studying in B-Schools, should not look for degrees and jobs only. They should be life-long learners. Even while studying their course, they should go the extra mile to increase their practical knowledge. They should meet industry people, look for latest studies and reports on the Internet and maintain a record of their learning. It is important to maintain the reading habit, even after they get the degree and a job.

• Management Schools

The Directors and the Professors of management institutes should be up-to-date with the latest problems in various industries. They should spend enough time understanding the industry's specific needs. This should be passed on to the students and practical solutions should be worked out. Industry experts should also be on the board of management institutes.

• Industry

The challenges of every industry are increasing and changing day by day. Industries like telecom, retail, finance, tourism, and others — through their respective associations —should make a list of the key result areas (KRA) that they would expect from their new managers. It is important to communicate this to the management institutes so that the students are trained accordingly.

• Individual Companies

When the new recruits fresh out of a B-School join an organisation, the management should acquaint them with the realities of the corporate world. They should mentor them by deputing a senior. This is not to say that the industries should be blind to the recruit's theories. Rather, after accepting and absorbing these, the industries should provide the student with insights into practical aspects.

Remember, the road between theory and practice can only be shortened by a deeper understanding and open communication. Each individual has to take the initiative to learn the know-how of the world by keen observation, open-mindedness, and a will to take up higher responsibilities.

145

Mixing up the Old and New

India, particularly the Indian corporate world, is going through a very dynamic change. Organisations and companies that have been in existence for decades are suddenly seeing a new way of doing business.

Technology, connectivity, globalisation — all have had a strong impact on the way business is being done. But, the most important change has been that a young work force joins the team to make decisions and scale up the businesses. The old with their experience and the young with their dynamism and new ideas can create a wonderful organisation.

Chanakya says,

"As between a newly arrived (army) and one that has come after a long march, the newly arrived would fight after learning about the region from others and being mixed with old troops." (8.5.4)

The older people in any organisation are basically soldiers experienced in fighting many battles. They know the region (market and customers) well and, therefore Chanakya suggests that the newly arrived army (the young generation managers) can do better if they learn from the experience of the previous ones.

This can be done easily:

• Be Open-Minded About Change

Just because it worked your way, does not mean there's no other way. Elders should be open to change. Look at how weapons have changed in wars today. The soldiers are different. Therefore, a different game plan also has to be adopted accordingly. In fact, the best thing to do is to learn from the young generation who are well-versed with the modern weapons — computers, internet, mobiles (technology that the young generation is good at).

• Be Ready To Learn

For the young generation, it's imperative that they learn from the mistakes and experience of the elders. What we are today is because of the hard work of the previous generations. We may have great ideas, but experience is very valuable. Just being with the elders and listening to the stories and their problems will change our approach to handling things.

• Mix And Match

A good mix and match of the two generations sets up a good organisation. Some of the best performing organisations have already done it. The top IT and consulting firms who provide solutions and ideas are better equipped to handle various multiple projects because of the mix of the elderly and experienced, along with the techno-savvy young generation.

Once a business leader noticed that the school children were quite well-acquainted with the computers in their school. Those were the days when PCs had just made an appearance and were proving difficult to understand for his generation. He had a brainwave. He brought in the kids as computer teachers for his senior managers. Hence, the first computer gurus for his company where not corporate trainers, but school children.

146

The Right Attitude

≈୬

In *Kautilya's Arthashastra*, a king's manager is referred to as an Amatya. He is a very important person. In the verse below, Chanakya gives us an idea of the right attitude and mental framework a manager should have.

He says:

"He should turn away from frightful (words by the king), and should not himself use frightful words to another, and should tolerate (such words) addressed to himself, being full of forbearance like the earth." (5.4.15)

The following three cases, along with their solutions, illustrate this verse:

Case I: The king (your boss) fires you!

* Solution: There are times when even the best boss will fire you. The reasons may or may not be known to you. You should turn away from "another frightful" exchange of words.

  This means that, if your boss is expressing his anger, it need not necessarily be towards you. Secondly, do not react with thoughts like, "I will leave this job", or "How can my boss do this after I dedicated 20 years of my life here?" etc.

Just be calm and let time pass. Then, with a cool head, analyse why he, or she, said what was said. It was probably a continuation of some previous event that affected his behaviour. Or, it could be that you did not do something that was expected of you.

Once you understand the reason, it will be easy to take action. If it was your mistake, then correct it and only then go back to the boss. Just go at a later stage ("turn away from... frightful" words).

Case II: Suppose you get angry

* Solution: Now this is a situation for anger management! Never aim your frustration towards others — this is very essential. It requires practice, but it's important to recognise when you are losing temper and try to remain cool.

Postpone every activity and thought till you are calm and quiet. Remember, your intellect may be a wonderful instrument, but it works only without disturbance.

Case III: Someone abuses you

* Solution: In such a case, Chanakya asks us to be as forgiving as Mother Earth. There are bound to be times in every manager's life when, despite doing one's best for the juniors and subordinates, they show an attitude of 'thanklessness'. It's very painful. At such times, remember your parents. You only have to look around to see how children constantly ask their parents, "What did you do for me?"

Never get frustrated or blame yourself with the thought, "What a child/worker I've got!"

Just remain calm, forgive them, and let life go on. Things return back to normal as all of us realise eventually that we need each other.

147

Learning Something New

≈૭

Almost all of us have had the bitter experience of picking up a new subject or language, only to give up on it soon afterwards. Why does this happen? The answer lies in our approach, or lack of it, when starting a new course.

To quote an example, I will draw from my own experience of having worked for years as a management consultant.

I have seen many businessmen and students start studying *Kautilya's Arthashastra* to apply its principles in modern businesses. But several hit a block in understanding the terminologies and words used by Chanakya.

To all such people, I have only one piece of advice — do not worry about the initial challenges, just keep going. New subjects are bound to have tough sections, but it's quite easy today to fish out their meanings.

Let us take an example. Chanakya had said:

"Between the eighth day after the full moon day of the Asadha and that of Kartika, ferrying (shall be provided). The workman should give a surety and should bring in the regular daily earnings." (2.28.27)

Most of this verse is already translated into English, except two words — Asadha and Kartika. These are months from the Indian calendar. So, first learn about the Indian calendar system. And then when you understand the entire verse, your interest in it will grow.

Now, how does one maintain this interest? Indeed, how does one go about learning any new project? Here are some tips:

• Develop A Positive Attitude

The first step for any student is to inculcate the right attitude.

If you start with negative thoughts like, "It's impossible", or "I don't have that much time", then there's no hope. You would have lost the battle even before you go to war. So start with a positive mindset. Only then will the battlefield be set for your entry.

* Seek Information

The next step is to find people who know what you want to learn. For example, if you want to know about the Indian calendar, your own grandparents or teachers are probably your best bet.

Make a few calls. Search for more information on the Internet and get the basic knowledge in place. As I've already said, it is far easier now to fish out additional information. But even if you have to go and meet people to clear any doubts, please take that extra step.

* Practice Makes One Perfect!

This is very important — revise what you have learnt till you master it. In Sanskrit, this is dealt with in *Abhayaas*, meaning constant repetition and practice. Then you start enjoying the whole process.

As you repeat a chore, it is memorised by your subconscious mind and you can recollect the information whenever required.

This is the only way we can study or adopt any new lessons. Continue to take inspiration from the past, work in the present, and attain a glorious future.

148

Expectations from a Manager

There are two key drivers in any organisation — the leader and the manager, or minister. The leader is called Swami in *Kautilya's Arthashastra* and the manager is called Amatya. One without the other is incomplete. While the Swami gives direction, it's the Amatya who will build the strategy and execute the work. In fact, Chanakya found the Amatya to be so important that he noted,

"All undertakings have their origins in the ministers." (8.1.22)

Here, 'origin' not only means beginning, but also planning, strategising, and executing. Hence, the role of any Amatya has many dimensions, especially in today's corporate world:

• Planning

This is a quality every manager is expected to have inherently. How well he plans a project will decide whether an assignment ends in success or failure. If you were to build a cricket team to win a tournament, the first step is to plan well — When is the tournament? How many days do you have to prepare? What are the conditions to be played in, and what kind of players will be required? How much finances will be required? What kind of training should be given? What equipment is required?

Find solutions from all different angles. The best way of doing this is to write down all your thoughts. Now, this step is called 'data collection'. Only after you have organised this required data, can we get into strategising.

• Strategy Building

This is different from the previous step, which was basically planning and listing the essentials for winning a game. But strategy building is deciding 'how' to win that particular game. Again, I will take cricket as an example to illustrate this.

Even in this 'gentleman's game', we find that every winning team is very good in strategising. They study the competitor very closely. They study the weather conditions, and the kind of moves required in different situations. This results in what we call the 'game plan'.

However, good strategies involve having alternative plans. Plan B should be ready to come into place if Plan A does not work. So strategising is about creating alternatives too.

• Executing

Finally, after all the required thinking, it's time for the actual execution in the field. All your preparation becomes useless if the action does not take place. Therefore, execution is the final key to success.

Ram Charan, the well-known Indian management guru, became world-famous because of his book by the same name — *Execution*. In it, he says, "Execution is the key through which every CEO opens his door to success." Without this, the goal cannot be reached. Even Swami Chinmayananda phrased it beautifully, "Plan out your work and work out your plan."

149

Are you really an Active Person?

So many people imagine themselves to be hard-working, sincere and 'active' — without understanding whether this is a fact, or a figment of their imagination. You do not become active if you are just running around and working.

Chanakya had a very simple definition of 'activity' in the *Arthashastra*:

"Activity is that which brings about the accomplishment of works undertaken." (6.2.2)

So, you should describe yourself as an active person only if you have completed all the projects you started. This is quite important, and let me tell you how.

Ask yourself if you have always achieved the 'results' that you started out for. So many of us — whether students, home-makers, office-goers, or managers — have this common complaint: "I work so hard, but nobody bothers to appreciate or understand me."

Let me tell you that if you finish your work and finish it well, you will be noticed. If you don't finish your assigned projects satisfactorily, it becomes a mere action, and not something 'active'.

Now, how can we plan an activity and achieve the desired results?

• Define Your Goal Or Purpose

Before you start, ask yourself questions like — Why am I doing this work?, What am I supposed to achieve by doing this? If you are not sure about the answers, take the help of seniors who can guide you better.

Achieving 'clarity' regarding the goal is important before we start any work. Do a goal-setting exercise before you start. It should be time-bound and specific.

• How Will I Do It?

Plan your work well with all the required details. Remember, if you fail to plan, you plan to fail! Also, understand the basic fact of life that you cannot do everything on your own.

So, if required, have a team around you, along with good advisors and consultants. Once the road-map is set, it becomes easy to reach our destination.

• Focus On Results, And Achieve It

As you begin your journey, remember to look at your road-map from time to time, or you will lose direction. Make sure you are proceeding towards the same place you started out for.

If you are a truly 'active' person, you will plan well, execute effectively, and achieve everything smartly. Several people can, and will, misdirect you. However, it's you who has to be careful and stick to your goal.

150

The Best in your 'Friends'

≈◠

Last week, I was sitting with my friend, Muulraj Chheda. We were discussing strategies for raising productivity in his company, with regard to his team and employees. Muulraj works in the energy sector, and manages various projects.

However, our discussion led to a different topic when he said, "Radha, at times when we 'discuss' strategies, some reservoir of knowledge in me opens up and I am able to tap a knowledge base I was not even aware of."

He continued, "Probably I had it in my subconscious mind but, as we discuss things, it comes back to me."

After that conversation, I went back to *Kautilya's Arthashastra* and found this verse where Chanakya said,

"Being constant — this is an excellence of an ally." (6.1.12)

The verse, together with my friend's observations, taught me two things — first, you don't need an expert around to consult, since even friends will do. Second, you need friends who are a constant part of your life.

It opened up a whole new world for me — how to work as a consultant, as a friend, even being regular in meeting up with your friends — for that's the real secret of success.

And to achieve this success, whether you are a consultant for people, or just a friend to someone, you need to follow certain rules:

* Be Constant

Chanakya had equated consultants and advisors with friends, referring to all of them as *Mitra* in the *Arthashastra*. That was centuries ago. This is valid even today when all kinds of management consultants in various companies need to first become a good friend in order to be a good consultant.

And how does one become a good friend? The answer to that is by being in regular and constant touch with each of our friends.

• Tune-Up Mentally

Several consultants have an 'I know more than you' attitude. This is wrong. Understand the fact that a consultant cannot be somebody who is somehow better or higher than anyone else. Rather, he has to be equal to the person seeking his advice.

For an advisor, the first key challenge is to 'tune-up' mentally to the other person. Once this is done, communicating becomes easy. Tuning into another person will never happen if you don't think like equals.

• Go With The Flow

Never be rigid. Don't be stuck with thoughts like 'only this way will work'. Both you and your 'friend' should act in a mature way and open up to bigger and better possibilities.

Go with the flow and see the 'transformation' that takes place within you. As I found out with the help of my friend Muulraj, teaching and guiding others to tap their own wisdom turns out to be a great learning experience for us too.

151

Advice for Modern Trainees

Today, India has over a thousand management institutions. With the Indian economy opening up, and Foreign Direct Investments (FDI) flowing in, there is a lot of demand for the students who graduate from these business schools.

Once recruited, the students feel they have achieved their goal. However, the real challenge is yet to start. The management student, who has now become a management trainee, is yet to show the results for which he has been recruited.

How does one work in an organisation which is an all-new environment for the new recruit?

Kautilya advises,

"Under the supervision of the officer, he should carry out the task assigned with special zest." (1.18.3)

No management trainee should consider himself superior because of the course that he has just completed. He might have a theoretical base, however, he has to go a long way to understand its practical applications.

A guide/mentor is required who can show him how to get things done. These can be seniors who have acquired knowledge and skills by gaining years of working experience. The senior may not necessarily be as qualified as the pupil, yet, the new recruit has approached him with humility in order to learn and benefit.

Steps for better on-the-job training:

• Under A Supervisor

The insights provided by a supervisor are invaluable. They have gone through their jobs the hard way to master themselves in that particular area of expertise. The trainee should accept his senior as his new teacher. Every teacher is happy to teach a willing and obedient student. In the end, the benefit will be a thousand-fold.

• Carry Out The Task

Whatever tasks the senior assigns, should be carried out. No work should be considered small or mediocre. It is only when one does small things perfectly, that one will be able to handle big responsibilities. Completion of any assignment within the given timeframe should be the first objective of a trainee.

• Special Zest

While carrying out the assignment, it is the attitude that matters the most. It has to be positive... with extra zeal. The enthusiasm, with which the trainee does his job, shows a lot about his mindset. The eagerness to learn, and the passion to get going, will determine where he will be placed in the future, or what new responsibilities will be given.

The training period is the toughest part. My friend, Venkat Iyer, who runs a company called Wealth Tree Partners believes in regular and continuous training. He says, "It is only a good student who will become a good teacher. After all, only a good subordinate will ultimately become a good boss."

A chartered accountant was hired by a successful businessman to manage his finances. The senior businessman was not even a graduate. Initially, the accountant used to have rebellious thoughts, 'This person is not even as qualified as I am. Oh! I have to work under such a person!'

One day he suddenly realised, 'Who pays whom?'

This boss had the ability to hire someone more qualified than himself, to work under him. The chartered accountant felt inspired, "Until and unless I learn all the skills that he possesses for running a business, I will not leave this company."

That should be your attitude.

Boss

152

Asset to the Boss

∾⋍⊃

When graduates fresh out of various B-schools join an organisation, there is a lot of enthusiasm and drive to prove themselves in the corporate world. They are eager to put into practice what they have learnt.

However, there is a lot, lot more to learn in addition to what one may have already gleaned from books. Real success, after all, will come only after they have proved themselves in the organisation they join.

For this to happen, the first step is to learn from your immediate seniors and bosses. Most important of all — try to be an asset to your senior, rather than a threat. Be part of their solution, rather than becoming a problem for them.

Unfortunately, more often than not, excitement is the root cause why new managers make their bosses uncomfortable and even leak out vital and confidential information.

Kautilya says,

"Just as a serpent, lying in hiding, emits poison at the place from which it expects danger, so this king, having become apprehensive of harm (from you), will ere long emit the poison of anger at you." (1.14.8)

Take care that you and your boss are always working for the same objective and not for conflicting objectives. Only then will you be able to grow in your corporate career.

Here are some tips for being an ideal subordinate:

* Watch His Mood

Bosses are always under pressure. Always try to reduce his pressure instead of adding to it. You may always want his time, but he may not have that much spare time (even if he wants to) when you really need to talk to him. Hence, whenever you want to tell him something — watch his mood. Don't just rush into his cabin and start talking. Wait for him to give his whole attention to you. Then raise your issues.

* Keep It Short

A subordinate went to meet his boss with a recommendation of 25 pages. The boss said, "Summarise the whole thing in one page. In case you cannot do it — that means you have not thought enough." Think about the issue from all angles. And when you present your ideas to him, make it short, and to the point.

* Make Notes

Instead of going to your boss every now and then, make a note of all the small issues. You can go to him either at the start, or at the end of the day. You can cover all the issues in one go. That way, your time and his will be very productive. You can plan a helpful discussion and he can take effective decisions.

Finally, let's be very clear on one thing. All this is not meant to please the boss, but to become a good subordinate who, in a short period of time, can understand the wavelength of the former's thinking — an important skill needed to grow in one's chosen career.

153

Identifying Potential Leaders

≈೨

'I shall not exist, but the work that I started should go on' — that's what a business tycoon once said. Now, for that work to 'go on', a lot needs to be done and that too, before we become non-existent.

Great leaders, as they slowly inch towards retirement, always focus on the creation of next-generation leaders. You should create your own photocopy to fill your position. If possible, someone even better than you.

That is what Chanakya says,

"He (king) should strive to give training to the prince." (5.6.39)

Leaders at the top should completely focus on developing potential leaders.

Who is a leader, and how can one identify him? This is a challenge by itself. One will realise that a person successful in one area can be a failure in another area. Or, one who is a successful leader in a particular group may be a failure while leading another group for a different task.

But, before we start training and creating leadership pro-grammes, it is important to identify the right leaders. You need to ask a few questions that will tell you whether the candidate will fit into the leadership framework.

Some of these questions have been listed below:

Question: Does he give credit to others when he is appreciated?

Objective: The answer will show if he is a team player. A good leader is a good captain. He takes his team along with him on the path to success. He knows that human beings have weaknesses and, still, all have to work together to achieve the common goal of the organisation.

Question: Is he firm in his opinions, or does he change his view point every now and then?

Objective: This is to understand if he has clarity in thinking — does he think through every step before taking up or executing a project? Does he get carried away by the politics in a company?

Question: How does he conduct meetings?

Objective: His planning skills — if he is good leader in meetings, he will have an agenda. He will be open to ideas, but will never let the meeting go astray.

Question: Does he command the respect and attention of his seniors?

Objective: To assess if he and his view points will be accepted by the top management as he takes up higher responsibilities — only a good thinker and a strategic person will be accepted by the seniors.

Question: Given a challenge, how fast does he complete the task?

Question: To understand his resource-management skills — how fast is he in getting things in place? A potential leader will not get stuck with the current problems. He will be a solution-provider, rather than a problem creator.

Most importantly, you should yourself be involved in the process of creating future leaders. After all, it is a question of handing over a company you created with your sweat and blood.

154

Remembering those who got you the Job!

≥

Of all the places, it's in the office where most people will concede that their success has come about due to the contribution and guidance of various people. Now it's our duty to never forget even the smallest assistance we have been given. Even the world's first management guru, Chanakya, says the same,

"He should gratify, according to his power to help, one who has helped him." (7.16.19)

But let's face it — the human mind is very unstable and in the long run we generally forget people and the things they have done for us. And in today's fast-changing world where there's hardly any free time, it is even more difficult to remember such things.

Practise these suggestions,

• Write It Down

Make a list of the people who have helped you and have been instrumental in shaping your life and career. Your first boss, the placement agency, the friend whom you always call up for any professional help you need — all of them. Treat this list as one of the most important documents of your life. Keep adding names to it, as more people help you.

• Make An Effort To Call People

When making the list, don't forget to add their contact details. The special dates in their lives would be a good addition too. These will give you a good reason call them and wish them on special occasions. If not on each occasion, just one call a year on their birthdays would be enough.

- Give Them A Gift

Chanakya, in his book *Arthashastra*, says that a gift is the most powerful medium that can influence anyone. Do not even waste time thinking about this! However, do not go out of the way to buy an expensive gift. As mentioned in the verse above — "according to his power", buy the gift according to your capacity.

- Be Ready to Help

Most of the above may even look superficial. But helping out, especially when needed, is the most valuable thing one could do for another person. The HR head of company put it beautifully, when he said, "Always help others get jobs — you never know when you will require one."

155

Do we take up the New Job?

Now that's a quandary all of us have faced at some time or the other. To continue in the current job, or move to a different company, to be in service, or start our own business, to keep working, or take a break for higher education — these questions haunt every person in the corporate world today.

Chanakya offers a solution for managing such conflicts,

"In case of two alternate routes, he should march in a region suitable to himself." (10.2.10)

This advice is self-explanatory. But the choice taken subsequently could either make or break us. And this does not apply to just choosing jobs.

Such a 'conflict management situation' can arise in any and every aspect of life itself. At such times, you have to think with your head and feel through your heart. Keep a check on your strength and weaknesses.

How does one do this? Well, here are some tips for you to follow when facing that tough decision:

* Ask Yourself

The first person you have to consider is yourself. Ask yourself if you are doing the right thing. If you feel that in the current company and industry your growth has stagnated, then, prepare for a change. It would actually be great to have an open discussion with your boss, or seniors, to get a new direction. If you still feel the solution is not forthcoming, then seek help externally.

* Speak To Others

You can consult experts in your field and check if you are capable of doing something better. If this is too difficult, look at the websites that can guide you in this matter. Join an online group of like-minded people and seek guidance and tips for better understanding of your situation.

* Follow That 'Gut-Feeling'

Finally, after all this analyses, what is important is to take a step in the direction where you want to be in the future. If you continue doing what you are doing, you will continue getting what you are getting. So if you want to be different from what you currently are, do something different. Once you take this first step, half the battle is won — provided you want to fight for something better!

Look, there are plenty of opportunities today. But only a few take risks. Only, those who take calculated risks with the right measures can succeed in achieving their long-term goals.

And please never regret a decision. Even, and especially, if it is a wrong move, keep going along the chosen path. You just need to follow the military maxim — 'Burn the bridges behind you.' That'll leave no avenue for retreat!

156

'Two' many Bosses?

≈Ͻ

This has happened, or will happen, to most of us. The problem with having two bosses is especially acute in those organisations where roles and organisational structures are not clearly defined, giving rise to a conflicting situation.

But what can we do when there are two seniors giving contradictory opinions and instructions?

Chanakya had a solution for employees facing such a situation:

"They shall obey the orders of one who proposes what is beneficial to all." *(3.10.39)*

So when faced with such a situation, the subordinate will have to sit down and think coolly. He will have to judge the situation and the attitude of the two bosses, and then decide on his own which order will be beneficial to all.

Now how does one practise and make a sound judgment in the above case? Here are a few tips:

• Be a Good Learner

The first and foremost quality of a good subordinate is the ability to learn from all possible people and then apply the same lessons. Be open-minded. Learn from everyone. Every person has at least one good quality which can benefit you. The more you can learn from your seniors, the better for you in your career. Make daily notes of what you have learnt and keep a file. Record your learning — it will help you in the long run and also give you that valuable experience with which you can decide which boss is good.

- Keep Cool

  The best strategy for dealing with conflicting situations is to remain cool and not rush to conclusions. Think logically and realistically. If necessary, take a sheet of paper and write down the issue or problem that you are facing. With a cool mind, think through and then reach your own conclusions. If you still find it difficult, talk to a friend — you will find this very helpful, even for tackling stress.

- Learn To Say 'No'

  A boss will never like a subordinate who says, 'No'. At the same time a boss also does not like a subordinate who always says 'Yes'. Then there's the 'Yes boss!' employee — he is a danger to the employer too. Initially, it may look like such a person is trying to impress the boss. But he is probably providing the wrong information. So, when dealing with your boss, learn to say 'No', but only when required. Never be rash — convey your inability to do a task, in a soft and peaceful manner.

  Just remember that, in the end, it is all about how you manage your bosses. A lady was once asked, "It must have been very difficult for you to report to two bosses..." The reply was, "No way! I always get two gifts on my birthday!"

157

How much Money should one ask for?

All of us, at one time or the other, have faced the dilemma of not knowing what remuneration to charge for our work. Whether it's the salary at a new job, funding for a business, charging a client for services, or even asking for donations for a noble cause, we always get stumped by the question — how much should we ask for?

Chanakya had a solution to this problem as well.

He said:

"He should ask money of the rich according to their wealth, or according to benefits (conferred on them), or whatever they may offer of their own will." *(5.2.35)*

So what Chanakya suggested was to first — even before you ask for any money —study the person you have to approach. People who master this art can easily succeed in any venture.

Let us split the above verse to understand it better:

• According To Their Wealth

Now this is very subjective. The definition of 'wealthy' differs from one place to another. For instance, the richest man in a village is just another man in a big city while your rich neighbour would be just another man according to global standards.

Therefore, Chanakya suggested that one should ask money from the rich as per their wealth.

• According To Benefits Conferred

A request along these lines is generally responded to positively. That's because you ask for remuneration in line with the favour you did to someone, or for the benefit gained by your association, or for just a recommendation or advice you had given. You can ask for payment in kind, or cash.

The perfect illustration of this would be what one of my clients once did when his doctor performed an operation for free. My client calculated the amount he would have spent on the surgery and then bought the good doctor a gift of the same value, as a small token of his appreciation and which the doctor could not refuse.

• As Per Will

Now there are certain situations where you cannot make a valuation. If you ask for more, you may get refused.

If you ask for less, the opportunity is gone. In such a case, let the person decide as per his will. You may actually end up getting more than you expected.

I once heard of a hotel which practises the policy of — 'Eat as much as you can, pay as much as you will'.

Surprisingly, customers are so happy with the service that the hotel owner makes more money than what he would have had he stuck to the prices on the menu card!

158

Working with a Powerful Person

In *Arthashastra*, you will find that Chanakya gave readers instructions on how power should be used, and even wrote about how to identify the misuse of power. At the same time, he also gave readers step-by-step instructions on how a person working under a powerful person must conduct himself.

Chanakya used an analogy to explain power:

"Fire, when it reaches another, may burn a part or (at most) the whole body, but a king might kill one along with sons and wife, or might cause one to prosper." (5.4.17)

This verse has a very deep meaning and, indeed, is one of my personal favourites. It tells you two things at the same time — a leader can destroy you, or help you prosper.

If you are rude to the king then, unlike fire — which can only burn your body — the king's resultant ire will destroy you completely, including your support system and all future hopes ("...along with sons and wife").

So how does one work with a powerful king/leader in today's corporate world? Here are some points to ponder over:

- Understand The King

This is the first step you should take before you work under someone. Unlike the old days of monarchy, we are fortunate enough now to choose our own kings or leaders. So it's important to choose the right leader.

Once you have selected the leader you would like to work with, it's important to understand him fully. Closely observe his likes and dislikes, and other such trends, as well as his personal and organisational goals.

Once this 'mental tuning' is complete, both the leader and the subordinate will have a long win-win association.

- Remember, The King's Men Are Stronger Than The King!

You have to remember this golden rule. Kings are always surrounded by advisors and information providers.

As you get close to the king, you will understand that any leader's system is dependent on these people. So, as you understand the leader, also try to understand the people who influence him.

It will then become easy for you to tackle any situation. If you become the king's man, you have an added responsibility to deliver the right information to him.

- Be Faithful To The King

After following the two steps above, it becomes extremely vital to be faithful to the king too. His power and influence in the society can be very helpful to you. It could also destroy you.

Keep in mind that a king will favour only those who have been sincere and dedicated to him. In any set up, 'trust' is a key element for getting favours from the king.

You see, leaders are great people who are surrounded by other great people. The sole link is faith and trust. Understand this, and become a great leader yourself.

159

Never Force Anyone

〜⤙

We all have to interact with so many people in our workplaces, or businesses. All of them are different, with different ideas and different thought processes. As an individual, I may have a certain mindset, ideology, or way of thinking. However, it may not be necessary that everyone else will be like me, or accept my ideas.

This is where the real challenge starts. But the good news is that if we learn the knack of dealing with all kinds of people, especially those who are different from us, success is virtually assured.

The trouble is, the reverse of this also holds true. You only have to look around to realise how much trouble 'imposing' an idea on others causes.

All too often, people resort to even physical violence to prove their point of view. But while describing the ways of violence, Chanakya warned that this is simply not acceptable:

"Touching, menacing, and striking constitute physical injury." (3.19.1)

Note that these three types of violence are considered a crime even by modern law.

• Touching

This is that type of violence which is usually not thought through. It's more of a reaction, like pushing, slapping, or even beating. It usually comes at the end of a prolonged argument which was full of 'ifs and 'buts'.

Basically, it's the transition from a verbal duel into a full-fledged physical fight. But it's important to understand how essential it is to control yourself in a hot-tempered discussion.

- Menacing

This means threatening. It may not be a physical fight, but Chanakya categorises it here as a physical injury since it can lead to one. For example, when you threaten someone with the words, 'I will take care of you later', the promise itself will pull you back into a fight and there could be blows and damage caused. So do not even think of menacing anyone.

- Striking

This is the worst act of all. Striking could mean hitting the person with weapons and other harmful objects. At times, the objective is even to kill the person, making it the worst form of physical injury.

Remember, arguments — even heated discussions — are unavoidable. But you can avoid imposing your views on others. If there's no solution, it's best to approach seniors to discuss and solve the problem.

Organisation

160

Self-Discipline

❧

All of us, at sometime or the other, have to do a job that we don't like. It's a universal truth and will remain an eternal truth. Therefore, self-discipline becomes the key to success.

Chanakya says,

"One doing whatever pleases him does not achieve anything." (7.11.35)

There are many things in life that we like to do but should not — eating junk food, sitting late in office even when it is not required, browsing through the Internet without a purpose — all these add up to make a person unproductive and inefficient in the long run.

Hence, discipline becomes a must, especially in an office. The source of discipline could initially be just 'external', like a boss guiding, directing, and controlling an employee. However, in the long run, external discipline should become internal discipline.

The following are some tips on how to self-discipline yourself with regard to work:

• Plan Your Day In Advance

Most employees do not have a purpose. Neither do they have an idea of what they are supposed to achieve when they leave their homes. It has become a matter of routine for them to travel to and from office. They hardly have any enthusiasm. To avoid all this, an employee needs to plan his next day before leaving the office. A good time-table will help tackle not only such regular activities as mailing, report preparation, calls, etc but also special activities like presentations and meetings which need to be looked at in detail. Keep one hour extra in your plan to accommodate unexpected events.

• Do Not Be Impulsive

Most problems happen when one is impulsive, especially when faced with a new or unexpected assignment. For instance, if you are doing a particular task and someone calls up, or comes to you for a different task, do not jump to pick up the new project immediately. Slow down. Complete the work in hand first before you take up the new task. Your original plan for the day is more important. In fact, you should keep track of what you have planned for the day on the hour, every hour.

• Be Proactive

Stepen Covey, in his book *Seven Habits of Highly Effective People* says that being proactive is the most important habit of a successful person. So do not wait for problems to crop up, find solutions even before they arrive. The more you get into the habit of 'right thinking' the more focused and sharp you will become.

Remember, discipline is not an inborn thing — it needs to be cultivated. We may fail many times but just don't give up, it is important to get up and keep going.

161

Knowing where to go for Shelter

∽◦◡

Everyone goes through tough times, especially businessmen. They venture into unknown territories, face financial problems, natural calamities, death, or the exit of a very important partner — all of which can strike at any moment.

A student of management once asked a very important question on this matter. And, in *Kautilya's Arthashastra*, this exchange gives us a reply:

"He to whom he may be dear, or he who may be dear to him — which one among these two should he approach for shelter? "(Chanakya's reply) He should go to him he may be dear. This is the best course of seeking shelter." (7.2.25)

We generally consider that, during difficult times, it's our near and dear ones who will help us. And here, as we are going to ask them for help (shelter), Chanakya makes us think! "Are you dear to that person, or is the person dear to you? Only approach the person who considers you as dear to him, otherwise you will be disappointed."

What's the difference? Let us see in detail:

• When You Are Dear To A Person

This is a great achievement. Swami Chinmayananda says, "To love and be loved is the greatest achievement of life." You may have touched the heart of someone in a special way, due to which they develop a special respect for you. If you are a teacher, you will understand this. If someone considers you dear to him, then there is no question of him refusing shelter to you during troubled times. His house may be small, and his pocket may not be deep, but he will go that extra mile to accommodate and help you. This person will always be ready to help you, whatever be the reason for your problem.

• When A Person Is Dear To You

This is generally a kind of one-way traffic. *You* consider a person to be dear to you. But does he also feel the same way? You are assuming something which may not be reality. Thus, you may consider a person very close to you, and you may even go to him for help. But you could come back disappointed as he never considered you dear to him. It's possible you had extended some help to him, but he may not consider that as something great. To know this difference is very important. Only then can you seek shelter from that person.

• It's Not Easy To Be Dear To Everyone

Yes, it's not easy to win everyone's hearts. How do you know whom you have become dear to? There is only one solution — during your good times, help everyone. Great people never close the door on any seeker. Probably during this process, without being aware, you might touch someone's heart. And it is nature's law that, during troubled times, this 'forgotten' person will give you shelter.

162

Cleanliness at Work

One should visit Ramoji Film City in Hyderabad. It's really an impressive place, with world-class facilities for film-making.

The largest film city in the world, Ramoji Studios offers a rich and varied choice in sets and locales — from Kashmir to Kanyakumari. What's more, it includes star-rated hotel accommodation and even a tourist bus service for film buffs.

And here's the best part — it's one of the cleanest campuses in the country. I even met some French people who expressed their astonishment at the obvious efforts taken to keep the place extremely clean.

Indeed, when a business establishment gives importance to keeping everything neat and tidy, you can be certain that it makes a very good impression on potential customers and visiting officials.

Chanakya had also highlighted this. He even advised penalising those who did not maintain cleanliness:

"For one causing damage to the wall of another's house the fine is twelve panas, double that in case of spoiling it with urine or dung." (3.8.22)

A very poignant statement, especially given our entire country's state today!

• But How Does It Affect Us?

Look all around you. Observe how each and every corporate office, or building is kept spic and span. Estimate the costs involved and only then you will realise how much importance business houses give to being neat and tidy.

Hanging a 'Welcome' or a 'Sale On!' sign is not everything. You have to also maintain a homely atmosphere which will make customers feel welcome and, the first step towards this is to clean up your act.

• How Do We Start Cleaning Up?

Start with yourself. There is a difference between physical cleanliness (outside) and personal purity (inside) — one needs to achieve both, and not just the latter. So when we say cleanliness, it means the way we keep our house, our office, our car etc.

And don't think you need to emulate the swanky private office complexes or showrooms. It hardly takes anything to pick up the broom yourself and sweep your store clean, even if it's got just a flagstone flooring.

There's another advantage — being neat and tidy also sows

the seeds of discipline in a person.

• Educate Others Too

Now, I do not mean that you must fight with those who spit all over the place. But a simple query like, "Why don't you spit in your own house?" would make others pause and think about what they are doing.

If not strangers, then just target your building/shop's watchman and liftman. After all, wouldn't you want your customers or clients to leave with a pleasant feeling from not only your office, but also from the gate of the complex where you work?

163

Hidden Wealth

≈৩

Recently, an investor friend of mine revealed to me that his grandfather recently discovered some share certificates tucked away in old files he had completely forgotten about. The current value of these shares, my friend claimed, is now 100 times the original value.

Most of us have heard such stories of unexpected wealth. Even Chanakya — the world's first economist — referred to it in the *Arthashastra*.

He said,

"What is lost, forgotten and so on is income from other sources." *(2.15.9)*

In any company, there are revenue streams that are factored in. It can be the sales of the product or services, or passive income from interest earned, lease, or rentals. Chanakya suggested that every company or person should put one more column in his balance sheet — 'wealth from other sources'.

That's because, at times, some unexpected money comes in and this has to be reflected in the income column too. In fact, not a single rupee in *Kautilya's Arthashastra* is unaccounted for.

But can we find income from unexpected sources too? Follow these steps to find an answer:

• Open Old Files

The modern world has us running so fast that we do not have time to look back. Life is all about time management now. However, it's important to take stock of our past as well. Take some time out and check your old files. You may be surprised by some proof of unexpected wealth waiting for you: An insurance policy, or an investment bond which has already matured.

It may also be worth your while to check with the accountant at your old work place to see if you have transferred or withdrawn every paise of your PF contribution, including the pension part. After all, the provident fund organisation is sitting on hundreds of crores of unclaimed money.

• Follow Up On Old Payments

When we are busy, we generally forget to collect some small, old payment. Do a little follow-up and you may end up collecting such outstanding amounts. It never hurts to give it a try, even if you had written off something.

Your final efforts could work, getting you extra income. If you do not have the time to do that, delegate it to someone who is working under you. But do it.

• Talk To Elders

From time to time, it's good to sit and listen to our seniors and elders. They will give you some ideas and tips that can solve your present problems. We grow in their wisdom. Also, purely from a financial standpoint, they will tell you where they have invested earlier and pass on the financial benefits to you.

But after all this, remember to develop your inner wealth as well. Chanakya said, "Wealth is not only what is with you, but it is also 'inside' you."

164

Individual becomes an Industry

≈⊙

All existing businesses, even the old shops round the corner, have been built by people who put in a lot of efforts to create a customer base. But now, with the entire world becoming one huge market, customers have a free choice. And they are exercising their rights too.

Customers are not the only ones who are changing. You will be quite surprised to learn that this 'open-market policy' — which most countries are adopting — is forcing even competitors to come together. Their aim is to make the entire market process smoother so that they do not have to face conflicts later.

Even Chanakya recorded something similar some 2,400 years ago when policies were made by various business owners for selling their goods in a specific market.

He said,

"Thus, (the sale of goods) in one's own territory has been explained." *(2.16.17)*

So even ancient India was acquainted with the spirit of co-operation.

But can this sutra teach us to co-operate with our competitors in this modern, globalised world?

• Create A Quality Product

The first requirement for a company that wants to be in a

position to negotiate is to be successful itself. For that, a businessman needs to have a good product or service, made as per the customers' wishes. So try to understand this need. Spend some time on research.

You will need a lot of hard work in this phase. You should be like a great leader with an undying spirit. This will be a good investment and will pay off in the long run if the process is right.

• Bring Competitors Together

After a point, we all realise that no market can have only one producer or supplier. Even if there's a monopoly, it will not last. Other players will enter sooner or later. But that doesn't mean you are under threat.

In fact, a competitor's entry is good news as it shows that the demand is increasing. And if more players enter the arena, the next best thing to do is to bring all of them together and form an association. Basically, you should transform yourself from an 'individual' to an entire 'industry'.

• Expand The Pie

Instead of fighting for a larger share of the market pie, try to expand the pie itself. There is enough space for everyone, especially if all players improve their services all the time.

Thus, the final phase involves all the players converting their individual businesses into a successful industry, not only serving their customers but also creating employment, building the society, and helping to achieve overall development.

165

Setting up Systems

Employees leave organisations for various reasons — higher

salaries, better opportunities, or because they are not getting along with the company's working conditions.

Now whatever the reason you have to join a new company or organisation, the switch will definitely bring new challenges for you. For one, you have to adapt to a new work culture. And if you are in a leadership position, you will have an additional challenge — to change and set new rules to make yourself and your team productive.

Chanakya had a suggestion for this situation:

"He should institute a righteous custom, not initiated before and continue one initiated by others; and he should not institute an unrighteous custom, and should stop any initiated by others." (13.5.24)

This sutra gives us a step-by-step process for a situation where you have just joined a new company and are asked to head a department,

• Start A Good System

First, study your team members and the current existing systems. As a leader, it's important to know each of your subordinates well, especially their strengths and weaknesses.

Make a list of abilities/tools that you think are missing. If you can't do that straight away, think of some good system that existed in your previous organisation.

For example, you can start a daily or weekly meeting, even a birthday celebration system — anything that will help create the 'impact' of your arrival.

• Continue Existing Good Systems

This is important. Each organisation already has in place some good systems. Now do not break that. Instead, encourage your team to continue with it and improve on it.

Let's say the accounting and reporting systems are very good in the new company. So, instead of changing it, use the same system to its full potential. In fact, you should try to upgrade or improve this existing system.

- Don't Start Anything Destructive

When in power, you will have the authority to start many new things. You can even experiment with your ideas. However, never misuse the power given to you.

You have to remember that you should never ever start anything destructive. If you are not sure if the process is right or wrong, consult other seniors and, after due diligence, implement any new ideas they suggest.

- Stop Anything Unproductive

You will also need to say 'no' to any wrong systems or processes you find. Using your power to stop wrong practices is as important as using it to start, or maintain, the right ones.

This is a leadership challenge — you will have to first learn to discriminate between right and wrong. After that, you need to have the guts to stop what is unwanted and unproductive.

Throughout the *Arthashastra*, Chanakya had emphasised these high qualities in a leader. Once you develop this, you will automatically be respected and honoured by your subordinates, and even superiors.

166

Migrate if you have to

A press release from the Government of India (Ministry of External Affairs, 2009) stated that about 1.30 crore job opportunities have opened up in Europe (thanks to the rapidly ageing European population) and will be filled by 2015.

Sensing an opportunity for deserving Indians, the Ministry of Overseas Indian Affairs (MOIA) wasted no time in inking a deal with the International Organisation for Migration (IOM) for the implementation of an European Union-sponsored legal migration programme.

When I read reports of this, I couldn't help but note that this is yet another case of Chanakya's management ideas in *Arthashastra* being applied worldwide. Chanakya had said,

"Settlement of people should be done by bringing in people from foreign lands." (2.1.1.)

Whether knowingly or unknowingly, Europe is doing something exhorted centuries ago in India. Still, there's no denying the fact that the visas being offered by European countries for working professionals is a huge opportunity for Indian teachers, artists, craftsmen, managers, and businessmen.

The vibrant expatriate Indian communities have already made an impact in the US, Middle East, and the UK. Now it's time for us to lead the rest of Europe.

But how do we do this?

• Don't Lose This Chance

This is an opportunity for working people to prove their worth in European nations. Hence, make it a point to check whether you are eligible for this programme. There are openings right from floor jobs in manufacturing facilities to vacancies in the government departments.

Let's be there before other populated countries join this global rat race. Europeans are developed economically, and we can learn a lot from their systems. It will open up a new world for us.

• Make An Impact

I suggest you go there, not as job seekers but as 'equal' partners. If they provide an opportunity to you, give them our traditional systems in return — family culture, spiritual knowledge, and the ancient sciences which are our strengths.

We can always instill Indian values and ethos wherever we are. And the best way to make an impact is by contributing your maximum through hard work and dedication.

- Learn And Come Back

Learn from the cleanliness, technology, economic policies, etc practised in these developed countries. However, do come back to share and apply the lessons back in India. Do invest in our nation and its growth.

This country requires you as much as others. Whether it's Europe or any other advanced country that's beckoning you, learn the best from that place and apply the lessons here.

167

Lost your Job?

Many people lost their jobs because of the recession in 2008-09. Even those who are still employed are spending sleepless nights in fear of being sacked, or finding out that their employer is a fraud! Everyone has one common question — are there better job opportunities out there?

My reply is a confident yes, thanks to constant enquiries from various firms, asking for people who can be recruited. In fact, I have even been asked to be part of the interview panel for several companies.

So, I am sure there are jobs even in these troubled times, possibly better ones!

Whenever I am involved in any recruitment process, I advise the top management with what Chanakya had suggested so many centuries ago:

"He (leader) should make new men well-versed in the knowledge of his ministers." (1.8.22)

So the first quality that recruiters should look for in a candidate when looking for employability is knowledge and a ready-to-learn attitude.

But what should the candidate do?

• Be Ready For Change

Some say that the recession is here to stay. Even though I do not agree fully, I know its impact has been very dangerous, at least for the time being, as many firms shrink their workforce.

So, if you are among those whose companies are seriously thinking of effecting job cuts — be ready to change. It's high time we rolled up our sleeves and moved onto a different path.

Come out of your comfort zone. Be ready to experiment.

• Try Smaller Companies

It's surprising that many SMEs (small- and medium-scale enterprises) are still going strong. They may not be big brands, but they have sound financials. These are companies that have a good work culture. Try to get yourself placed in these organisations, where they will welcome you. Look out for ads in newspapers and job sites.

• Think Long-Term

Youngsters just don't do this! In times of recession, they (and indeed all of us) need to learn one important lesson — life is not all about the good times, but also the tough times.

So always think about the long-term in your career. Look out for companies that will give you not only the temporarily fat salaries, but will also help to give your talents an expression.

Finally, remember that a career is not just about the money, but about finding your true 'inner' calling and being happy.

Let the recession help you discover yourself. All the best.

168

To be or not to be?

∾

At the top level it is all about making decisions. A delay in timely decisions leads to loss of not only time and money, but also mental energy.

Managers have to be very careful while making decisions. The first step is to collect the right information from the right sources. The Chief Executive spends a lot of time collecting and analysing various information. Such information is categorised by Kautilya as three types:

"The affairs of a king (leader) are (of three kinds, viz.,) directly perceived, unperceived and inferred." (1.9.4)

- Directly Perceived

This is the most authentic form of information one can gather. Seeing is believing. A study of sick factories revealed that, various labour problems happened when the production manger spent more time in his cabin than on the shop floor. In Japan, a manager who spends most time meeting people in the workshop is highly respected.

Directly meeting people in 'their' work area gives one the best insights into the real issues the employees may face. It exposes one to ground level realities and also gives an opportunity to meet every one on a personal front. As they say, the best leaders are the ones who know their employees by their first names.

- Unperceived

What is communicated by others is unperceived. As human beings we have limitations. We cannot be at all places at the same time. In areas we are not able to reach directly, we may gather information from other sources. Technology can also help us

gather more such information

However, this may not be a very authentic source. A lot of contradictory information may also be floating around. Therefore, one has to be very careful while studying the source of information.

• Inferred

Forming an idea about something that has not been done with the help of something that has been done is called 'inferred'. For example, if a manager who has been highly productive comes up with a suggestion to improve productivity, one can 'infer' from his high productivity that his suggestion could be valuable.

Keen observations and lots of experience go into making good decisions. A mature leader can analyse any given situation within moments. He acquires the 'knack' of quick decision making.

What about those leaders who are still learning the tricks of the trade? How does one know if the decisions taken are correct? Once a successful businessman was asked this question, he replied, "By taking wrong decisions."

The most important factor in decision making is 'clarity' about what one wants to achieve. As Ben Stein, a famous American lawyer, law professor, economist, actor and White House speechwriter once said, "The indispensable first step to getting the things you want out of life is this — *decide what you want!*"

Everything else follows.

169

Migration: To accept Job Seekers?

Migration is a natural process. Animals and birds migrate in search of food and shelter. All of us are aware that even human beings migrate. Some migrate for money, some for education, while some for a better lifestyle and comfort. But from the angle of governance, or even that of an employer, it is important to check the credentials of each migrant or candidate.

Migration does not automatically convert people into assets in the new place.

Chanakya says,

"And he should not allow in the city 'outsiders' who cause harm to the country. He should cast them out in the countryside or make them pay all the taxes." (2.4.32)

This shows how particular Chanakya was in keeping a watch over each person coming into his kingdom. If you read the above verse carefully, you will realise that several centuries after Chanakya's time, this became a formal visa process.

The sutra can even help you choose whom to accept when potential candidates migrate to your organisation:

• Check Your Requirement

Firstly, be clear what your company, organisation, or country's requirement is. Based on that, allow migrants to come in. Many migrants add value to a new place. The labour class of India migrated to the Middle East and became a cheap but efficient labour force. Indian doctors and engineers who migrated in the 1960s added great value to countries like USA and UK. A nation like Singapore, which values human capital, has created intellectual assets from migrants.

So can your organisation, provided you know what you want and make that synergy work.

• Check Their Requirement

Understand the need of the person seeking migration or a change in job. It could be economic, security, and even safety. War-torn countries displace entire generations to neighbouring nations.

In the corporate world too, companies that suddenly close down, end up generating a huge pool of talent looking for work. Even otherwise, growing companies and multinationals talk of global talent than just national talent.

But, even if that candidate migrating to your firm has this talent, you should be clear about what that person's needs are and whether this can be fulfilled.

- Win-Win, Or 'No Deal'

All those seeking migration need not be productive. Just be aware that both — the one migrating to you as well as your firm which may accept him — should benefit from the change. Therefore, it is necessary to have a win-win deal. Or to put it in the language of management guru Stephen Covey, "No deal!"

Also remember that you have to be open and tolerant since — be it in nations or companies — people who migrate not only come with suitcases but also bring along their culture, habits, and mind-sets. Therefore, be ready to adapt.

Advice

170

The Correct Advice

Consultants are required by every company in various departments, activities, and also in the boardroom. They play the very critical role of beacons, illuminating the right path and bringing focus to achieve the organisation's goals and objectives.

Whenever a new venture has to be started, a person with knowledge in that particular field is required for guidance. His tips and insights can help us avoid many pitfalls and save a lot time and effort. Such a person is a consultant. Kenichi Ohmae, the author of the famous management book, *The Mind of a Strategist — The Art of Japanese Business* says, "A consultant plays the role of a strategist and a mentor at the same time."

Kautilya in the *Arthashastra* offers step-by-step instructions for identifying the right consultant and how to work with them.

"All undertakings should be preceded by consultation. Holding a consultation with only one, he may not be able to reach a decision in difficult matters. With more councillors it is difficult to reach decisions and maintain secrecy." *(1.15.2,35,40)*

• Do Not Proceed Without Consultation

In business and in other aspects of life it is important to accept the fact that 'I require guidance'. Proceeding without the advice of experts can lead to serious mistakes. A consultant has years of experience and knowledge, based on which he can give valuable suggestions.

• Do Not Consult Only One Person

After knowing that one requires a consultant, however, it should also be understood that the ultimate decision and course of action should be based on one's own discrimination and judgment. Complete dependence on one person can narrow the viewpoint. Only different persons can bring variety and freshness to perspective. Therefore, there should always be more than one guide.

• Do Not Consult Too Many People

While it is important to look at different perspectives, this should not be overdone. Getting too many people involved can create confusion. Just as too many cooks spoil the broth, too many ideas can complicate matters, making it difficult to hit the right course. Moreover, if more people come to know about a project, its plan could be compromised to rivals. It is important to announce a project only when all the ground work is complete.

• Consult With The Mature

"Therefore sit and counsel with those who are mature in intellect." *(1.15.21)*

After one has identified these few right people, about two or three of them, the next step is to sit along with them. 'Sitting' means listening to their insights, imbibing from their deep knowledge of the subject and vast experience. They should be people who are mature in intellect. It means those who are experienced, deeply analytical, and possess an intellectual and practical knowledge of that particular subject.

Chanakya himself was such a consultant who advised Emperor Chandragupta Maurya on strategies in war, diplomacy, statecraft, and economy during one of the most important periods in Indian history.

171

Advice of Consultants

Let's face it — a consultant is required in every organisation. Why? Because, he has a lot of experience and can look at the problem objectively and unemotionally and then offer a simple solution. This is the role of a management consultant. Therefore, before making any action plan for your company, it is necessary to take the advice of a consultant.

Chanakya advises,

"He should ask the councillors concerning a matter exactly similar to the undertaking he has in mind, 'this work was like this, or, if it were to happen like this, how then should it be done?' As they might advice, so should he do that work." (1.15.24-25)

Here, Chanakya suggests that when a company takes a management consultant on board for advice and suggestions, it should be with an open mind.

Here are a few tips:

• Choose The Right Consultant

There are many consultants offering their services in the

market. However, you should be clear about what kind of expertise you want. Choose a person who is experienced and has a thorough understanding and knowledge of that particular field. He should not only have theoretical aptitude, but also practical know-how of the problems you are facing or may have to face in the future.

The consultant should be a person who not only gives advice, but also makes sure that you are benefiting from it. He should be able to explain the problem with simple examples.

• Sit And Listen To Him

Having chosen the right consultant, it is important to sit down with him and explain what you want from him. As already pointed out, don't forget to ask, "What should be done?" The right questions will give you the right answers. His insights are very essential for building your strategy.

• From Advice To Application

After getting the necessary advice, many companies usually think that the work of a consultant is over. But wait! Think through every possible angle. Having a consultant in an advisory capacity is just the beginning. You should try and involve him in the application process as well. Let him also be a part of the process to apply these ideas and get the desired results.

Remember — the consultant has to be a part of your team throughout the duration of the project. If and when the need arises, you could and should go back to him before starting another project.

172

Power behind the Kings

~⁌⁊

I was once conducting a workshop on strategy for a group of chairmen from various companies. I asked them, "Who according to you is the most powerful?" Most replied that it was the person who held a high position, like the president, chairman of a large company, etc.

But when we analysed this deeper, we all ended up agreeing that it's the 'chair', or the position a person holds that represents true power, and not necessarily the person himself.

We also referred to a verse from the *Arthashastra*:

"He who sees policies as being interdependent plays as he pleases, with kings tied by the chains of their intellect." (7.18.44)

Ever notice the secretaries, PAs, and even key ministers who keep buzzing around VVIPs? These are the people who can guide and control power, even when they are not in powerful positions themselves.

These men, through their 'sharp intellect', guide kings and leaders. But they have not gained their proximity to the highly visible public figures just like that.

Rather, these people were already connected to the rising stars in various roles. Still, it's vital that choosing them is a carefully analysed process:

• Advisors

No powerful person will take any decision without the consent of his advisors. These advisors are always present behind the scenes and may hardly be noticed in public.

But a piece of advice can make or break any king. These advisors can turn the way a nation or organisation runs. So it's important that one is guided by good experts in each field for effective decision-making.

• Gurus, Or Teachers

World over, and especially in India, teachers play a very important role in a person's life. We may call them our spiritual gurus, or religious guides.

Whatever they may be known as, seek their opinion when you are in any moral dilemma. By virtue of their experience and value of their guidance, these people can highly influence a powerful person's thinking.

• Friends

Finally, we have the group of old friends that any powerful person spends his time with. In the *Arthashastra*, they were called Mitra. A leader has to be very careful when selecting a friend, for there are good and bad people out there. After all, these people will become the king's men, and will become more powerful than the king himself.

Remember, "Power can destroy, and power can create. But the question is to understand who really influences the powerful people."

173

The Greatest Opportunity

≈つ

A management graduate was once asked during his interview, "What is the greatest lesson you have learnt about management?" He replied, "An ability to understand and communicate future business trends." When asked how he would go about this, he answered, "By studying past business trends and applying it in present situations." He got the job.

After all, a strategist learns from past mistakes, experiments in the present and innovates for the future. But to survive, you have to create a team and inspire them to fight for you.

For this, Chanakya advises,

"Being devoted to the training of the troops, he should arrange signals for the arrays by means of musical instruments, banners and flags, when halting, marching, or attacking." (2.33.11)

Here, training is for the future, musical instruments denote inspiration, while signals denote communication.

Once Bill Gates was asked, "What is your biggest success?" He replied, "It's yet to come." Mature leaders and businessmen understand this. What you have learnt, is only the past. Your success is the present.

So one should always be alert because the next big idea that can scale up your organisation is yet to come. On the flip side, if you're unable to communicate the dangers of the future, you can be totally ruined.

Let's see some action points for this:

- Study Past Successes

If you want to know what will work in the future, first understand what worked in the past. This is an important base to start from. Now how does one do that? Simple, either get the information from elders and seniors who were part of the process, or read books and reports that document the relevant facts and figures.

- 'Observe' Demands

After having equipped yourself with past knowledge, look around you. What are the products and services that people are using, or want to use? What are the demands, and is it possible to supply this? What are the needs of the people of our generation? What would make them complete? Put these questions to others and also to yourself. Seek these answers. Keep your eyes and ears open.

- Now 'Create' The Future

The good news is that once you do the previous two steps, you can shape the future yourself. For example, if you find that there is a need for trendy college clothes — *you* can create the next trend by creating a line of clothes that appeals to them. Therefore, the key in strategy is to 'create' and 'direct' the customers to your products and services.

It's easy to create the future, if you can look into the past. Because it is nature's law that what was in the past will become the future in some other form.

As was written by Hermann Hesse in the Nobel Prize winning book *Siddhartha*, "What goes away from you, comes back to you..."

174

Career Persons must Conserve

All of us spend so much time running around to build a career that we don't even stop to think about what kind of legacy we will leave behind. I am not referring to a monetary legacy. Rather, I am hinting at the state of the environment in and around our city. And if you, dear reader, are thinking about what you can do, let me tell you that the answer is *a lot!*

In case you are too busy to save the mangroves or whatever mission all the 'green' activists are on, you can at least save a little electricity or, better still, water. In fact, you will be surprised to know that we already have well-documented solutions to our current conservation problems in our ancient books, including rainwater harvesting. *Kautilya's Arthashastra* — primarily a treatise on economics — also gives suggestions on how to preserve water.

Chanakya had said,

"In conformity with the appearance, he should give exercise to the gentle and the dull (elephant), and to the animal with mixed characteristics, in various types of work, or in accordance with the season." (2.31.18)

This highlights how water — as a natural resource — should be allowed to run free with no one allowed to have a monopoly on it. Then again, we need to utilise this great resource effectively with minimal wastage. But how can we do this as individuals in today's corporate world?

• Understand Our Strength

As a nation, we have been blessed with various perennial rivers. Countries like UK still have to recycle a major part of their water. Now let us do something at a corporate level to save water.

We should spread awareness among our colleagues about not wasting water and plan for the long-term. Water not effectively used today will worsen the scarcity problem tomorrow. Do we want our future generations to go thirsty?

• Community Development

Despite our great rivers, water is scarce in many parts of India. Many farmers have committed suicide for want of any effective irrigation system. You can spare some time or money with some leading foundation or trust that is trying to reorganise things in these affected areas. If your firm already supports, or runs a project, as a part of its Corporate Social Responsibility (CSR) role, you can get even more involved at the personal level.

• Individual Development

This is most important. Take steps in your own private life to stop water wastage — like closing the tap while brushing your teeth, getting leaking pipes fixed immediately, etc. If you see water wastage in public places, call the authorities immediately and make sure it is addressed.

You see, we live in a nation where pure and safe drinking water is still a 'privilege' for a majority of the citizens. Problems may persist at the level of local authorities, but the solution lies with each individual.

175

Applying the knowledge from *Arthashastra*

ॐ੭

The knowledge in *Arthashastra* needs to be used in practical life too. The most frequently asked question is — how will these ideas help my business?

I quote Chanakya for an answer:

"In this way (by following ideas given in the Arthashastra), the kingdom continues in the succession of his sons and grandsons, free from the dangers caused by men." (5.1.56)

A study of *Kautilya's Arthashastra* guarantees tools and techniques by which you can create a business model which will exist beyond you. It will make your system good and permanent, with people following you for generations. Look at how we still follow Chanakya!

Another query that's often put to me is for 'step-by-step instructions' on how to benefit from these ideas.

Well, this is the best way:

• Stay In Touch

These ideas are the simplified version of the original *Arthashastra*. You can write to us for more information about how to study the text and get more knowledge. Mail us at *info@spmfoundation.in* and also visit our website *www.spmfoundation.in*

- Gift A Copy Of This Book

  As an author I do not want you to 'buy' this book. I want you to gift a copy of this book to others. If you gift this to others, watch a miracle happen. Someone will gift it to you. Let the knowledge spread to maximum people across the globe.

- Apply These Models

  The book may have come to an end. But after understanding the theories now you need to start applying it. Chanakya's ideas have worked for over 2400 years. It will work for you as well. Try it.

  No theory is good till you benefit from its practical application. The same is the case with *Kautilya's Arthashastra*. You have to be your own judge.

- Teach It To Others

  The best way to learn anything is by teaching it to others. So whatever you have learnt, teach it to others. If you are a boss, teach these principles to your subordinates. If you are a teacher by profession teach it to your subordinates. If you are a trainer use these techniques in your training sessions. Why keep knowledge to yourself? It grows if you share it.

- Let's Meet Soon

  I have personally trained over 20,000 people across the globe. Yet, I still get excited about meeting new people every day. I love to understand how different people think and behave. I love human psychology and how differently each one of us thinks. And I love to understand the different aspects of the most beautiful creation of God — human beings.

  So I am looking forward to seeing you soon over a cup of coffee, or may be as a participant in one of my training programmes, or public lectures. Do check my schedule on our website *www.spmfoundation.in*

JAICO PUBLISHING HOUSE

Elevate Your Life. Transform Your World.

Established in 1946, Jaico Publishing House is the publisher of stellar authors such as Sri Sri Paramahansa Yogananda, Osho, Robin Sharma, Deepak Chopra, Stephen Hawking, Eknath Easwaran, Sarvapalli Radhakrishnan, Nirad Chaudhuri, Khushwant Singh, Mulk Raj Anand, John Maxwell, Ken Blanchard and Brian Tracy. Our list which has crossed a landmark 2000 titles, is amongst the most diverse in the country, with books in religion, spirituality, mind/body/spirit, self-help, business, cookery, humour, career, games, biographies, fiction, and science.

Jaico has expanded its horizons to become a leading publisher of educational and professional books in management and engineering. Our college-level textbooks and reference titles are used by students countrywide. The success of our academic and professional titles is largely due to the efforts of our Educational and Corporate Sales Divisions.

The late Mr. Jaman Shah established Jaico as a book distribution company. Sensing that independence was around the corner, he aptly named his company Jaico ("Jai" means victory in Hindi). In order to tap the significant demand for affordable books in a developing nation, Mr. Shah initiated Jaico's own publications. Jaico was India's first publisher of paperback books in the English language.

In addition to being a publisher and distributor of its own titles, Jaico is a major distributor of books of leading international publishers such as McGraw Hill, Pearson, Cengage Learning, John Wiley and Elsevier Science. With its headquarters in Mumbai, Jaico has other sales offices in Ahmedabad, Bangalore, Bhopal, Bhubaneswar, Chennai, Delhi, Hyderabad, Kolkata and Lucknow. Our sales team of over 40 executives, direct mail order division, and website ensure that our books effectively reach all urban and rural parts of the country.

SINCE 1946